Race, Class, Power, and Organizing in East Baltimore

Race, Class, Power, and Organizing in East Baltimore

Rebuilding Abandoned Communities in America

Marisela B. Gomez

LEXINGTON BOOKS
Lanham • Boulder • New York • Toronto • Plymouth, UK

Published by Lexington Books
A wholly owned subsidiary of The Rowman & Littlefield Publishing Group, Inc.
4501 Forbes Boulevard, Suite 200, Lanham, Maryland 20706
www.rowman.com

10 Thornbury Road, Plymouth PL6 7PP, United Kingdom

British Library Cataloguing in Publication Information Available

Library of Congress Cataloging-in-Publication Data

Gomez, Marisela B., 1965–
    Race, class, power, and organizing in East Baltimore : rebuilding abandoned communities
in America / Marisela B. Gomez.
        p. cm.
    ISBN 978-0-7391-7500-2 (cloth : alk. paper)—ISBN 978-0-7391-7501-9 (ebook)
    ISBN 978-1-4985-1161-2 (pbK : alk. paper)
    1. Community development, Urban—Maryland—Baltimore. 2. Community
organization—Maryland—Baltimore. 3. East Baltimore (Baltimore, Md.)—Race relations.
4. East Baltimore (Baltimore, Md.)—Social conditions. I. Title.
    HN80.B3G66 2013
    307.1'416097526—dc23
                                                                                    2012034903

Printed in the United States of America

This book is dedicated to the community of Middle East Baltimore:

past, present, future

May you always be well.

Contents

Part III: The Future of East Baltimore: Race, Class, Power and Organizing as Causes and Consequences in Rebuilding Abandoned Communities

List of Figures

Chapter 1

Chapter 2

Chapter 3

Chapter 4

Chapter 6

Chapter 7

Chapter 9

List of Tables

List of Boxes

Chapter 3

Chapter 4

Chapter 5

Acknowledgments

There are many individuals and organizations to thank. Some prefer to remain anonymous. Therefore I would like to thank everyone who will remain nameless, in the many ways you each contributed to this book coming together. Here are a few acknowledgments: for all those who readily and reluctantly told their stories; for all those who reviewed and offered comments, some twice; for those who believed that telling this story will help us move toward more just ways of rebuilding our most vulnerable communities. I hold deep gratitude to all of you for your wisdom and right action.

> As a beautiful flower
> without fragrance is disappointing,
> so are wise words
> without right action.
>
> As a beautiful flower
> with a delightful fragrance is pleasing,
> so is wise and lovely speech
> when matched with right action.
>
> Dhammapada

Introduction

WHY TELL THIS STORY?

We rarely acknowledge the history of racism and classism as reasons for urban poverty and decay in U.S. cities. Usually we blame the current residents for deterioration. Seldom do we consider the role of developers in contributing to future urban decay, benefiting from it through public-private development projects. Usually we see them as "saving" a neighborhood's residents from themselves. And seldom do we include the residents of the area in the process of rebuilding their community. Usually we remove the people, rebuild the place, and invite people with power—from a different race and class—to live, work, and play in the renewed community. And we do all this without ever addressing the root causes of poverty in the process of rebuilding a healthy community.

The urban renewal of the mid-1900s is now widely recognized as an ineffective way to do community renewal. Yet it continues, under different names, to be the way we rebuild communities today. This story is an example of a current urban rebuilding initiative, with the same ingredients past ones had, and an opportunity to make future initiatives more just and equitable.

The community changes described in this book occur in a historically African American community in East Baltimore. It is therefore about race, class, and power in the setting of communities organizing against unfair rebuilding processes. It is my aspiration to offer a perspective from "inside" the community: one that is seldom recorded in detail. The purposes of this book are to: document how past systems of race and class oppression created disinvested communities and continue unequal approaches to rebuilding abandoned communities which obstruct community-directed rebuilding processes; record a history of organized communities, revolutionaries, and witness an often forgotten and hidden aspect of rebuilding inner cities through

1

examples of struggle and victory, side by side; reveal the systems of power supported by public-private partnerships that challenge sustainable community-directed rebuilding by using the example of the Johns Hopkins Medical Institutions' (JHMI) continued expansion in a disinvested and abandoned Baltimore neighborhood; link the effects of racial and social segregation in creating and sustaining unhealthy communities; offer direction for improving current and future practices in rebuilding processes. It may also offer insight into participants in this story and into the ways we are similar or different on our own path of individual and societal change.

The intended audience of this book are diverse: residents attempting to gain insight into determining their community, community activists, organizers, urban planners and policy makers, community development professionals, housing and health policy analysts, current students and teachers of sociology, urban planning, community development, history, public health and medicine, political economy, ethics, law, anthropology, geography.

This book is organized as follows: the history of racial and class segregation and its impact on creating abandoned and decaying communities while setting the stage for the growth of power in white and wealthy communities is presented first. Historic and current examples of how these abandoned and disinvested communities are rebuilt, with no community participation, and the challenges and successes in organizing for participation follows. An analysis of the current rebuilding project is next with examples of other rebuilding projects in the U.S.A. (referred to as "America" and the "United States" throughout the text) and abroad and the structural effects on individual and community health. A summary and discussion of next steps in the current rebuilding project closes this book.

The organization of this book mimics the framework of any good community organizing effort: we must know the history and use it to understand and inform the organizing process, organize with clear goals rooted in community participation, decision making and transparency, and analyze our process continuously to adjust for ongoing changes from intended and unintended outcomes. Chapters 3 through 6 can be used as a practical tool for those directly involved in organizing communities in general and communities facing displacement and demolition in specific.

It is my hope that this book will benefit not only the current process in East Baltimore, but all rebuilding processes seeking to encourage equity—fairness or justice—in the midst of oppressive power.

THE STORY: REBUILDING MIDDLE EAST BALTIMORE

In the year 2000, in the mid-eastern area of Baltimore—Middle East Baltimore—the community was primarily African American, low-income residents. Its social, economic, and health characteristics, among the worst in the city, included a majority of unoccupied houses, high rates of crime, drug dealing, high unemployment, overgrown vacant lots, lead poisoning, heart disease, strokes, cancer, diabetes, and other chronic health conditions.

The community had been abandoned. It had been allowed to deteriorate to this level of blight (decay) with little or no systematic process to address the abandoned houses or the increasing crime and trash that come secondary to increasing abandonment and decreasing tax bases and public city services. This outcome had been decades in the making: the Middle East Baltimore community had been designated an area of urban blight, an urban renewal area, for more than 50 years.

Once an area is deemed an "urban renewal" area, private and public investment decreases and the local residents are left on their own to stem the flow of continued decay. This continued decay is provoked by abandoned and vacant houses—sometimes blocks—becoming fire risks and havens for drug trafficking and use, prostitution, crime, trash dumping along with further decrease in public services to address the increasing conditions of decay. Urban renewal became synonymous with "Negro removal" in the 1950s as it resulted in largely poor and African American communities being displaced to other similarly disinvested areas, the land often used for development of private interests or public-assisted housing.

The argument underlying this book is that if sufficient community participation is present in the planning, implementation, and evaluation of the processes of rebuilding an existing community (the place and the people)—constructing and rehabbing homes so displacement is minimal, demolishing buildings to minimize hazards to health, relocation practices which assure minimal stress and maximum benefit, assuring increased economic and social stability through opportunities in the rebuilt and relocated place, assuring that historic residents will not be forced out due to unaffordable rent, property taxes, products and services in the rebuilt and relocated place, and evaluation of all this—then the likelihood of equitable benefit to all stakeholders is increased. While the main rebuilding project presented to highlight this argument relates to the 2001 rebuilding of East Baltimore, the history of rebuilding in East Baltimore over the previous century is presented to highlight how and why the systematic result of past urban renewal strategies affect the current rebuilding project.

The 2001 community rebuilding process in Middle East Baltimore begins with a plan, not by the affected or targeted community but by several stakeholders whose primary vision was to address the effect on them as neighbors to a disinvested and abandoned community. This plan would require relocation of approximately 800 occupied households—more than 2,400 people—and demolition of the entire neighborhood of more than 1,500 houses to build a biotech park and new houses. The major stakeholders of this plan—Johns Hopkins Medical Institutions (JHMI), city and state government, and foundations—intended to use the powers of eminent domain (the legal right of the city government to acquire private property for public benefit) to take the property of approximately one-third homeowners and two-thirds rental occupants and several businesses and churches. Reminiscent of racial segregation, the first plan allowed relocation assistance only if residents, businesses, and churches moved to adjacent neighborhoods with similar socioeconomic indicators as Middle East Baltimore. Demolition of homes began with no regard for the health and safety of nearby residents. Construction of moderate and market rate homes were planned to assure that this urban renewal project of the twenty-first century would guarantee a gentrified community for the safety and benefit of the prestigious Johns Hopkins Medical community—to live, work, learn, and play. Public support in the form of tax credits, subsidies, grants, and bonds—guaranteed by the poverty-stricken condition of the community—invited private developers to come and grow their assets on this abandoned community. There was no plan for the historic residents to participate in the rebuilding of their community, remain in their community, or return to the rebuilt community.

After residents organized and challenged this "Negro removal" process, the relocation benefits changed, the plans for housing construction changed, and the demolition activities were delayed until health and environmental experts assessed adequate practices were in place. This all occurred while the community was organized, demanded equity as a collective voice, and maintained consistent pressure on the quasi private-public entity directing the rebuilding process (East Baltimore Development Incorporated, EBDI) and before they were displaced. Today, after displacement of most of the 800 households, the memory of the powerful stakeholders have fallen short of promises—verbal and written—made to the local community when they were still in residence. Promises by EBDI and their partners in regard to community-engaged processes, construction of affordable housing, a funded plan for right of return for those displaced, and employment and local hiring from the community have all been forgotten as a third master plan confirms that the Science and Technology Park at Johns Hopkins will continue the history of serial community displacement and gentrification in East Baltimore.

This type of continued displacement of racially and socially separated or stratified communities has occurred mostly unchallenged in the rebuilding of disinvested communities in America. On the occasions when they are challenged, the demands by residents for equity goes mostly unheard due to insufficient power of the organized residents, lack of relationships of support (bridging relationships) with outside organizations, political representatives and governmental agencies (planning, land use, transportation, housing and community development, health, social services). It occurs because the disinvested communities have little power to challenge the powerful developers whose allies include all levels of government—as is the case in past and current redevelopment projects in East Baltimore. These stakeholders have the power to make community rebuilding a more democratic and equitable process to benefit local community residents. A majority white group of stakeholders, they continue to live and enact the deception of "separate and equal" from the past when racial segregation sowed the seeds of current separate and unequal communities across America today. They ignore the connection between current-day poverty of communities like Middle East Baltimore and growth of powerful institutions like JHMI: that expansion of institutions are dependent on their power to access land and displace the members of disempowered nearby communities. This book will document how this skewed understanding of history results in non-community participatory rebuilding processes, continued community displacement and gentrification, gross inequity in benefit to the affected communities, and continued segregating of those displaced into already disinvested and unhealthy communities. Confronted with the power of organized resistance it reveals how changes are possible but inconsistent and easily reversed when the collective voice is absent.

HEALTH OUTCOMES

Socioeconomic and political oppression of African American people throughout the history of America has directly resulted in the creation of neighborhoods of urban decay and poverty in the twenty-first century, which in turn affects the health of individuals living in these neighborhoods. The unequal and discriminatory laws and policies resulted in disinvestment and marginalization of communities in which majority African Americans lived leading to unhealthy physical environments of unsanitary, abandoned, and run-down streets, schools, parks, health clinics, recreation centers, stores, and houses, and high crime. The consequences or effects of living in such disinvested neighborhoods help to determine exposure to different levels of stress faced daily by individuals living, playing, working, and learning in these communities as well the internal and external resources available to address these stressors in a healthy way.

The effect of having a low-paying job or no job, being African American or part of a racial minority, and education below high school level independently and together affects the health of an individual. These socioeconomic factors or social determinants increase the likelihood of an individual having a variety of physical and mental illnesses and a shorter lifespan.

The neighborhood effects and social and economic characteristics of individuals living in East Baltimore, together and individually, resulted in East Baltimore being characterized as one of the least healthy communities in America.

Community rebuilding efforts must therefore assess the community's health history and assure that the processes of rebuilding are participatory and not hierarchical as has been the intention and practice of EBDI and its partners. Rebuilding with input and direction from those living in the community can begin to change the historic oppressions that have directly and indirectly contributed to creating unhealthy communities. Assessment of the health impact, as well as the economic, social, educational, environmental, and political impact, on the people affected by community rebuilding processes must be included in an analysis of "benefit for whom."

For those who organize and challenge the powerful stakeholders for more equitable rebuilding processes, the consequent health impact of increased stress must be assessed in light of the already existent stress resulting from living in abandoned and disempowered communities. These types of analyses must be incorporated into the strategies for rebuilding communities like Middle East Baltimore in order to address the historic damage and narrow the gap of unequal benefit to the stakeholders involved today. Such comprehensive analyses will begin to address the power imbalances which serve to widen the growing disparity in health between communities with differing degrees of resources and which are separated by race and class.

THE THEORY

Community Rebuilding

In theory, community rebuilding describes an intention and process of neighborhoods developing and changing to benefit those who are living in them. This improvement may directly and indirectly benefit the surrounding communities.

The extent to which a rebuilding process directly benefits the community is determined by the degree of participation by its members—residents, businesses, and religious institutions—in all aspects of planning and implementation. A relationship of trust must be built, much like a bridge, between the members of the community and the various outside stakeholders, or interests, participating in the community rebuilding process. These outside stakeholders can include the neighboring associations or businesses (universities, hospitals, markets, other retailers); city, state, and federal governmental departments involved in different aspects of rebuilding (planning, housing and relocation, demolition and construction, transportation, preservation, health, social services, parks and recreation, evaluation); and nongovernmental interests such as foundations, development organizations, schools, and nonprofit organizations.

Community Organizing

Participation of residents, religious institutions, schools, and businesses in a rebuilding process is determined by how well the community is organized. An organized community, or community organizing, involves sufficient bonds, or connections, between members of a community. These bonds or connections develop from common desires and goals to benefit the community, and they lead to trust.

An organized community can include neighborhood associations, block clubs, issue-specific organizations, and groups sponsored by religious institutions. Issue-specific organizations may form spontaneously in response to an issue or exist continuously to address or prevent known problems. Over time, these relationships become systems of support for individuals in the organizations, often extending into the larger community. Though one may not be directly involved at any one moment, knowing that a community organization is available when an issue arises offers a sense of security for individual members of the community.

Healthy community bonding—organized relationships—establishes a base of trust, transparency, and support from which residents can negotiate for their collective interests with organizations outside their community. This type of relationship, between community organizations and entities or organizations outside the community, is sometimes referred to as a bridging relationship. Community organizing involves a healthy degree of bonding relationships between members of the community and healthy bridging relationships between the community organizations and the external institutions and organizations that may support the local communities' interests.

Healthy community organizing during rebuilding processes is essential. It involves open communication among the members of the community about planning, implementing, and sustaining the rebuilding process. These relationships must be maintained after the rebuilding of the physical structures is completed, to ensure that the historic community has opportunities for housing and jobs in the rebuilt community and improvement in living conditions in the relocated communities.

Equally important is the bridging, or associating, that must occur between the residents in the community being rebuilt and the outside stakeholders. If the common interests being brought to the table, as well as the ones not in common, are not clear, challenges and disconnects arise. This can lead to mistrust, nontransparency, and a silo effect, in which each group or interest is unaware of the intentions and actions of the others.

Community organizing in East Baltimore over the past 100 years is described in this book. The organizing which occurred during the first 10 years of the current rebuilding project is presented in detail to offer the reader a step-by-step process of the challenges and successes.

How Rebuilding Occurs

While community rebuilding efforts can begin from the community's initiative, they do not always begin this way. Efforts may begin at the initiative of others when there is no collective voice, no organized base of residents, representing the interests of the existing community.

Such poorly organized communities seldom maintain the power necessary to motivate government and private stakeholders to participate in a collective rebuilding effort. Perhaps one or two individuals may speak on behalf of the community, but because there is not an organized base, there is little opportunity for authentic participation within the larger community. Without an organized base, there is a lack of healthy bridging relationships with organizations and institutions outside the community. This absence results in isolation and lack of connection with external social and political organizations or movements.

When there are poorly organized efforts in a community, as there were at the time of the planning of the rebuilding process in Middle East Baltimore, it is easy for outside interests to develop plans to rebuild the community without participation and control by residents—and more likely that they will.

The rebuilding effort in Middle East Baltimore was initiated by outside stakeholders through a public-private partnership. With the support of the local, state, and federal housing and planning agencies; political leaders; and local and national foundations, the outside developer of the Johns Hopkins Medical Institutions planned and directed the removal of the Middle East Baltimore community for construction of a biotech park and the structures to support it. In this example, to build the anticipated structures required acquiring existing houses (occupied and unoccupied), businesses, and churches. As it did in Middle East Baltimore, this type of rebuilding may result in the displacement (displacement and relocation are used interchangeably going forward) of residents of a community while providing little or no direct benefit or causing them harm (displaced to areas of greater poverty, no social networks, disruption of existing social networks, stigmatization, continued segregation, economic challenges, negative health consequences of displacement). In the case of the current rebuilding process in Middle East Baltimore equitable benefit to historic residents and major developers such as JHMI and other private institutions is lacking with no current intention to remedy this inequity.

The initiation of community rebuilding can come from city planners or housing and development departments. Often the rebuilding processes of public-assisted houses and apartments are such government-driven initiatives. Here as well, when initiatives are not clearly informed and directed by residents of the rebuilt community, outcomes for residents are less positive and more likely to serve the interests of outside stakeholders.

Using a critical analysis of the history and theory of community rebuilding and the practical way it has and continues to occur in Middle East Baltimore we can begin to identify aspects of the process that move us toward—and those that move us away from—building a more just society.

WHO IS TELLING THE STORY

And why am I telling this story? I spent 14 years as part of the Johns Hopkins Medical Institutions (JHMI) community, as student, research fellow, medical resident, and instructor, and 17 years as part of the East Baltimore community, as resident, volunteer, community organizer, health advisor and consultant, health care provider, board director, and cofounder and executive director of community organizations.

My journey with Baltimore City began in 1990, when I relocated from New Mexico to attend graduate school at the Johns Hopkins Medical School. The medical school is part of the JHMI, located in the eastern part of Baltimore, called East Baltimore. The residential communities surrounding the JHMI are low-income and primarily African American, reflecting the changes and consequences of growing abandonment over some 50 years.

My introduction to the community surrounding the institutions came at the formal orientation for graduate and medical students. During the presentations, we were warned about the dangers of venturing into the community surrounding the JHMI. For example, it was suggested that we park in the garages affiliated with the institutions and not on the streets, to ensure that we were safe.

While this was the official position of the JHMI, it was not a view supported by all. Many people employed by, and other affiliates and students of, the JHMI held differing opinions: "Of course there were safety issues, like any other area that is struggling; one had to be aware of their surroundings." Many of the housekeeping and kitchen service staff also seemed to have a different way of looking at this issue of safety in the area surrounding the JHMI. It was the community that many of them returned to after their work at the medical campus. Still others suggested that the responsibility of the Hopkins community was to provide factual information to its members. To this direct recipient of this information, the bias in the way the information was delivered was clear.

The perception of separation between this renowned health care, research, and teaching institution and the surrounding community rapidly became clear. Inside the walls of Hopkins, there was fear of the neighbors. This fear intensified the separation and justified continuing and increasing it. As the local community residents would say, Johns Hopkins had "set up" the surrounding community as the evildoers and itself as the savior. From the point of view of the medical institution, it was the institution's responsibility to address the reality of the results of poverty—crime, unsafe environments, increasing drug use, and abandoned buildings—and their effects on the community.

The die had been cast long before my arrival in 1990. I became an observer of and participant in the interactions of these two changing communities.

Over the first year, I slowly met the community surrounding the JHMI. Though warned about "venturing" out into the community, I felt I knew this community of people: people who were survivors of a system of disinvestment and who became branded as the inner city, low-income people of color, responsible for their destiny. My own history as a person of color growing up in a disinvested community helped me to identify the similarities, even while I had ventured into a privileged community of higher learning. I parked on the streets about 4 to 5 blocks away from the research building I was affiliated with. Slowly, the neighbors on my walk to and from the car became my friends. We knew each other's names, and they reminded me when I was working too late at night. They invited me to sit on their stoops and share a conversation, to enter their homes and gush over the new photos of grandchildren.

I patronized a car-repair shop and a hairdresser around the block. It was a community I enjoyed being with each day, before and after being with my other community of Johns Hopkins for graduate training. As I shared time with the residents of East Baltimore, I heard a story unfold: their story of living in East Baltimore, their parents' and their grandparents' lives in East Baltimore when it was a different type of community. It was healthier then, clean, not boarded up and abandoned. They talked about their fears and what was important to them: being safe and being healthy, their children and their grandchildren, their aspirations and their joys, and their right to determine the destiny of their community. Their stories really were no different from the ones I shared inside the JHMI.

Another thing the two communities had in common was that neither community spoke with one voice and everyone had an opinion.

I was also interested in community organizing as a tool for peaceful and equitable means to community change. To this end, I sought out the different community organizations in the area surrounding the JHMI. I volunteered with them and participated in different types of health services the JHMI offered the community.

During my second year in East Baltimore, the walls between these two neighbors were being built higher and higher. This happened directly and indirectly, through increased security forces, incomplete and inaccurate information about the surrounding community given to the JHMI community, and the lack of equal opportunity for construction jobs with fair wages and training for community residents.

Students and staff at the JHMI formed an organization to address these growing walls. It was called Bridges not Walls (BNW). Supported within the different schools of the JHMI, BNW spoke out strongly in challenging the "official" position of continued separation from the surrounding community through consistent demonization of our neighbors. We formed coalitions with existing East Baltimore community organizations and represented the different voices from each community to the other, attempting to bridge the divide.

As the years went on, I became more active in community organizing in East Baltimore. When stepping across a single street meant crossing from poverty to wealth and wealth to poverty, accessing both in the span of 30 seconds, it was difficult to be comfortable with either. The clear separation between these two communities I was a part of greatly influenced my path.

It was challenging to accept that one community was on a path of growth while the other was on a path of decline. It became clear that they affected each other's paths in more ways than crime and health care. The very existence of one type of community contributed to the path of the other, and vice versa. Participating in both, I observed this seemingly inevitable result of gain and loss by these communities, which were perceived as being so separate.

While my time within the JHMI was invaluable in teaching me about medicine, biomedical science, public health, and prevention, the communities surrounding the great institution provided training in the causes of individual and community health. Though the classroom of the streets and community meetings was not part of the schedule of my formal training in medicine and public health, it was in the homes of residents, at rallies, in community meetings, and in the streets that I learned about the social factors that affected individual and community health and illness. The processes that determine the social context in which individuals carry out a healthy or an unhealthy lifestyle are in the daily activities of the community, the process of community change, the development of community organizations, and the cultural norms of communities imprinted by their histories. These directly and indirectly affect the origins of individual and collective health outcomes. These were the lessons of the residents and spaces of East Baltimore.

During the early 2000s, a plan to redevelop the more than 80 acres just north of the JHMI—called Middle East Baltimore—without any input from the existing residents was announced. I became fully involved in the community organization, Save Middle East Action Committee (SMEAC), formed to represent residents affected by this plan—variously serving on the board of directors, as a community organizer, and as executive director. The work of this organization was challenging and intense: there were too many battles, not enough support for the affected community, a powerful force of private and public support of the plan, and time pressure imposed by the schedule of those with power.

Six years into the redevelopment process, it was clear that community building for real transformation, without adequate internal transformation, results in limited understanding and vision for equitable and sustained change. It was also clear that the stakeholders involved in the community rebuilding process in Middle East Baltimore had not challenged themselves deeply about their own transformation. Yet we were all "experts" in social transformation and we expected change to flow according to our own limited ideals.

The first phase of relocation of residents was nearing completion at this point, and those doing the developing were renegotiating the second phase. The developing entity continued to "tell" the local community how the changes would be good for them. Yet, its communication in other matters was not clear, its promises were open for change, its sincerity was in question, and trust was lacking on both sides. After some reflection, I decided to leave the process for 1 year and look into other models of community building.

In October 2006, I left East Baltimore to seek a different and more contemplative understanding of community change, leaving so I could return. One year turned into several and I spent more than 3 years living in monasteries and contemplative communities in and outside the United States—in solitude, in silence—to learn about peace inside myself and how this affects peaceful and equitable means in community building, organizing, change, and existence. Time away, reflection, and study and practice with communities attempting to live in understanding and harmony offered insight into individual and social transformation.

During the past 20 years, the communities of the JHMI and East Baltimore have been my home. Both equally beneficial to the understanding I now have, they together revealed the extremes of wealth and poverty and the results of this imbalance. Moving in different roles and capacities between the formal institution of higher learning and the streets of higher learning has offered me a view from the middle, a bridge between these two extremes.

The opportunities for experience and study with communities practicing in the direction of more intentional and concrete spiritual means of community building and living enhanced this understanding. They highlighted the need to understand the differences that must be bridged in moving toward the middle: a middle that holds both the differences and the similarities with equity and dismantles the separation in attitudes and actions that promotes continued health and wealth disparity.

In 2009, residents affected by the East Baltimore rebuilding process suggested that a history should be written. I returned to East Baltimore and listened again, to people directly and indirectly affected by the rebuilding process in Middle East Baltimore. While much of the information for this story comes from interactions and relationships with stakeholders involved in the rebuilding process, the prior years in the neighboring communities of East Baltimore and the JHMI offered much insight into and understanding of the history, framework and context.

Formal interviews with more than 100 individuals directly and indirectly involved in the current redevelopment of Middle East Baltimore inform the story, as well as information collected from newspapers, texts, private and public references, and Internet sources. The historical sections are summarized from the texts, periodicals, and newspapers of the Maryland Department of the Enoch Pratt Free Library in Baltimore. Brief notes are used in the text of the story; a listing of resources used directly as references and a list of those that may be of interest for further reading follow the final chapter. Direct quotations from individual interviews appear in the text in quotation marks (""). Quotations from written material are included in quotation marks and followed by their source in parenthesis.

SUMMARY OF CHAPTERS

The first chapter focuses on the history of Baltimore and East Baltimore and the role of race, class, power, and separation as contributing factors to current-day East Baltimore. This chapter recounts how the civil war and the Jim Crow era resulted in the growth of power imbalance between whites and African Americans in housing, employment, education and all social systems in American cities—racial stratification. It describes racial and social stratification effects on changes in population in East Baltimore since the early nineteenth century and the establishment and growth of the Johns Hopkins Medical Institutions relative to these stratifications.

Chapter 2 describes community development in East Baltimore in general and specifically focuses on two major development projects of the 1950s and 1960s and introduces the current 2001 development which is the focus of the remainder of the book. These two previous community development projects highlight the role of the powerful medical institutions of the Johns Hopkins campus and its close partnership with local, state, and federal government in acquiring public and private land for its expansion. Development of the JHMI in East Baltimore and the emerging separation or stratification between the institution and the neighboring community is discussed. Chapter 3 focuses on past community organizing and its successes and challenges in East Baltimore from the perspective of the local resident organizations. This rich history of local community development and organizing sets the framework for discussion and analysis of the current rebuilding project of 2001. It informs the reader of the challenges to organizing presented by the history of abandonment and disinvestment and the presence of a powerful institution as neighbor expanding and displacing residents. The organizing process that occurred as a result of the current rebuilding project in Middle East Baltimore is elaborated upon, offering the reader an understanding of why the organization was successful in changing aspects of the plans for displacement of residents and demolition of houses, businesses, churches. The development of a community organization, leadership, and processes of transparency and democracy is reported in this chapter.

Chapters 4 through 6 detail the current rebuilding process through the challenges and successes of organized community residents demanding participation and decision making in the planning, processes, and outcomes of rebuilding Middle East Baltimore. Chapter 4 focuses on how targeted community residents act on and are acted upon by the different powerful stakeholders driving the rebuilding effort even while attempting to build a sustainable organization. It describes the challenges faced by residents in negotiating for equity, respect, and shared control in all aspects of the rebuilding process; including displacement, demolition, and construction. Chapter 5 focuses on the roles of the various stakeholders involved and the degree of transparency in which each represents their expectations and benefit from the rebuilding process. Chapter 6 summarizes the challenges, successes, and evolution of community organizing through the first 10 years of the current rebuilding of Middle East Baltimore. The role of community organizing as the tool for residents to challenge the powerful stakeholders driving the rebuilding of Middle East Baltimore links chapters 3 through 6. It provides the data necessary for the analysis and understanding of who benefits from current top-down approaches of rebuilding abandoned communities like Middle East Baltimore.

Chapter 7 offers a framework for assessing how the current rebuilding process in Middle East Baltimore is an example of redistributive justice gone awry through government taking of private property for the benefit of more powerful private corporations. Redistributive justice typically refers to the use of government powers to benefit those deemed more needy. In light of the use of eminent domain by the city of Baltimore to take the homes of private owners and demolish them for a Johns Hopkins Science and Technology Park and new housing and retail businesses, and no formal plan to assure residents can afford to return or stay in the rebuilt area, the balance of public and private benefit remains unclear. The benefit to JHMI of rebuilding Middle East Baltimore is clear. This chapter highlights the question of "for whom the community is being rebuilt" through a discussion of how each type of funding benefits its recipient and whether there is absolute or relative gain for each. For example, detailing how the tax subsidies to the developers and corporations increase their assets 5, 10, 20, and 50 years later must be compared with how the relocation assistance for residents increases their assets 5, 10, 20, and 50 years later. If a stressful rebuilding process negatively affects the health of residents, both acutely and chronically, how does this "benefit" the historic community? Do the JHMI's gains in prestige and power have a dollar value, in return on research grants, patients, scholarly publications? How does this "wealth gain" compare with the "wealth gain" for residents forced to relocate to accommodate this expansion that will foster the institution's perceptions of "safe neighbors"? Has this rebuilding project widened the gap between the rich and the poor of East Baltimore? Chapter 7 will address these questions.

Chapter 8 highlights several rebuilding processes in America and abroad. It compares and contrasts different aspects of rebuilding in Middle East Baltimore with each example and focuses on the role of community direction and participation and public-private partnerships where applicable.

While chapter 9 focuses on the health impact of rebuilding abandoned communities, the factors determining what makes up a healthy community must be held in mind throughout the reading of this book. After all the aim of rebuilding unhealthy abandoned communities is to rebuild healthy communities. The health of a community is determined by the economic, social, political, and environmental factors affecting the individual and the community. The history of East Baltimore presented in the first three chapters emphasizes that these systematic or structural factors have all contributed to a disinvested community—in housing, schools, recreational centers, businesses. The individual health consequences of abandonment of communities which then become at risk for increased drug use, prostitution, gangs, violence, lack of sufficient and adequate nutrition, lack of areas for sufficient and adequate exercise, and havens of environmental risks factors such as lead-painted houses, rodent-infested vacant houses and land, and asthma-inducing conditions are described. The consequences of the social factors of race and class on individual health are described and the pathways leading to the disparate health outcomes between white and racial and ethnic minority groups are presented. The negative physical and mental health impact on individuals and communities, resulting from uprooting families from their social networks through mass displacement, as occurred in Middle East Baltimore over the past 80 years is discussed in this chapter.

Chapter 10 offers a framework for change in the current rebuilding process in Middle East Baltimore. This chapter challenges all the stakeholders to define their roles and needs as a way to positively change the current recipe being used for rebuilding Middle East Baltimore. For example, before future changes in the rebuilding plans are publicly announced they must include strategic planning informed by all stakeholders using indicators that allow evaluation of whether benefit is distributed equitably. A different type of accountability, transparency, engagement, planning, and evaluation is necessary, to ensure that rebuilding communities today is different from the "Negro removal" processes of yesterday and today. With transparency and acknowledgment of the historical way the powerful stakeholders have controlled community development in East Baltimore, a more healthy way of rebuilding with a focus on shared equity and decision making by all stakeholders could inform a comprehensive plan addressing the roots of abandonment and poverty. Addressing the roots could help to nurture realistic actions for rebuilding a thriving Middle East Baltimore from the inside, one that historic and new residents alike would feel is theirs to determine.

I

RACIAL AND CLASS OPPRESSION AND A CENTURY OF BUILDING AND REBUILDING EAST BALTIMORE

1

Race Separation in Historic East Baltimore: Yesterday and Today

" . . . always been a Master . . . just different faces . . . look, the plantation still sits up there . . . we still the slaves." —East Baltimore resident

"we cannot dismantle the master's house with the master's tools . . ." —Audre Lorde

This chapter describes the history of Baltimore and East Baltimore from a racial and social context and its general effect on power and access. It further develops the racial and social character of the Middle East Baltimore and Johns Hopkins communities which is the focus of the 2001 rebuilding project. It closes with a discussion of the decrease and growth in power of these two communities, geographic neighbors, as a result of past and current racial and social separation and inequality.

RACIAL SEGREGATION ESTABLISHES BALTIMORE

Race and class continue to dominate the social, economic, and political direction of Baltimore and East Baltimore, as they did in the 1700s. Therefore, a short history of race and class in Baltimore and the region is necessary to understand the context of rebuilding this community.

Maryland was founded in the 1600s, Baltimore in the early and mid-1700s. At the start of Baltimore's settlement, the majority of the population was white. This included a mix of immigrants from Ireland, Scotland, Germany, Poland, Bohemia, and Italy. A small percentage of the population was African American farmers who had migrated from the South.

While Maryland was founded on the economy of tobacco and enslavement, Baltimore itself had few enslaved people. In Baltimore before the Civil War, though

African Americans lived peacefully near whites, "each was treated as a slave in some respect".[1] This included the social norms that treated the African American person as inferior to the white person in all respects.

Maryland was declared neutral during the Civil War, with many of the enslaved people recruited for the Union army. Still, for Union troops to occupy Maryland and its regions without being attacked, supporters of enslavement were held under arms in Baltimore. It was not until 1864, one year before the Civil War ended, that Maryland changed its constitution to outlaw enslavement.[2] Several months later, the Emancipation Proclamation was issued, followed by the outlawing of enslavement in the United States, when the Thirteenth Amendment to the Constitution was ratified. After the Civil War ended, the pro-enslavement states of the South could no longer secede as confederate states of the union and had to abide by the ratified constitutional amendment regarding "possessing or owning" another human being as a slave. African Americans who had been enslaved were set free from their enslavers' plantations. Some migrated to cities to their north, seeking opportunities to work.

Following the end of the Civil War, Maryland maintained a tyranny of active and organized white supremacy. In Baltimore during this time, the city's Democratic Party ran on a ballot proclaiming Baltimore as a "white city," an attempt to assure white voters of their continued supremacy over African Americans.[3,4] Baltimore immediately moved to ensure that all schools, churches, hospitals, eating establishments, and employment places were segregated.

This post-enslavement period of overt racism throughout the country, which resulted in mass segregationist tactics, was known as the Jim Crow era. These practices maintained whites and African Americans as separate and unequal, setting patterns then that continue today. Baltimore fully supported Jim Crow, in unwritten policies and overt actions that dictated patterns of housing, employment, worship, recreation, transportation, entertainment, and education. This ensured that opportunities for African Americans remained substandard and public and private services disinvested from African American communities.

As more African Americans migrated to Baltimore after the Civil War, whites migrated out of the city into growing counties. This continued into the early 1900s, during World War I. By the 1920s, this migration pattern resulted in a trend toward a growing African American population in the city and a majority white population in the suburbs, or counties. The migration of African Americans from the South to Baltimore, cities north of the Mason-Dixon Line, and other industrial cities of the United States continued after World War II and well into the late 1900s.

As African Americans continued to move from the South, pockets of East Baltimore slowly opened up for African Americans to rent. The existing locals termed these "highly entertaining negro settlements."[5] The neighborhoods slowly changed, becoming and remaining segregated by color in East Baltimore and Baltimore. Within the communities of color in East Baltimore, different classes of people lived together. During these times, there was no choice. By the 1970s, Baltimore and East Baltimore had become majority African American.[6]

RACIST AND CLASSIST REAL ESTATE AND EMPLOYMENT PRACTICES IN EARLY BALTIMORE

These types of segregationist strategies grew after the Civil War ended. During these times of enforced segregation, slum landlords benefited richly from investment in houses in the alleys, where African Americans were forced to pay higher rents due to a lack of adequate housing elsewhere. These neighborhoods were marked with aging buildings, inadequate upkeep, and continued racially motivated neglect by those allocating city and state resources.

Early Baltimore had no remorse in maintaining a rigid racial and social class structure in all systems. In 1872, the expensive prices at which landowners sold property forced builders to build houses for higher-income people. These classist practices prompted reports by a newspaper article of that period, of a society that supported further separation of the rich and the poor: "The present law makes the rich man richer and the poor man poorer."[7] Baltimore's social class structure recommended that "a stable neighborhood was one where every house was owned by its occupant," as it ensured the least disorder among its members.[8] As the city's poverty and African American population both grew in the late 1800s and early 1900s, the rich continued to move to the spacious and growing counties, distinguished by their lack of low-income residents and of African Americans.

The elite also embraced a rigid class distinction in schooling, determining that old or rented facilities were suitable for African Americans and newly migrated Germans and reserving newly constructed facilities for the middle class and the elite. Similarly, the more expensive churches were situated in areas of higher income. And new institutions such as libraries, museums, and hospitals dedicated by the wealthy also maintained different levels of services, providing better services to those in the higher class.

Baltimore was a leader in particularly vicious racist real estate practices. Following the official end of the Civil War, citizens initiated an organized attempt to maintain racial oppression in the form of real estate practices of blockbusting and scare tactics in white neighborhoods.

Blockbusting consisted of convincing fearful white owners to sell at low prices because African Americans were moving into their neighborhoods, suggesting that as soon as one African American family moved into a neighborhood, it would deteriorate. These same houses, bought cheap from fearful white owners, were then sold to African Americans at two to three times the price the blockbusters had just paid for them. Scare tactics included forming neighborhood associations in white neighborhoods to prevent African Americans from buying into these neighborhoods; intimidating households; and violating property lived in by African Americans in primarily white neighborhoods.[9,10,11]

Orchestrated in Baltimore, these practices were endorsed and enforced by cultural, commercial, and government institutions, becoming the model for other cities in the United States to replicate. One example is the 1910 law officially segregating housing between African Americans and whites. Baltimore was the first U.S. city to pass such an ordinance. This resulted in several cities establishing similar laws ensuring separate and unequal rights to acquisition of land and rental housing.

These socially and legally entrenched racist strategies were substantially reinforced by the lack of fair lending laws and practices over the next century. Banks, mortgage lenders, real estate brokers, and housing departments nationwide continued these segregationist practices without legal or ethical oversight.

When African Americans could afford to buy a house, they were forced to buy in neighborhoods profiled by race and income, often with substandard housing stocks. It took a greater portion of their income to maintain these substandard houses. And houses in such neighborhoods grew in value at far slower rates than did houses in white neighborhoods. African Americans could not accumulate assets in their homes as their white counterparts could, which guaranteed that they had less savings for education and future opportunity for increasing assets in generations to come.

During the Great Depression of the 1930s, federal housing lending programs rated African American neighborhoods as risky places for loans, marking them out, or redlining them.[12] Federal grant and loan programs would not lend money to whites if they chose to buy in these "risky" neighborhoods. These racist practices further guaranteed housing segregation and deterioration of the housing market in African American neighborhoods. With less income available for improving housing, African American neighborhoods became neighborhoods of decreased housing value, as well as lower-income neighborhoods. These areas, gained the name "blight" and "slum" in the 1930s, and further migration out of white and upwardly mobile immigrants and the migration in of working-class African Americans.

When increasing numbers of African Americans did buy into middle-income neighborhoods that were substantially white, these neighborhoods experienced a flight of white residents. This pattern existed more than 100 years ago, and continues its legacy of marginalizing the majority of African Americans into areas of lower-priced housing stock.

One result of redlining was that racist speculators offered loans to African Americans if they would buy in such neighborhoods. These loans had markedly higher interest rates than those offered by banks and other lenders to buyers in white neighborhoods. And for those unable to maintain their payments and taking additional loans to prevent foreclosures, these speculating firms charged even higher interest rates on loans, deepening the cycle of debt.

In the 1940s and 1950s, under the GI Bill, the federal government provided loans for housing to soldiers returning from war. Once again, the distribution of federal loans favored white homebuyers; loans were not accorded equally to African American soldiers.

This gap between whites and African Americans, in the opportunity to buy land, in its commercial value, and in the amount they paid and owed to maintain it, continued into the 1970s and the current housing and real estate market.[13]

For those renting, often the housing stock was in need of repair and landlords bypassed the laws requiring remediation. This pattern contributed to the continued disinvestment from and subsequent deterioration of a neighborhood as more African Americans move in.

This history of racist and unfair housing and real estate practices has fueled a cycle of decreased housing value and the consequences: higher housing cost and higher interest rates causing a greater portion of income to be used for housing costs, less income for housing improvement, less income for saving and education.

These unfair housing strategies become more significant in light of the historic and current unfairness in employment practices for African Americans. In the past, African Americans were relegated to menial work, and they were paid less for these tasks than whites were. With consistent lower incomes because of unequal pay, and having to use a larger percentage of their income for housing, African Americans had less money available to save for college. Discriminatory laws and social practices governing education also contributed to lesser likelihood of attending college for African Americans.

Meanwhile, their white counterparts maintained employment with higher incomes, used less of their incomes for housing costs, and were able to accumulate assets in their homes to afford higher education. Even without an examination of discrimination in regard to accessing and remaining in institutions of higher education, these examples illustrate how the gap between whites and African Americans in access to higher incomes, better housing, higher education, and business ventures grew.

WHERE IS MIDDLE EAST BALTIMORE?

The part of Baltimore described as East Baltimore, approximately 300 acres, is bordered by Fayette Street on the south, Aisquith Street on the west, North Avenue on the north, and Erdman Avenue on the east. Locals, and those familiar with the neighborhoods there, also call this area historic East Baltimore. The community referred to as Middle East Baltimore, approximately 88 acres or 20 square blocks, targeted for rebuilding in 2001, sits within East Baltimore.

Several other neighborhoods or communities loosely defined by geographic boundaries also sit within East Baltimore. They include Madison East End, Broadway East, Milton-Montford, Oliver, Rose Street, McElderry, Port Street, Douglass Homes, East North Avenue, Duncan, Gay Street, Collington Square, Lakewood, Ashland, and Ashland Mews. Other, smaller communities or neighborhoods are located within these neighborhoods.

Within East Baltimore, the Middle East Baltimore community is bordered by Madison on the south, Broadway on the west, the Amtrak railroad tracks on the north, and Patterson Park on the east, as seen in figure 1.2.

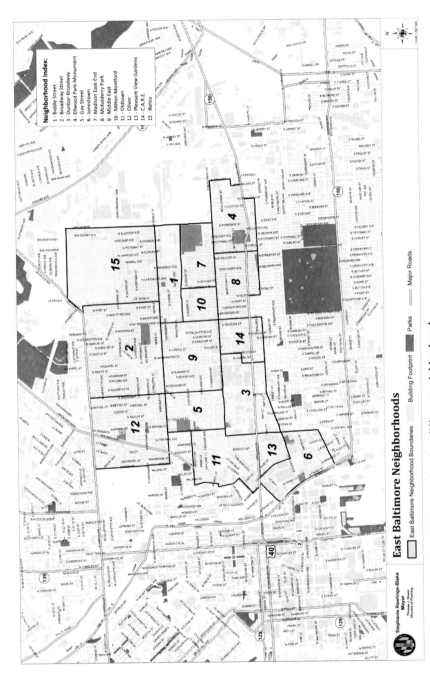

Figure 1.1. Map of East Baltimore showing different neighborhoods

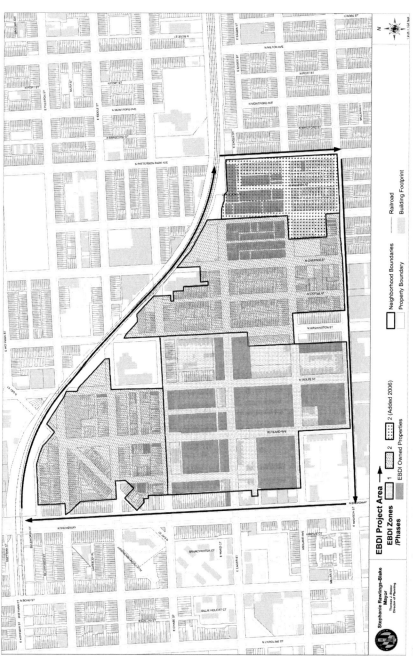

Figure 1.2. Map of East Baltimore with Middle East Baltimore and rebuilding phases highlighted

This figure also shows the proposed rebuilding area, labeled as Phase 1 and Phase 2 to illustrate the timing of community relocation, acquisition, and demolition and rebuilding of structures. In 2001, when Middle East Baltimore was targeted for rebuilding, more than 2,000 individuals and approximately more than 1000 families—approximately eight hundred households—lived there.

SOCIAL AND ECONOMIC CONDITIONS IN EAST BALTIMORE: COMING INTO THE PRESENT

In cities like Baltimore, with discriminatory governmental oversight and disinvestment, communities like East Baltimore became prone to greater poverty and abandonment by governmental services, unfair housing policy, and continued speculation.[14,15] In the early 1900s, Middle East Baltimore became one of these "planned disinvested communities," designated an urban renewal area; there were five others in the city of Baltimore alone. The United States' institutionalized pattern of racism in housing and employment in the nineteenth century guaranteed racialized urban poverty in the twenty-first century. It is the bridge that connects the century of blight of the East Baltimore of yesterday to the East Baltimore of today.

Like many cities of the United States, Baltimore lost many high-wage factory and shipyard jobs between the 1940s and the 1970s, when the national and regional economies shifted from manufacturing to services. This resulted in more white flight to the suburbs, and an increasing majority African American population in Baltimore. And its neighborhoods segregated even more along lines of race and class. Communities like East Baltimore, whose residents were primarily working class and African American, were devastated by lack of employment of their residents.

While more African Americans had bought into Middle East Baltimore, with the increasing unemployment and the high costs already discussed, they had little income left for maintenance. Renters also fared poorly, preyed upon by speculators who had seized on abandoned properties for cheap and rented high. Many unmonitored landlords took risks in renting houses that were not up to code and did little or nothing to improve the structure of the houses they rented.

Over the years, this persistent unemployment and out-migration of residents who could afford to move elsewhere resulted in increasing abandonment: by people, a tax base, and public services. A cycle of increasing numbers of vacant and abandoned houses, along with increased housing density, or crowding, of those who remained in the occupied houses, occurred.[16]

The history of racism in Maryland and Baltimore that produced the segregation of East Baltimore also ensured that the area's communities would be more prone to continued disinvestment by governmental systems in housing structures, street maintenance, school upkeep, recreational facilities and parks, community centers, and health care facilities. The churches in these neighborhoods supported low-income residents and the unemployed but could not address the systematic effects of poverty: deteriorating houses, speculation, lack of adequate public services, high rates of unemployment, inadequate opportunity for education and other services guaranteed to white and middle class neighborhoods.[17]

Between 1990 and 2000, the population in the Middle East Baltimore community had decreased by almost one-half (45 percent), the greatest decline of any part of the city of Baltimore. In 2001, the reported rate of abandoned houses in East Baltimore was 13 percent, with rates as high as 80 percent in the Middle East Baltimore community. This decrease in population left only approximately 3 out of 10 houses occupied in the Middle East Baltimore area. Walking from block to block, one could see the emptiness of the area evidenced by boarded-up and open vacant houses and trash piled high in the backyards and thrown around inside vacant houses and lots. Some compared the area to a postwar zone.

Race and class oppression had determined the health outcomes for this community—in place and people. Middle East Baltimore had many unhealthy features that are typical of disinvested and abandoned communities which increased the risk of poor health: a strong drug trade, violence from the effects of increased drug use and traffic of nonresidents buying drugs, illegal dumping, rat infestation, few or no safe places for children to play and for adults to congregate socially, no place for regular exercise, underfunded schools that could not afford to offer after school programs for children, and poorly organized residents. It had the highest rate of houses with lead-based paint in the state and the highest rate of crime in the city.

The supermarkets that stayed, and the corner groceries with their barred and caged windows for service, offered food that was least expensive and least nutritious. Liquor stores proliferated on street corners, as did the small churches, and desperate youths ruled the street. The police passed through frequently, though not frequently enough or fast enough when calls for domestic violence or theft were made. Fear was a driving energy in Middle East Baltimore, and the stress of living a daily life of poverty in these social conditions took its toll.

Middle East Baltimore residents boasted some of the worst health indicators in the United States; such indicators as death rate from HIV, homicide, accidents, diabetes, and infant mortality exceeded those in the city and the state.[18] Rates of chronic illness were high. Hypertension, coronary heart disease, strokes, asthma, lead poisoning, depression and anxiety disorders, sexually transmitted diseases, and substance abuse were at the top of the list.[19]

Currently, the legacy of disinvestment is seen in the public schools in Middle East Baltimore which enrolled more than 70 percent of children qualifying for the federally assisted free and reduced-price meals. Forty-nine percent of Middle East residents have not completed high school, compared to 25 percent in the city of Baltimore.[20]

This is also reflected in the average income of each household reported as approximately $29,0000, compared to approximately $55,000 in the city of Baltimore.[21] The rates of unemployment and underemployment in communities in East Baltimore continue to be some of the highest in the city of Baltimore. For example, 12 percent of East Baltimore residents are unemployed, compared to 6 percent in the city of Baltimore.

These conditions did not occur suddenly—acutely—in 2001. They were the signs and symptoms of a chronic life of poverty and racial discrimination and the outcomes of deep-rooted social causes of illnesses (discussed further in chapter 9). They are comparable only to the conditions in other low-income communities of color in the United States.

COMMUNITY LIFE IN MIDDLE EAST BALTIMORE

That said, Middle East Baltimore had its rituals of community life, its flow. Each day Ms. M could be seen sweeping the block across from St. Wenceslaus Church on Ashland Avenue. Two blocks down, Mr. H had bought several row houses adjoining each other, in early 1990, with the intention of opening a school for training neighborhood children in gourmet baking. On Washington Street, Mr. J and Mr. L could be seen greeting passersby going to and from work each morning and evening. Over on Caroline Street, Ms. G held meetings for those who cared to attend, a place for outsiders and residents alike to find out what was going on in the community.

Sweet Prospect Baptist Church, on North Durham Street, had a regular congregation, as did Greater New St. John Baptist Church, on Wolfe Street. There was indeed a lot of sweetness offered and received in the congregations, no discrimination. Charlie's garage, Central Auto Repair, passed on from his uncle, was the place in Middle East Baltimore to get a car repaired for cheap—until he had to close down when Johns Hopkins terminated his lease. The property remains boarded up today, 8 years later. The car wash was live on Wolfe Street, and a haircut was still $10 on Madison Street, at Razor Cutz. And every five or six blocks, snowballs—shaved ice decorated with flavored syrup—could be had to beat the heat in August.

There was community in Middle East Baltimore, amid the crime and the grime. Residents alive during the early 1900s talked nostalgically about a time when they felt safe in their neighborhood: leaving their doors unlocked, sitting outside in the dark without fear of being attacked, sitting and sleeping in nearby parks when it was too hot to be inside.

In the 1990s, there still were social networks, rooted from generations before. They ran deep and held the oral history of a people who came from the North and the South and together formed their spaces of hope. Jackie could go to work because Ms. J could watch her kids two blocks down. Ms. O, with chronic lung disease, could walk to the Northeast Market, five blocks away, resting on a stoop on each block along the way, catching her breath and chatting with her neighbors. She was known and she felt safe in her community. And there was Johnny, who would run to the store, make sure the kids didn't fight, or sweep the stoop for Ms. J on the corner.

"Damont the Dealer" said "Good morning" to Ms. J on his way to the next sale. As in many neighborhoods in similar conditions—and not so similar—some neighbors looked out for each other. Some knew when to turn their heads the other way. Some had gone to safety inside and did not know their neighbors.

Residents knew who the dealers were, who the addicts were, who had a good job with the government or worked at the "plantation" of Johns Hopkins, who the preacher and the teacher were, who could afford the rent each month and who could not. When furniture was put out on the street for late rent, there were no nods of surprise or pride, only comments of, "Hope she finds a place for those kids." There was a social network, and this allowed residents to feel safe in the midst of unsafety.

The community had adapted to the changing norms and built networks within their 88 acres. Folks would let you know in a minute that their community was neglected by the government, that outsiders had opinions about them that were wrong, and that they knew very well that each child born into the neighborhood was at risk for jail. But the perseverance and insight of the elders of the community who knew a time past which was better, and of times past that were worst, brought a commitment to surviving and thriving in the midst of challenge. Middle East Baltimore residents knew they and their ancestors had been given the scraps of the table of the United States for more than a century and learned how to make do with these scraps in hard times and reach for better when times changed.

JOHNS HOPKINS HOSPITAL

A history of Middle East Baltimore cannot be told without a discussion of its neighbor just south, the Johns Hopkins Medical Institutions.

The historical relationship between these two neighbors is an important part of this story of community rebuilding in Middle East Baltimore. In fact, the story of rebuilding Middle East Baltimore would not be a story to tell without the presence and power of this institution. Likewise, the rise to power and grandeur that this institution has accomplished has been directly and indirectly affected by who its neighbor has been over the decades: a low-income African American community.

Now known as the Johns Hopkins Medical Institutions (JHMI), the campus in East Baltimore covers more than 21 square blocks. In 1877 the philanthropic Quaker Johns Hopkins donated funds for the construction of a hospital that would serve its neighbors as well as "the indigent poor without regard to sex, age or color and without charge".[22] During the late 1800s, the area today known as Middle East Baltimore and East Baltimore was populated by new immigrants from Italy, Germany, and Poland. It was mostly a working class community, stable in its housing. Immigrant communities north of the hospital lived in clean and tidy row houses, proud of the marble steps leading to their homes.

Hopkins dictated that the hospital should be built on 13 acres of land previously housing the state mental health facility, nearly a full square block. But he died while the project was still in the planning stages. His trustees then purchased the land. They convinced several owners of adjacent property on Broadway Avenue to sell their homes, stables, and a small cemetery, thereby acquiring a full square block, a final 14.5 acres, for the construction of the hospital. This first block was bordered by Broadway Avenue on the west, Monument Street on the north, Wolfe Street on the east, and Jefferson Street on the south.

The Johns Hopkins Hospital opened in 1889 and served the communities its benefactor intended it to serve. In the early 1900s it was one of only two hospitals serving the most disenfranchised and African Americans in the city of Baltimore.

During that same period, the area just west of "Hopkins Hospital" on Wolfe and McElderry Streets was known as "the Street," with almost all resident houses hosting maids answering doors in stiffly starched uniforms. It was a social gathering space, with high tea for the families of the doctors at the hospital. Almost all the houses in this area were occupied by doctors or students of the Hopkins Hospital and schools of medicine and nursing. Many of their wives were also employed in some capacity by the Hopkins institutions.

By 1926, the hospital had expanded into its 14.5 acres with 21 structures, not including the schools of public health and medicine. That same year, it was beginning the city's largest building program, set to expand with a dormitory for nursing students and the Wilmer Institute.[23]

The year 1946 found the Johns Hopkins Hospital seeking public contribution of $3 million for two additional buildings to accommodate its increasing patient population.[24] These buildings would accommodate more moderate-income patients, who could afford to pay for services in private and semiprivate rooms, offsetting the cost of services offered at lesser cost. The institutions' officials reported that income from paying patients was not covering the cost of operating the hospital: more than 60 percent of its patients were paying less than the cost of treatment and another 30 percent were paying only the cost.

In addition to these two buildings, they planned an extensive expansion over the following 10 years, with a funding goal of $15 million in public support.[25]

Johns Hopkins' request to his trustees in 1873 detailed these instructions:

> You will also provide for the reception of a limited number of patients who are able to make compensation for the room and attention they may require. The money received from such persons will enable you to appropriate a larger sum for the relief of the sufferings of that class which I direct you to admit free of charge, and you will thus be enabled to afford to strangers, and to those of our own people who have no friends or relatives to care for them in sickness, and who are not objects of charity, the advantage of careful and skillful treatment.[26]

The hospital was attempting to fulfill its benefactor's original dictate of serving the disenfranchised.

DISPARATE GROWTH OF TWO NEIGHBORS
IN THE MIDST OF DISTRUST

The Johns Hopkins community physically located in East Baltimore is many things: community, university, corporation, complex, and medical institutions. It has continually expanded since the establishment of the first buildings in the square block that housed the hospital, an emergency care unit, and several wards. Today it stands in much grandeur in approximately 21 continuous square blocks in East Baltimore, and it includes the initial hospital; dormitories; schools of medicine, public health, and nursing; the Kennedy Krieger Institute; a children's hospital under construction; cancer centers; ambulatory care centers; an eye institute; several research and administrative buildings; a security administrative building; and parking garages: the JHMI of the twenty-first century. And now, a biotech park or life sciences building.[27]

Technically the schools of public health, medicine, and nursing—though physically located in East Baltimore—are part of the Johns Hopkins University, which is in the northern part of Baltimore city. The institution uses the term Johns Hopkins Medicine to describe all its medical enterprises under the directorship of one executive officer. According to the institution's website, these consist of "separate employers which include three acute-care hospitals, a school of medicine, 16 primary health care physician offices, home health care, health insurance administration, and an internal staffing agency." The internal staffing agency includes medicine, allied health, administration, and security services. The majority of these entities are physically located not in one area but across the state of Maryland.[28] While the schools exist physically in the medical complex of East Baltimore, each maintain separate deans and are directed by a president of the university. Two board of trustees and directors oversee the running of the JHMI and the university, with some individuals serving on both boards.

To support the growth of this institution it has expanded by slowly acquiring properties in the communities surrounding its original boundaries. This continued expansion of the institution has contributed to its being referred to by those in the neighborhoods surrounding it as "the elephant": its large size allows it the power to sit where it chooses and do what it chooses. It has also seeded and watered the fear in residents of the area, as parents and grandparents tell of "Hopkins taking the neighbor's house to pay for his hospital bill." Many residents report that "Hopkins would eventually take the land, one way or the other . . . you can't fight them." At the time of the announcement of plans to rebuild the 88 acres just north of the JHMI in 2001, the institution owned more than 100 of the approximately 1,000 vacant or abandoned properties on that land.

While this grand institution of health care teaching and services has continued to grow and to expand its mission, its neighbor to the north has continued to deteriorate in housing, services, employment, and safety. The stark inverse relationship between these neighbors, one growing rich and one growing poor, has contributed to the history of mistrust by the community.

Residents and businesses in East Baltimore question whether JHMI would have been able to continuously expand if its neighbors were more economically stable. Would it have been so easy to acquire the land of middle class, upper middle class, and white citizens? Residents of Middle East Baltimore feel strongly that "They do it because they can, because we're poor and we're black." The JHMI's continued acquisition of property during the times of in- and out-migration of residents in East Baltimore has facilitated the institution's movement into the surrounding communities. Residents of past years report how "the man from Hopkins" would come to ask about buying a neighbor's or family's house nearby. That it acquired 100 of the 1,000 vacant houses planned for demolition in the first 33 acres of the current rebuilding effort supports such claims.

It is clear that to grow from 1 square block to 21 square blocks the institution must have acquired property, through either direct purchase or government-assisted acquisition of land for its rebuilding efforts (this will be discussed in chapter 2). This powerful institution's bridging relationships, public-private partnerships, with governmental and political leaders have directly and indirectly supported the growth of the institution.[29] That the diminishing community of Middle East Baltimore and East Baltimore has not had similar ties is a legacy of the discriminatory real estate practices and public policy and services of Baltimore.

The assets set forth to establish the institution were gained through a legacy of separate and unequal laws and covenants. Its continued expansion has been supported directly and indirectly through its relationships with other powerful stakeholders in Baltimore, in Maryland, and across the United States. These relationships of social networks are the result and fuel of continued asset development: powerful people know other powerful people. High level executives of the Johns Hopkins Institutions sit on boards of banks, private financial and other investment corporations, nonprofits, foundations, development, insurance and law firms, and public contracted economic and community development corporations.

Besides the continued fear they will eventually lose their homes, East Baltimore residents report other reasons for distrust of their medical neighbor. Residents today tell stories, whether myth or reality, of experimentation by the institution on their neighbors, and they remain distrustful of the institution for medical services. The well-known Tuskegee Study (1932–1972), in which African American men with syphilis remained untreated with the most appropriate treatment of that time, so researchers could discover the cause and cure of the disease, is an example of the types of racist practices in health care and research that have plagued the relationship between East Baltimore residents and the JHMI.[30] The 2001 judgment by Maryland's Court of Appeals comparing a lead-based paint study, conducted by JHMI on children in East and West Baltimore, to the Tuskegee Study add to this distrust of their neighbor.[31]

Residents in East Baltimore report stories told by their parents or grandparents, of going to the hospital and not receiving any care, but just "being watched like they did them in Alabama." Others report stories of having relatives who went to the hospital in good health dying or not returning. Children were warned to stay clear of the hospital after dark for fear that the "researchers" would "take them for experiments." There was even a van seen regularly at night, making the rounds to "pick up anyone looking drunk and take them back to the hospital."

The recent book documenting that cancer cells from an African American woman in Baltimore were used, without consent from her or her family, by researchers at Johns Hopkins Hospital has not diluted the fears of unethical practices. Today these cells remain one of the cell lines most used to study vaccines, infectious diseases, cancer, and pharmacological agents.[32] These stories, some proven and some not, continue to nurture the community's deep-seated distrust of its powerful neighbor. Even while many residents of East Baltimore seek health care from the hospital and its many affiliates, some say "I rather go across town than there."

Adding to this history of distrust is the continued use of the communities of East Baltimore to study new treatments for diseases without providing information on research findings to the participants. Residents have continuously complained that "They just take your blood and tell you nothing." Others report going for treatment for high blood pressure or diabetes for 6 months, "then nothing, no call, no paper, no nothing . . . they done their study." These ways of doing research in East Baltimore have left residents feeling "On my body they teach their fancy students." In light of a history of growing separation, trust has not been easy to grow in these circumstances.

Having a community nearby who could be easily accessed to study diseases, without having to provide long-term services, has been a benefit to the JHMI. Having a renowned teaching hospital nearby, where they could access state-of-the-art medical care by some of the brightest minds in medicine and public health, has been a benefit to residents of East Baltimore.

While the JHMI has benefited from its neighbors, it has also benefited them, as Johns Hopkins intended it to. From its inception, it has continuously served its neighbors, initially white, working class immigrants, then middle-income and low-income working class African Americans, and now primarily low-income and working class and uninsured or underinsured African Americans. Available data for Johns Hopkins Hospital revenue and costs in shown in table 1.2 and dollars spent by the Johns Hopkins Hospital for community services are shown in table 1.1.

Employees and students of the medical institutions volunteer throughout the year for different services in the community. The JHMI has also been the biggest employer in Maryland. And, as it grows, it remains a major employer in Baltimore, employing residents from the East Baltimore community.

In regard to its formal educational benefits, there has been no record of residents of East Baltimore entering or graduating from the university.

While hospitals in general offer ready access for health care to its neighbors, when its neighbors are primarily poor this poses a challenge. Medicaid reimbursement decreased in the 1970s and resulted in hospitals serving a large percentage of unemployed and low income populations with Medicaid, no insurance, or insufficient insurance being challenged financially. The future remains uncertain as to how

Table 1.1. Johns Hopkins Hospital community benefit activities 2009

Community Benefit Activities	U.S. Dollars
Community Health Services	$5,534,085
Medical Education	78,228,639
Mission-Driven Health Services	18,428,285
Research	75,000
Financial Contribution	1,070,637
Community Building Activities	4,740,002
Community Benefit Operations	228,061
Charity Care*	37,024,000
Total	$145,328,709

*Number of cases = 33,740
Source www.hopkinsmedicine.org

continued changes in medical reimbursement and public cuts to social programs will affect the viability of such hospitals when other sources of income are not present.[33] Hospitals like JHMI had to make decisions in regard to surrounding itself by majority poor and low-income communities who received health services through Medicaid insurance or were uninsured. In response to this, one solution is for the hospital to change its location to another setting where they are not surrounded by neighborhoods with high poverty and high Medicaid insurance. The other is to change the currently surrounding community so it is not majority poor. The JHMI choose to do the latter and with support of city and state government has consistently moved towards gentrification or changing its surrounding neighbors to a more gentried class.[34] The city and state government would be challenged if the largest employer and financial contributor in Baltimore city relocated itself into the county.

Another neighborhood effect of hospitals is their impact on the physical environment. Increasing expansion of institutions like JHMI result in increased traffic patterns affecting the quality of life for local residents and business. Constant traffic noise and movement diminishes the quality of life and makes it unsafe for children to play on streets in front of their homes. In neighborhoods like East Baltimore with unsafe playgrounds and a lack of adequate recreational facilities, this poses a regular challenge for local residents. Due to the the increased number of workers at hospitals, greater competition for parking and greater surveillance for parking violations occur which poses a daily nuisance to local residents. The nature and height of the physical structures often block sunlight from neighbors resulting in increased heating bills in the winter and lack of gardening in the summer.[35] The tunneling effect of wind forced to find a path between tall structures also causes homes to experience colder temperatures in the winter and increased energy cost. The presence of lights from hospitals and its facilities results in neighboring homes having lights continuously interrupting their night time sleep. During construction of new hospital buildings the continuous dust and debris pose a health risk and without preventive measures

Table 1.2. Johns Hopkins Hospital health services cost 2007– 2008

	2007		2008	
	Johns Hopkins Hospital	State Average[6]	Johns Hopkins Hospital	State Average
Net Operating Revenue[1] ($)	1,241,915,775	203,732,785	1,336,839,058	218,251,804
Uncompensated care rate[2] (%)	6.58	8.07	6.87	8.29
Operating Profit (Loss)[3] ($)	35,167,112	6,716,479	42,215,610	5,526,568
Non-operating Profit (Loss)[4] ($)	25,451,783	5,171	27,432,276	-2,313
Revenue per admission[5] ($)	21,531	11,742	22,700	12,221

[1]Total of net patient revenue plus other operating revenue, not-collected debt or charity care
[2]Uncompensated care includes charity and bad or uncollected debts. The rate is calculated by dividing the gross regulated operational revenues by the cost of charity and/or bad debts. Gross operational revenues include net operating revenues plus cost of charity and bad debts. JHH ranked 22nd and 23rd (out of 31 hospitals in the metropolitan areas of Maryland) in uncompensated care in 2007 and 2008 respectively
[3]Profit or loss from the normal occurring regulated and unregulated operations; JHH reported the highest Profit/loss of all Maryland hospitals for both years
[4]Investment incomes, extraordinary gains, research and other non-operating gains or losses; JHH reported the highest non-operating profit/loss of all Maryland hospitals
[5]JHH reported the 4th (out of 49 Maryland hospitals) highest revenue per admission for both years
[6]State average is determined by dividing the state totals in each category by the number of hospitals used to generate the sum total.
Sources:"Disclosure of Hospital Financial and statistical information for hospitals with fiscal year ending June 30, 2008, August 31, 2008, December 31, 2008". Health Services Cost Review Commission. July 1, 2009
http://www.hscrc.state.md.us/documents/Hospitals/ReportsFinancial/ Accessed January 2011.
http://www.hscrc.state.md.us/documents/HSCRC_PolicyDocumentsReports/AnnualReports/Disclosure/HSCRC_DisclosureReport-FY08.pdf Accessed January 2011

can result in exacerbation of chronic lung diseases, allergies, and greater rodent and insect infestation. These neighborhood effects of a hospital or medical institution's presence are reminders of the challenge to current and future local residents who must live next door to future expansions.

SEPARATE AND UNEQUAL: CAUSE AND CONSEQUENCE OF DISPARATE COMMUNITY CHANGE

Still, while the hospital has grown to be the most prestigious hospital in the nation and has ranked at the top of its class for 10 years in a row, the surrounding communities have grown poorer in wealth and health, with some of the most severe indicators of poor health in the state and the country.[7] Why this disparity between these two neighbors? It is clear that communities do not exist in isolation, little islands onto themselves, separate from their neighbors. While communities may have clear physical boundaries, and inhabitants that can be defined and identified by different social and economic aspects such as race, education, job status and income, health status, lifestyle and behaviors, and other determinants, they still exist relative to each other. This is the case in East Baltimore. The Middle East community and the Johns Hopkins medical community are geographic neighbors within East Baltimore and can be clearly distinguished as being different from each other: the two extremes of the social and economic characteristics of society.

To the superficial and unknowing eye, they would appear to be on separate paths of their own doing. A keener eye would delineate the contrast in the growth of strong bridging public-private relationships this powerful institution has with government and generous private benefactors and the growth in weak bridging relationships the neighboring poor African American communities have with the same government and wealthy benefactors over time. Through the means that government provides— the subsidies, tax-credit status, and acquisition of land—this private institution can continue to expand and accumulate wealth and benefit unequally.

These inverse relationships, though seemingly disconnected, are not separate in the matrix of power acquiring more power while the disenfranchised continuously lose what little they have; one grows at the expense of the other, widening the gap of rich and poor. The history of race and class segregation and the laws and practices in real estate, housing, employment, education, and health care established the conditions necessary for creating separate and unequal communities. These laws directed and interpreted the way that African Americans and whites should live separately from each other even while equality in the school structures, houses, hospital services, and employment did not exist: in the past and the present.[36] Such understanding, supported by law and practices, rooted the norms of a society that segregation was okay even while it turned its eyes on the unequal legacy of such separation.

This acceptance in a history of inequality has offered present-day society many blind spots in critically assessing the effects of racism and classism in creating and rebuilding poor communities today. Acknowledging this unjust history would introduce a fragmentation to the accepted norm by the white and privileged majority that the outcome of these laws contradicted the constitutional rights of all Americans for equal opportunity and access. This false truth of separate and equal allowed growth of two very different types of neighboring communities in East Baltimore without concern for this growing inequality.

The greater the perceived difference in these neighboring communities, the easier it is to separate the expectations of each and assume that those with power and wealth should determine the outcome of communities they do not live within or know. This paternalistic attitude drives the process of rebuilding abandoned and disempowered communities and assures that those with power and privilege acquire what they perceive is equal benefit, reminiscent of the law of the land started during the Jim Crow era. As in the rebuilding of East Baltimore over the years, the abandoned community is provided minimal if any benefit and this is perceived as consistent with the illusion of separate and equal: why change now?

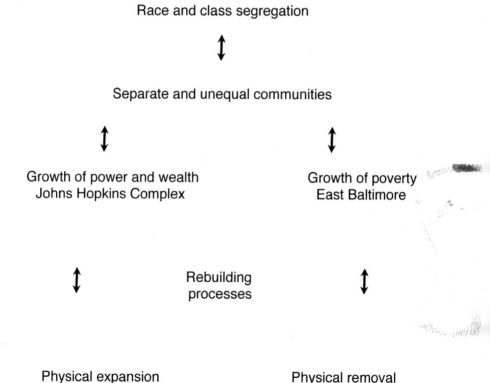

Figure 1.3. **Historic and current rebuilding practices**

Cushioned within a larger economic system of capitalism, powerful institutions maintain individual power through growth and competition by exploitation of the less powerful. The resultant disempowered communities from past segregation, strong public-private partnerships, and paternalistic and oppressive non-community participatory rebuilding practices continue to be the perfect fuel for continued growth of more powerful institutions like JHMI.

Figure 1.3 shows a diagram of how this relationship continues the cycle of power and wealth disparity and segregation. The continued dispossession of low income communities, through displacement into other communities of disinvestment, continues the cycle of segregating the disempowered and recreating deteriorated and unhealthy places to live, work, worship, and play.[37]

The next chapter will provide specific examples of this type of exploitation in community development and displacement in East Baltimore.

NOTES

1. Olson SH. (1997) *Baltimore: The Building of an American City.* The Johns Hopkins University Press. Baltimore, MD.

2. Hesseltine WB. (1962) *The Tragic Conflict: The Civil War and Reconstruction.* George Braziller, NY.

3. Pietila A. (2010) *Not in My Neighborhood: How Bigotry Shaped a Great American City.* Ivan R. Dee, Chicago.

4. Olson SH. (1997) *Baltimore: The Building of an American City.*

5. *Baltimore Sun.* July 9, 1929. "Across town."

6. Olson SH. (1997) *Baltimore: The Building of an American City.*

7. Olson SH. (1997) *Baltimore: The Building of an American City.*

8. Olson SH. (1997) *Baltimore: The Building of an American City.*

9. Pietila A. (2010) *Not in My Neighborhood.*

10. Olson SH. (1997) *Baltimore: The Building of an American City.*

11. *New York Times.* 1910. "Baltimore tries drastic plan of race segregation."

12. Pietila A. (2010) *Not in My Neighborhood.*

13. Harvey D. (2000) *Spaces of hope.* U California Press, CA.

14. Pietila A. (2010) *Not in My Neighborhood.*

15. Harvey D. (2000) *Spaces of hope.*

16. Harvey D. (2000) *Spaces of hope.*

17. Harvey D. (2000) *Spaces of hope.*

18. Gomez MB, Muntaner C. (2005) "Urban redevelopment and neighborhood health in East Baltimore, Maryland: The role of institutional and communitarian social capital." *J Critical Public Health.* 15:83.

19. Gomez MB, Muntaner C. (2005) "Urban redevelopment and neighborhood health in East Baltimore, Maryland."

20. EBDI. (2009) "The Workforce supply and demand characteristics of the East Baltimore Development Inc. redevelopment effort."

21. EBDI. (2009) "The Workforce supply and demand characteristics of the East Baltimore Development Inc. redevelopment effort."

22. Chesney AM. (1943) *The Johns Hopkins Hospital and the Johns Hopkins University School of Medicine. Vol 1. 1887–1888.* Johns Hopkins University Press, Baltimore, MD.

23. Power Pictorial & Gas Graphic #6. April 1926.

24. *Baltimore Sun.* November 18, 1945. "Hopkins hospital seeks $3,000,000."

25. *Baltimore Sun.* November 18, 1945.

26. Chesney AM. (1943) *The Johns Hopkins Hospital and the Johns Hopkins University School of Medicine.*

27. www.hopkinsmedicine.org/about "About Johns Hopkins Medicine." Accessed June 2011.

28. www.hopkinsmedicine.org/about. Accessed November 2010.

29. *Indypendent Reader.* Summer 2006. "#1 Baltimore: A conversation between David Harvey and Marisela Gomez."

30. Centers for Disease Control. "U.S. Public Health Service Syphilis study at Tuskegee." www.cdc.gov/tuskegee/timeline.htm. Accessed March 2011.

31. *Washington Post.* August 24, 2001. "My kids were used as guinea pigs." www.gwu.edu/~pad/202/readings/lead-hopkins.htm. Accessed November 2010.

32. Skloot R. (2010) *The Immortal Life of Henrietta Lacks.* 2010. Random House, New York.

33. Bostic RW, Lewis LV, Sloane DC. (2006) *The Neighborhood Dynamics of Hospitals as Large Landowners.* community-wealth.com/_pdfs/articles-publications/anchors/. Accessed March 2011.

34. *Indypendent Reader.* Summer 2006. "#1 Baltimore: A conversation between David Harvey and Marisela Gomez."

35. *Philadelphia Neighborhoods.* March 4, 2010. "Nicetown-Tioga: Temple hospital changed the neighborhood and not necessarily for the better." sct.temple.edu/blogs/murl/2010/03/04/nicetown. Accessed March 2011.

36. Brown NLM, Stentiford BM. (2008) *The Jim Crow Encyclopedia: Greenwood Milestones in African American History. Vol 2.* Greenwood Press, San Francisco, CA.

37. Wallace R, Fullilove MT. (2008) *Collective Consciousness and Its Discontents: Institutional Distributed Cognition, Racial Policy and Public Health in the United States.* Springer, NY.

2

East Baltimore's Community
Rebuilding History:
Abandonment and Displacement

"The City [government] does not have a tradition of doing a bottom-up approach but only a top-down approach; to change this mindset is revolutionary and is what inspired the movement of the Civil Rights time . . . breaking that pattern is what brings in transformation, a bottom-up approach." —East Baltimore stakeholder

"Apartheid results in the loss of the collective memory." —Nelson Mandela

This chapter describes growth of communities of blight in Baltimore and East Baltimore and the beginning of large-scale city-led community development and displacement in East Baltimore. The development of the Johns Hopkins Institutions are described followed by examples of two major city-led community development projects in the 1950s and 1960s. It introduces the current 2001 rebuilding project and discusses how these three community development initiatives are similar and different and why.

ABANDONMENT, GROWTH, AND DISPLACEMENT: BALTIMORE SETS THE STANDARDS OF COMMUNITY REBUILDING IN THE EARLY 1900S

In early 1900s Baltimore, when businesses required space for expansion, such as for railroad warehouses, African Americans living nearby were forced to move—at times, 200 or more households.[1] Those doing the displacing did nothing to identify or construct new houses for these displaced families, and no laws or housing policy were in place to address this injustice.

No new subdivisions or houses for African Americans were being built during this period when the social factors discussed earlier were increasing the ghettoization of living for African Americans. There was no relocation plan or community participation in deciding how families would be accommodated. There was no due process of inclusiveness. Instead, a legal and tightly enforced process for exclusion of African Americans in the city was another of the factors that produced the high population density, cramped spaces, poor housing conditions, and insufficient resources that became the norm in many primarily African American communities in early 1900s Baltimore.

By the 1930s, the problem of blight and slum neighborhoods became increasingly clear as institutionalized and individual racist and classist practices continued to shape those communities. Poor and overcrowded communities existed before many African Americans moved to Baltimore. And blight was present in all communities that had little or no income, unreliable employment, and insufficient city and state resources to maintain adequate services. But the term quickly became synonymous with the African American neighborhoods blighted by the factors that sank them into poverty and abandonment.

And, just as quickly, "slum" and "blight" came to be associated not only with the places, but also the people living in these neighborhoods. It was socially acceptable to attribute "slum" and "decay" as inherent characteristics of being African American which would naturally result in the communities they inhabited becoming slums and decayed. This convenient assumption allowed the growing inequality of segregation to be ignored and instead blamed the victims of these laws, policies, and practices. Residents of segregated disinvested and abandoned African American communities were exemplified as the cause of the social conditions, inseparable from the consequent of unfair institutional policies of segregation, housing inspection, health services, employment, pest control, transportation and voting rights. This accepted and racist belief system continues today with current residents of communities like East Baltimore still blamed for the demise of their communities.

By 1934, a housing study for the Real Estate Board declared six areas as "blight" in the city of Baltimore, each 35 to 60 acres.[2,3,4] The majority in each of these communities was African American families. Within these neighborhoods labeled blighted, 50,000 houses were determined to be in violation of the housing code. The study recommended that such areas be demolished or thinned out through targeted block redevelopment. In 1947, eight areas in the city were identified to undergo possible redevelopment.[5] By the 1950s, 55,000 houses were recorded as substandard in Baltimore. Six years later, after a "slum clearance program," the total number of substandard houses remained at 55,000, with an additional 78,000 predicted to require some type of rehabilitation within the following 20 years. These slum areas housed 350,000 people, with increasing numbers projected as the postwar and industrialization of agriculture, particularly in the southern states, resulted in continued migration of whites and African Americans.

In 1957, the Baltimore Urban Renewal and Housing Agency was formed and charged with the administration of an urban renewal program targeting three of those six previously established areas in need of renewal. These three urban renewal areas encompassed approximately 45 percent of the area of Baltimore. The agency's goal was to complete these renewals in 20 years, at a cost of $900 million. East Baltimore was included in this plan.

This bold plan called for greater input from residents than earlier plans did. But during the period of the first renewal projects it became clear that residents were seldom informed or sought out for their input. And the provision of adequate houses for African Americans was poorly planned, which often resulted in shortage for them and other low-income residents in the renewal areas—or anywhere else.

Racial discrimination in renewal or rebuilding efforts was becoming clearer, as described by one historian in a series by the Catholic Reporter:

> There's not much, legally, that the housing agency can do about this. The private developer can simply state that the Negro families were out of his price range and he is not to blame for that. . . . Frankly, this is another way of pointing to the complicated racial problems which have been injected into the general problem of urban renewal. . . . We will have to change our thinking a great measure if this particular facet of the problem is to be solved. Greater living space will have to be provided in the center of the city. Living space, housing, which will have to be unrestricted—in a sense a free market open to both Negro and White. Financing for this housing will have to be provided on equal terms without consideration of color.[6]

THE MAJOR DEVELOPER IN EAST BALTIMORE: JOHNS HOPKINS HOSPITAL, 1912–1950'S

The expansion of the Johns Hopkins Hospital and its medical institutions offers one model of community rebuilding in East Baltimore. The community of Johns Hopkins was never deemed "a slum," "blighted," or "in need of clearance." In fact, its rebuilding was based on its desire for more space, to enlarge itself and its mission. The Johns Hopkins community was regularly declaring the importance of its role locally and the growth of its role in the international community and the world, in the fields of research, public health and preventive and curative medicine.

In 1935, the Johns Hopkins Hospital began a campaign of soliciting public assistance to raise $200,000 to accommodate the cost of health care it offered to the "poor" of Baltimore and Maryland. Numerous stories supporting this solicitation were published in a local newspaper, detailing the large debt that was being incurred due to the charitable care it offered to the citizens of Baltimore. The language of the solicitation pamphlet directly called on the public of Baltimore to support its "responsibility to the hospital."[7]

Again in 1945, Hopkins looked to the public to finance the building of two structures in addition to its existing facilities. This time the amount the fundraising campaign asked for was $3 million through direct pleas in the newspaper: "Solicitation of funds for a $3,000,000 building program at the Johns Hopkins Hospital, which will reach its climax in a general public appeal next June, already has begun among large corporations and individuals interested in the hospital . . . , chairman of the board of trustees, said yesterday."[8]

In addition to this campaign for $3 million, the chairman announced that the hospital would seek a total of $15 million over the next 10 years for continuing expansion. By June 1946, a final plea printed in the Baltimore Sun on behalf of the president of the board of trustees of the hospital reminded the public, "Well-being is the universal desire of men and all must share in the processes which combine to achieve it, because all are beneficiaries of it." The hospital's trustees publicly announced the need for renovation of obsolete buildings and expansion of new buildings with such explanations as, "There must continue to be growth at Johns Hopkins Hospital because it is a vital force in our community and in the nation."[9]

Another reason offered for why the public should support the hospital was its increasing debt resulting from its service to the poor and needy of Baltimore. The new buildings would accommodate a growing "paying" patient population and offset these increasing debts. A brochure issued in connection with the campaign pointed out that "support of the hospital appeal has a vital bearing upon the community's health problems".[10] Within 1 year after the announcement of its campaign, it had raised more than half of its targeted amount. In 1951, construction began for the second building of the $3 million campaign.[11]

By 1953, Johns Hopkins's physical presence had expanded from one square block housing a hospital, in 1889, to eight square blocks that contained nine additional specialty buildings or clinics; schools of hygiene, medicine, and nursing; and a dormitory with more than 300 separate rooms for nursing students.[12] Since the construction of the nurses' dormitory in the late 1930s, several additions had been built onto the original. The majority of the cost for the expansion since then was contributed by the federal government—$97,000—the remaining contributed by Johns Hopkins Hospital—$20,000.[13]

In 1957, plans were publicized for a new research building on the northeastern boundaries of Johns Hopkins Hospital, the $5 million cost "financed almost entirely by governmental and private gifts."[14] Alongside these plans were announcements of construction of a children's medical center. The path of growth and power for this prestigious health and research institution was clear, consistent, and supported by the public and wealthy private communities (as seen in figure 2.1).

BROADWAY REDEVELOPMENT PROJECT IN EAST BALTIMORE: 1950–1961

Before the 1957 Urban Renewal plan was enacted, two areas were undergoing redevelopment after the Baltimore Redevelopment Commission designated them areas

Figure 2.1. Johns Hopkins past and present

2.1a.   1885. Land bought by Johns Hopkins for hospital construction

2.1b.   1889. Johns Hopkins Hospital

Hopkins' changing footprint

Johns Hopkins buildings and
their dates of construction:

Buildings to be demolished

Meyer psychology, neurology 1982

Nelson/Harvey, general patient beds 1977

Phipps 1913

MRI, radiology 1984

Laundry

Broadway garage

Pathology, clinical labs 1923

Weinburg, cancer 2001

Carnegie, operating rooms 1927

Jefferson St. building

Blalock, operating rooms 1954

Brady 1915

Park, emergency pediatrics 1973

Maumenee, eye 1981

Children's Center, pediatrics 1961

Marburg, urology 1889

Billings 1889

Wilmer, eye 1889

Woods, eye 1959

Note: Many buildings, including those without other labels, contain administration and research labs.

North Castle St.

East McGerry

East Jefferson St.

North Washington St.

Fayette St.

Fairmount St.

North Wolfe St.

Future children's community health center

Ann St.

Children's tower

Public health

New parking deck, loading dock, power plant

Broadway

Medical school

Detail above

Weinberg building (cancer center)

Planned patient and family pavilion

Medical school

Cardiovascular, Critical Care tower

East Orleans St.

Broadway Overlook Housing

Bond St.

Research, present and future

Fayette St.

Research

Outpatient center

North Caroline St.

Public health

Research, present and future

Pratt Library (to be built by Hopkins)

Medical school

East Madison St.

East Monument St.

Garage

Dumbar High School

Baltimore City

Map area

Source: Sun research
SUN STAFF

2.1c. 2004. Johns Hopkins Medical Institutions

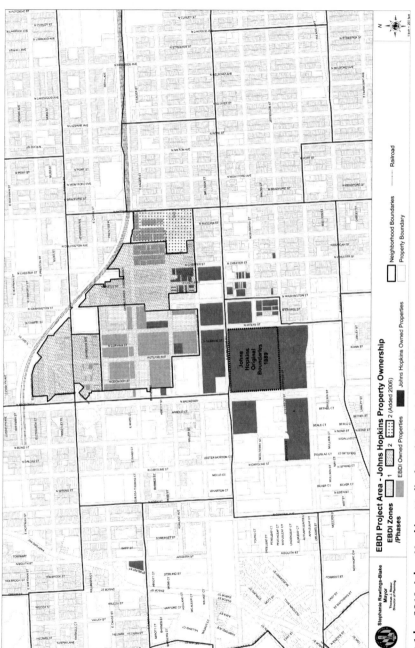

2.1d. 2010, Johns Hopkins Medical Institutions in East Baltimore

"acutely in need of corrective treatment" and "slum-clearance projects." An additional 9 areas were "designated as areas in need of corrective treatment."[15] Both projects had displaced African American residents without relocating them back to the redeveloped area. One was the Waverly community, and the other was the Broadway area, termed the Broadway Redevelopment Project, just west of the Johns Hopkins Hospital. In both, the majority of displaced residents was African American: 75 percent in Waverly, 90 percent in Broadway Redevelopment Project. These residents had no opportunity to return to the redeveloped area.

The 1950s redevelopment in the Broadway neighborhood followed patterns similar to those of the current development in Middle East Baltimore. Then, the 39 acres were home to 1,062 families, 90 percent of whom were African American. The initial plan called for extensive clearance, including all dwellings. Remaining would be a high school, Chick Webb Recreation Center, the Colored People's First Baptist Church, and the residence hall of the Johns Hopkins Hospital School of Nursing.

According to a newspaper account, the mayor supported the plan and called for ready approval, pointing to "the pressing problem of the spreading blight in the city, and the opportunity to relieve some housing problems of the Hopkins Hospital and Medical School".[16] The plans gave the developer approval to accommodate the residential needs of the Johns Hopkins Hospital and medical campus in the area directly facing the hospital, between Broadway Avenue and Caroline Street.

However, the original plan presented by the city of Baltimore for the Broadway Redevelopment project did not boldly proclaim it was a plan to accommodate the needs of the Johns Hopkins Hospital. The original housing plan approved in early 1950 for this Broadway Redevelopment project dictated housing as follows: "328 for white families, 178 for Negroes." Included in these numbers were dormitories for 250 "Hopkins students." This plan was the first time that "new apartment buildings of modern construction had been offered to Negroes in the city of Baltimore." The chairman of the Redevelopment Commission stated, "If this 'experiment' is successful . . . it can be repeated in other redevelopment areas later".[17]

Three years after approval of this original plan by the Planning Commission, after relocation of more than 1,000 families and demolition of 800 buildings (as seen in figure 2.2), it was announced that financing was not available for affordable residential construction for the historic residents of the Broadway Redevelopment Project—for neither whites nor African Americans.

The cleared land sat vacant for 4 years, until the city Planning Commission produced and voted on a revised plan in 1955 (as seen in figure 2.3a). The federal government approved that plan for funding in 1956.[18]

The new, 1955 plan for the Broadway Redevelopment Project deviated substantially from the initial plan approved by the city council in 1950.[19] The African American community voiced its disapproval of the new plan, which provided no new residences for them.[20] All the residences were being constructed to serve the Johns Hopkins community. When community members criticized this lack of adequate housing for displaced residents, various city agencies responded that they had no

Figure 2.2.   Historic residents relocate to accommodate changing plans, 1955

control over who the private developer chose to sell or rent to. In the case of the 39 acres of the Broadway Redevelopment Project, the developer—Johns Hopkins—controlled the housing redevelopment, and the resulting housing was affordable only to medical and nursing students and staff.

The historic merchant community also protested the new plan, which differed significantly from the initial plan proposing 12,000 feet of stores, "to serve the Negro garden apartment development." The 1,160 families of potential customers were moved out and, though initially promised a right of return, would not be returning due to lack of accommodations. Instead, a new retail shopping center was proposed, to serve the needs of the expanding Hopkins community.[21]

Response to these protests came from the bankers unwilling to finance the new plan because of the major changes that had occurred over the previous 5 years. They stated, "the city had changed the street pattern in the area, and obtaining federal financing for rental apartments for 'whites or Negroes' was impossible."[22] These were the publicly stated reasons for changing the initial housing plan for the Broadway Redevelopment Project. The result of the change was that developers would purchase land, build on it, and rent and sell the buildings in accordance with what the market was willing to pay, driving the design of a new plan. The free market then was driven by those who could afford the cost of the new housing. One newspaper reported the

Figure 2.3a. Past: Broadway Redevelopment Project with cleared land sits for 4 years, 1954–1958

Figure2.3b. Present: Cleared land sits in East Baltimore development after displacement and demolition, 4 years, 2008–2011

changes in the plan as follows: "One large section is to be relinquished by the developer to Johns Hopkins, for development by Johns Hopkins itself with substantial loss of taxable basis to the city. . . . The fact is that the plan formally agreed to and approved, and on the basis of which the city spent $4,412,000, has been junked, and that after all these years there is still no substitute."[23]

The new plan was amended twice before it was made public and the city declared its role in it completed in 1959.[24] The scale of the project had increased from 39 acres to 54 acres after the city of Baltimore relocated the residents of, acquired, and demolished two more blocks of homes—for resale to Johns Hopkins Hospital for its future development—demolished an armory, widened two streets, and closed one street.[25] The budget for the revised and final plan had gained $3.5 million in support from the federal government—totaling, after a 9-year process, $5.4 million. The city government contributed more than $1.5 million; the remainder came from sale of properties to the local urban renewal agency.[26] The mayor reported, "The new structures will replace one of our worst slum areas with necessary facilities servicing the world-renowned Johns Hopkins medical institutions and a community center for East Baltimore that will improve the living environment".[27] Figure 2.4 shows the ground-breaking ceremony for the new student complex, supported by the Johns Hopkins representatives, the developer, the mayor, and other government officials.

Figure 2.4. Breaking ground for the construction of a dormitory for Johns Hopkins medical students (1956) on the land previously intended for new housing for historic residents

The final construction of buildings in the Broadway Redevelopment Project was projected for completion in 1961.[28] In total, it produced a residence hall for Hopkins' unmarried house staff and students, the Broadway Shopping Center, the Baltimore-Sheraton Inn—built primarily for the families of out-of-town patients treated at the hospital—an 11-story medical office building containing 150 apartments and professional offices, the Eastern Health District Building, a new elementary school, expansion of the play area of Dunbar High School, two newly constructed churches—Church of Our Savior and St. Philip's Lutheran Church—and a new parish hall annexed to the Colored People's First Baptist Church.[29]

It remains unclear whether there ever was any intention to fulfill the original plan to accommodate the historic residents of the area. Residents of East Baltimore today remember this project and refer to it as "the same ole Hopkins land-grab going on today" (figure 2.3b). In the Johns Hopkins Magazine, in 1952, it was made clear that the planned redevelopment of the Broadway community was not intended to meet the needs of the existing poor and African American residents of the "slums." Instead, it says, this was the intention from the beginning: "The Hopkins-Broadway project is, therefore, planned primarily to be a residential campus for Baltimore's world famous medical center" and "deterioration of the neighborhood surrounding hospital and school could have serious effect upon their prestige."[30]

In an effort to inform the planned Hopkins expansion, in the Broadway Redevelopment Project, surveys were conducted within the Johns Hopkins community to assess the housing, entertainment, shopping, dining, and other social needs of permanent staff, student body, and visitors. No surveying of the community of primarily poor and African American residents and their merchants occurred before or after the initial plan was put together for this project. The rebuilding effort aimed to remove the blight—of people and place—from the Johns Hopkins community's sight. What it did was allow public dollars, public policy, and private power to concentrate poverty even more, just out of sight of the expanding powerful institution.

GAY STREET I PROJECT IN EAST BALTIMORE: 1965–1975

The neighborhoods in East Baltimore continued to deteriorate, boarded-up houses increased, and urban renewal targeted the Gay Street community in 1963.[31] The sting from the Baltimore Redevelopment Project remained fresh and activated residents to organize for decision making and control of the rebuilding process. The Gay Street I Urban Renewal Project began its planning process for this 20-block area in 1964. The Baltimore Urban Renewal Agency worked with residents from the area to learn what they wanted to see in rebuilding their neighborhood, how to demolish as few houses as possible so as to displace fewer people, and how to build affordable houses in the neighborhood to allow people who chose to stay in the neighborhood to do so with just one relocation.

Figure 2.5. The "Compound": housing for Johns Hopkins Medical Institutions' community built on land where local residents were displaced during 1950s urban renewal project.

This area of East Baltimore sat at what was then the northwest boundary of the JHMI. The residents were still angered by the results of the Broadway Redevelopment Project, which area residents called "The Compound" because a high fence had been erected around it "as protection from vandals" (figure 2.5).[32]

Today residents in the Middle East Baltimore community still remember "The Compound" and the hurt it caused them to have their neighborhood taken from them and then to be prohibited from walking through the area where they used to live. The Urban Renewal Agency, also feeling the sting from the recent renewal project in East Baltimore, declared it had learned a lesson from the Broadway Redevelopment Project and other projects, that urban renewal "must be about people, as well as buildings." It determined that this new project would be a "people-run" project.[33]

The Gay Street I project began early to seek out resident participation in and ownership of the redevelopment process. Community residents became active in the planning process individually and collectively after forming an association, the Citizens for Fair Housing (CFFH), which took the lead in working with city planners, developers, and other government agencies. Two years earlier, its predecessors, the Congress of Racial Equality and the local Community Action Agency, had started to bring attention to the deteriorated housing conditions in the area. Residents of the area, later organized as CFFH, participated in designing and carrying out surveys of the area's needs, seeking information on housing expenses, income, education, employment status, age, attitudes and physical conditions of the area's current residents.

Using these results, planners and developers hired by the city completed an initial plan in 1967.[34] In initial meetings, residents voiced their fears and demanded that city planners stop JHMI from taking over their community:

> Calling the Johns Hopkins Hospital an "oasis" [one resident declared] "Our fear is Johns Hopkins—that's our ultimate fear." Recalling that the hospital was permitted to block off Bond street [the resident said] "That made me feel like we're saying, this is where civilization ends and this is where the wilderness begins. . . . It's high time of six people to stop deciding for 2,000. It's high time for 2,000 to decide for 2,000. . . . One hundred years of promises is too long." Urban renewal planners said they intended to give residents nearby housing while rebuilding was going on. They explained that they wanted to keep through traffic out of the area. They offered hopes for nonprofit housing and for keeping the Hopkins from expanding.[35]

After 40 meetings with residents, business owners, and property owners in the area and three formal presentations of a plan, the residents accepted a final draft. "The people are telling the architects what to do rather than the other way round . . . one way to liberate the ghetto from external domination," was the way a resident organizer described this urban renewal project in East Baltimore in 1968.[36] There was still disagreement on details of the plan, but consensus was reached after the disagreement was documented in writing. Representatives of the residents accepted the plan: "This is a good plan. One of the reasons it's good is the people in the neighborhood actually designed it. This is what they want."[37] The "black lifestyle" was taken into account. For example, four bedrooms instead of two was determined to be the size of an apartment to fulfill the "black community's needs."[38]

The particulars of the plan were informed continuously by residents. When it came time to demolish a block of houses, the community rejected this out of concern for the displacement of the residents. Instead, houses were built on the southern end of the project area first, to accommodate those having to move. The project proceeded in this way, intent on minimizing demolition and relocation and optimizing rehabilitation when possible, through assistance from the Federal Rehabilitation loan and grant program. Parks and a recreation center were also constructed, and part of Gay Street was closed to minimize traffic through the neighborhood.

As the project went on, disagreements remained, between the planning agency and residents and between different resident associations. Still, the process was considered a success: "not only because of the agency, but because of the enlightened and consistent pressure from neighborhood groups and the willingness of the agency to go along. And the neighborhood is prepared to maintain an eternal vigilance to see the plan is carried out."[39]

Planning for a new school began in 1969 through a 14-hour-a-day, 2-week charrette (a planning process often used in land use and urban planning to engage residents along with multiple stakeholders) for assuring community participation and decision making. Outside consultants were invited in to ensure an objective process and gather residents input regarding but not limited to a curriculum, possible school sites, and joint services to be offered at the school. The local paper headlined the planning event as "an extraordinary way to plan a school" and described it as follows:

> . . . The charette was people . . . It was ordinary people who have spent their lives in East Baltimore's slums, with little hope for a better life for their children and even less hope for a better life for themselves. It was people who have felt, with justification, that their lives are ordered by members of the white establishment who often arbitrarily decide "what's good for the black man." Mainly, the charette was a chance for people to show what they could do when, for a change, they had a major role in planning for a big new community high school and the neighborhood facilities that will be built along with it.[40]

When the Gay Street I project was complete, a nonprofit housing corporation consisting of Gay Street residents and the Interfaith Housing Corporation designed and sponsored the construction of two housing complexes, consisting of 61 units: Harrymills Terrace-Odessa Courts. The local community owned and operated the complex.[41] The Harrymills Terrace townhouses fronted the surrounding streets, while the Odessa Courts apartments were located on the interior part of the complex. Parks, playgrounds, a new community high school, and stores were placed in areas convenient to the flow of the community, and houses were built to meet the income level of the residents. A newspaper headline read, "Renewal with a difference: not just another white-run innovation, the Gay Street Project gives residents a voice, making it a people-run project."[42]

ROUNDING OUT COMMUNITY DEVELOPMENT IN EAST BALTIMORE IN THE 20TH CENTURY: 1975–2000

After the Gay Street I project was completed, rebuilding of East Baltimore occurred through smaller initiatives directed at targeted blocks. In the 1970s the East Baltimore Community Corporation (EBCC), which initially came together as community members forming and directing the East Baltimore Medical Center, negotiated with the city to be the go-between in buying and rehabilitating 20 houses between Patterson Park Avenue, East Preston Street, East Federal Street, and East Hoffman Street. After rehabilitation, houses would be sold to low- and moderate-income residents. Similar types of small-scale initiatives were carried out by the EBCC and other East Baltimore community groups between 1975 and 1990.[43] The Ashland Park Mews, 252 units of new and rehabilitated houses, was targeted for completion by 1983 through a $3.3 million grant to the EBCC's affiliate, Central Ashland Housing Associates.[44]

These types of rebuilding projects, along with the smaller initiatives carried out since the 1970s, attempted to rehabilitate the most deteriorated areas a house or a block at a time. However, the pace of decay in the East Baltimore community continued to defeat the attempts to slow or stop it. Today five communities within East Baltimore are still designated as urban renewal areas, since the 1960s.

In the 1990s, the walled-off institution of JHMI began to feel the threat of the decaying surrounding community. After several crimes which impacted their student and faculty, security became a challenge and the institution started seeing the need to address the decaying effects of disinvestment and unfair rebuilding in their neighboring community, for their own benefit. One local paper headlined this new effort with: "A neighborhood hospital; Hopkins: The world-class medical institution is shedding its imperial image of indifference in favor of neighborly involvement in the East Baltimore community. It's not a matter of altruism."[45] The leader of one community organization reported, "Crime that is touching everybody today is touching Hopkins. . . . It's no longer a neighborhood problem. . . . They got involved because they just looked around, and they saw this neighborhood is falling apart. Crime is a real problem for Hopkins employees and for their visitors and their patients. . . . It's everybody's problem." One JHMI administration said, "People look at Hopkins, and they see this big research institution on the hill, and we realized we needed to change the perception."[46]

This renewed effort for rebuilding East Baltimore resulted in formation of the Historic East Baltimore Community Action Coalition (HEBCAC) in 1994, a partnership between the city, state and the JHMI and took the lead in carrying out targeted rehabilitation of houses through the Federal Empowerment Zone Initiative.[47] "The [mayor] also said it would help Baltimore retain the Hopkins medical institutions, which have a combined budget of more than $1 billion a year and have more than 11,000 faculty, students and staff . . . 'Both {the city and the state} are concerned about whether Hopkins is going to stay and flourish,' the mayor said."[48] The president and CEO of the hospital and health systems stated: "Hopkins is providing seed money for the organization because "we are an integral part of this community. We're interested in seeing further development around the hospital."[49]

Four to six years later and after $13 million had been spent, less than 10 percent of the targeted number of houses rehabbed and an increase in the number of vacant properties, deterioration of the neighborhoods in East Baltimore continued. According to the U.S. Congress's Government Accountability Office report of the effect of this federal initiative, no one had analyzed the effects on poverty and it had done little or nothing to address the blight of East Baltimore.[50,51]

In 1998 Hopkins attempted to expand into two square blocks just north of their Madison street boundary, "by redeveloping the area and offering subsidies for home-closing costs, Hopkins is encouraging more of its employees to live closer to its medical campus."[52] The expansion would result in displacing 200 families. JHMI attempted to buy properties directly from residents for prices some felt were unacceptable as reported by a local paper's headline: "Homeowners angered by Hopkins bid".[53] One resident who was approached by Hopkins for purchase of her home stated: "Hopkins wants to be in control of the community, of everything, . . . They're just trying to push everybody out . . . they made me an offer I could refuse. I was so mad."[54] But without condemnation by the city, residents were not forced to move from their homes. Of the two square blocks presented to the city for condemnation, one square block was approved and construction of the Kennedy Kreiger Institute—an affiliate of JHMI—occurred.

During the last quarter of the twentieth century, the Johns Hopkins campus continued its own rebuilding, slowly accumulating individual properties, boarding them up or leasing them, until it had enough to rehab or construct a new garage, administrative building, or research and teaching space. When it had no more houses adjacent to demolish and develop, residents were not selling for cheap, and the city council did not condemn the houses and force resident displacement, it was aided by the larger displacement and demolition projects of urban renewal. The current—2001—one in Middle East Baltimore was the next large scale expansion.

MIDDLE EAST BALTIMORE REBUILDING PROJECT: 2001 TO PRESENT

The majority of residents of the Middle East Baltimore community first learned about the 2001 plan to redevelop up to 88 acres of their community when they read an announcement in the Baltimore Sun.[55] This plan announced the acquisition of more than 1,700 houses, 1,000 of which were vacant at that time; relocation of approximately 800 households—owners and renters—and of businesses and churches; and demolition of the entire area. To be built in their place was a community equipped with a bioscience park, houses, retail shops, and green space.

There was no mention of understanding poverty: the racist and classist policies and practices that had shaped the community and the effects of the resulting poverty. The description of the project focused on removing "blight and slums," as did most of the attempts at urban renewal in the previous 60 years. The intention behind the plan was to remove the signs and symptoms of poverty: remove the—black—people and the structures that had come to be associated with poverty in Middle East Baltimore and replace them with those—white—not associated with poverty.

With the Office of the Mayor and the city's Office of Economic and Neighborhood Development spearheading the initial effort, the city government would use its power of eminent domain to acquire the homes in the area. Under a 1949 federal law (Title One of the Housing Act of 1949), the city has the power to acquire nonpublic property, using eminent domain, for the improvement of the overall neighborhood or community.[56] In other words, it has the power to take land if it will allow the city to improve the community and benefit the "public good." Under this law, federal funding can be used to acquire the property, relocate families, demolish the now unoccupied buildings, and prepare the land for the next owner.

The intention of the law is for new owners/developers to buy the land back from the city and rebuild the community with new housing and businesses, thereby making it a thriving community with a stable tax base. This stable tax base is supposed to result from the construction of houses and apartments for owners and renters with higher incomes than the previous residents had and business and retail structures to attract new businesses. These communities are expected to bring increased income; increased taxes from sales, property, and income; and employment opportunities and to result in a thriving community. This is considered community growth and progress, based on the ability to be self-sufficient and require minimum government assistance.

The plan to use eminent domain to rebuild the Middle East Baltimore community had no real community-informed process and no way to incorporate participation by residents. As in the formation of the 1950s Broadway Redevelopment Project, there had been no community input in putting together this plan. Unlike the 1960s Gay Street I Redevelopment project, in which the Baltimore Urban Renewal Agency worked with residents for 4 years before an initial plan was presented, this plan received last-minute nods from one or two community leaders before it was announced publicly. After the plan was announced, residents demanded accountability and the details of this plan. It became clear that there was no process in place to change the plan, and if there was to be a change in how this rebuilding would occur, residents would have to organize and force their way to the table.

This failure to engage residents in the rebuilding of their community set the stage for how the current rebuilding of Middle East Baltimore would occur and for whom it was intended. From the beginning, it was clear that the people deciding it was time for a grand redevelopment project did not value resident participation. The plan to rebuild came hand-in-hand with a plan to remove residents, thereby making the 88 acres adjacent to JHMI northern borders more safe, not an eyesore to the visitors and potential students and faculty who came for interviews. The medical school continued to lose potential faculty and students to other prestigious universities, some secondary to the perception of safety in the neighborhood. Some wanted to live near their work and East Baltimore did not appear to be such an area for them. There were no nearby restaurants and shops to satisfy the professional population the institution sought to attract who could go to competitive prestigious institutions with these amenities nearby. A redevelopment plan aimed at clearing 88 acres under the guise of rebuilding Middle East Baltimore to establish a biotech park and new housing could address all this. Because the JHMI had made public promises to the community to not develop beyond their current northern boundaries, it would not publicly announce that it was expanding or dictating how redevelopment would occur—initially. Instead the city could put forth such a plan and reported that the institution would be the anchor and participate in the direction and implementation of the development.

The conveners of this initial plan included city government planners, developers, Johns Hopkins Medical Institutions (JHMI) interests, city council officials, the housing authority, foundations, and nonprofit entities. The implementation of the plan began through the formation of East Baltimore Development Incorporated (EBDI) the following year, 2002, advised by the Baltimore City Office of the Mayor. EBDI was established as a public-private partnership, structured to maintain consistency through changing governmental administrations.

A board of directors had oversight over the actions of this functioning body, which was supervised by a chief executive officer (CEO). Various stakeholders were represented on EBDI's board: it had one seat each for the mayor's representative, the governor's representative, and the city council representatives; two seats for the JHMI; and seats for various foundation representatives and financial and development corporate interests. There were no seats for community residents on the board.[57,58]

The process of the first 10 years of implementing this 2001 plan to rebuild Middle East Baltimore will be detailed in section 2 (chapters 4–7). The focus from the community residents organizing and challenging the process for a more equitable process and outcome will be presented in these chapters.

Theses three large-scale rebuilding projects offer examples of two types of community development processes in East Baltimore (as seen in table 2.1).

The Broadway Redevelopment in the 1950s and the current 2001 project are similar in their massive displacement of a historic African American community. In both redevelopment projects, approximately 800 households and businesses were displaced. They were both projects aimed at renewing the place, not the people-place based initiatives. Both projects began with the city of Baltimore presenting a plan for redevelopment with little or no input from the local community. Both plans changed after residents were relocated allowing the land to sit after acquisition of houses, demolition of houses, update of infrastructure, and clearing of land. And both projects announced a greater role for JHMIs—and direction by—after relocation of residents in the form of new or revised plans that were informed by surveying the JHMI communities and communities similar to them. Neither surveyed the

Table 2.1. Comparison of three major urban renewal projects in East Baltimore 1950–2011

	Broadway Redevelopment Project	Gay Street I Project	Middle East Baltimore Project
Year	1950–1961	1967–1975	2001–current
Size	54 acres	30 acres	88 acres
Displacement	1,062 families—~800 households—90% African American	Minimal	~800 households[1] 99% African American
Resident participation in planning	No	Yes	No
Organized resident base	No—before No—during No—after	Yes—before, during, after	No—before Yes—during (first 7 years) No—currently
Plan for return of residents	Yes—changed during project	Yes	No
Affordable housing for local residents	No	Yes	In law and policy, not in practice
Jobs for local residents	Not targeted	Yes	In law and policy, not in practice
Johns Hopkins Medical Institutions expansion	Yes	No	Yes
Public:private partnership	Yes	No	Yes[2]
Type of rebuilding initiative	Place Based	People and place based	Place based

[1] Many households had more than one family living in them; this number does not reflect those families who remained in their homes after rehab or moved into a rehabbed house in the project area.

[2] Besides the Mayor's office partnering with JHMI in planning, eminent domain for acquisition of land, tax subsidies, grants, bonds to assist private development.

historic East Baltimore community to learn the needs of this community, before, during or after the relocation of residents. Both projects changed plans to construct affordable housing to accommodate return of residents by citing lack of sufficient financial resources to construct affordable housing.[59] Both projects highlight the strong bonding public-private partnership between government and JHMI through city-funded infrastructure updates, acquisition, demolition and preparation of land for the private developer to eventually lease or own, and public subsidies.

The second type of rebuilding presented in this chapter is the Gay Street I people-lead community development. Residents were organized and insistent that the broken promises and lack of transparency of their city and state representatives and their prestigious neighbor which shut them out before, during and after the redevelopment project was not going to happen again. This redevelopment project resulted in less people displaced, more affordable housing built, and resident participation in all aspects of planning and implementation—a people- and a place-based initiative. It was the same urban renewal strategies, same housing policies, but with community participation before a plan was put together and it maintained consistent community input through organized pressure from residents. What was missing in this people-based initiative was long-term economic opportunities—employment, training, business opportunities—for wealth gain for the residents of the rebuilt place.

Another major difference in these two types of rebuilding projects—both led by city government—is that Johns Hopkins Medical Institutions did not participate in the planning or owning or leasing of any resultant construction in the Gay Street I area. They had no direct stake in the rebuilding and still benefited from having a neighboring community which was not as blighted and unsafe as before completion of the project.

The presence or absence of organized residents demanding decision-making and JHMI demanding decision-making affected the process and outcome in large-scale rebuilding efforts of the mid- and late 1900s in East Baltimore. These first two chapters have described the growing power of JHMI and its influence in the city of Baltimore in receiving public and private support for its expansion. The next chapter will describe organizing efforts and challenges of disinvestment, abandonment, and unjust rebuilding policies faced by residents of East Baltimore during the mid- and late 1900s and their effect in determining community change and empowerment.

NOTES

1. Olson SH. (1997) *Baltimore: The Building of an American City.* The Johns Hopkins University Press, Baltimore, MD.

2. Olson SH. (1997) *Baltimore: The Building of an American City.*

3. *Baltimore Engineer.* January 1934. 8:6.

4. Baltimore Council of Social Agencies. (1937) Frances H. Morton. "Social study of Wards 5 and 10 in Baltimore Maryland."

5. Commission on City Plan. (1945) "The Hubbard Report: Redevelopment of Blighted Residential Areas in Baltimore."

6. Sherry G. (1957) *Catholic Reporter.* "Part 1 Urban renewal project concerns all citizens."

7. *Baltimore Sun.* April 22, 1935. "City urged to aid Hopkins campaign."

8. *Baltimore Sun.* November 18, 1945. "Hopkins hospital seeks $3,000,000."

9. *Baltimore Sun.* June 11, 1946. "Your debt to the Hopkins."

10. *Baltimore Sun.* June 11, 1946. "Johns Hopkins Hospital drive underway."

11. *Baltimore Sun.* July 19, 1951. "Hospital addition being built."

12. *Baltimore Sun.* April 27, 1953. "Hemmed in, hospital grows up."

13. *Baltimore Sun.* July 16, 1943. "Johns Hopkins Hospital Hampton House."

14. *Baltimore Sun.* September 6, 1957. "Hospital plans include motel, shopping unit."

15. Department of Housing and Community Development. July 15, 1968. Information Services.

16. *Baltimore Evening Sun.* May 24, 1950. "Slum clearance projects here approved."

17. *Baltimore Evening Sun.* May 24, 1950.

18. *Baltimore Sun.* March 16, 1956. "U.S. approves of Broadway Project fund."

19. *Baltimore Sun.* January 18, 1955. "Broadway slum housing plan unsettled."

20. *Baltimore Sun.* April 6, 1958. "Unit defends relocation of Broadway families."

21. *Baltimore Sun.* January 18, 1955. "Broadway slum housing plan unsettled."

22. *Baltimore Sun.* January 18, 1955.

23. *Baltimore Sun.* January 20, 1955. "The Broadway: Pig in a poke."

24. Department of Housing and Community Development. July 15, 1968.

25. *Baltimore Sun.* February 11, 1958. "Development near Hopkins Hospital hits council snag."

26. *Baltimore Sun.* July 1, 1959. "City renewal check paid."

27. *Baltimore Sun.* March 16, 1956. "U.S. approves of Broadway Project fund."

28. *Baltimore Sun.* September 1960. "Ground broken for $2,000,000 Hopkins building."

29. Department of Housing and Community Development. July 15, 1968.

30. *Hopkins Magazine.* February 1952. "Hopkins-Broadway area getting tailor-made reconstruction."

31. Baltimore Urban Renewal and Housing Agency. 1967. "The Residents. Their characteristics, houses, needs, attitudes. Gay Street I."

32. *Baltimore Sun.* December 15, 1968. "Renewal with a difference."

33. *Baltimore Sun.* December 15, 1968.

34. Baltimore Urban Renewal and Housing Agency. 1967. "The Residents. Their characteristics, houses, needs, attitudes. Gay Street I."

35. *Baltimore Sun.* March 9, 1967. "Residents in renewal area voice fears about project."

36. *Baltimore Sun.* December 15, 1968. "Renewal with a difference."

37. *Baltimore Sun.* December 15, 1968.

38. *Baltimore Sun.* December 15, 1968.

39. *Baltimore Sun.* December 15, 1968.

40. *Baltimore Sun.* March 9, 1969. "An extraordinary way to plan a school."

41. *Baltimore Sun.* August 15, 1982. "East Baltimore Community Corp. make things happen on the Eastside."

42. *Baltimore Sun.* December 15, 1968. "Renewal with a Difference."

43. *Baltimore Sun.* August 5, 1978. "Group Plans to Buy, Recycle 20 Houses."

44. *Afro-American*. May 15, 1982. "East Baltimore Community Corp. make things happen on the Eastside."

45. *Baltimore Sun*. April 8, 1998. "A neighborhood hospital: Hopkins."

46. *Baltimore Sun*. April 8, 1998.

47. *Baltimore City Paper*. May 31 2000. "Testing ground."

48. *Baltimore Sun*. February 7, 1994. "Renewal set for East Baltimore."

49. *Baltimore Sun*. February 7, 1994.

50. *Baltimore Sun*. October 15, 2000. "Eastside loses ground in effort to stem blight."

51. *Baltimore Sun*. December 26, 2004. "Goals met but not hopes: Development."

52. *Baltimore Sun*. April 26, 1998. "Homeowners angered by Hopkins bids."

53. *Baltimore Sun*. April 26, 1998.

54. *Baltimore Sun*. April 26, 1998.

55. *Baltimore Sun*. January 16, 2001. "City plan for troubled area alarms some residents divided over plan to raze homes near Hopkins."

56. Johnstone, Q. "Federal Urban Renewal Program" (1958). Faculty Scholarship Series. Paper 1896. digitalcommons.law.yale.edu/fss_papers/1896. Accessed January 2011.

57. *Baltimore Business Journal*. September 16, 2002. "City names Hopkins Biotech Park board." www.bizjournals.com/baltimore/stories/2002/09/16/daily42.html. Accessed January 2011

58. *Baltimore Sun*. January 16, 2001. "City plan for troubled area alarms some residents divided over plan to raze homes near Hopkins."

59. *Daily Record*. July 28, 2011. "Residents rebuke EBDI developer."

3

Organized Communities and Resistance in East Baltimore's Past and Present

"... the collective memory is lost to the cult of individuality ... have to create systems and institutions, not programs and services ... has to be community-owned and -controlled ... collaborating, thinking through the situation." —Baltimore activist

"If you want justice, you had better strategize and organize for power." —J.S. Mill

The presence of functional community organizations helps individual residents participate in the activities affecting their community. They provide a vehicle for residents to access, participate in, and be informed about the processes which are continuously changing as communities grow and evolve: whether a clean-up of a block, opposing unhealthy demolition practices, or rebuilding of a community. Community organizations and associations also provide a social network which connects members of a community around their geographic location. Social networks, broadly and loosely interpreted as social cohesion or social capital, are a major structural or social factor determining the sense of feeling a part of a community and supporting the health of community members. This chapter will describe the growth of community organizing and resistance in East Baltimore from the mid-1900s to current times. The challenges faced by the effects of race and class segregation and continued unfair real estate public policy and public-private partnerships are presented along with examples of organized resistance by community members. The 2001–2010 community organizing against community displacement for the private benefit of the Johns Hopkins Biotech Park is presented in detail, providing the context for the remainder of the book.

ORGANIZING TO ADDRESS DISPARITY
IN MID-1900S EAST BALTIMORE

The dynamics of abandonment and disinvestment resulted in continued housing deterioration and unsanitary conditions in East Baltimore in the early 1900s. As JHMI grew so did the blight in the neighborhoods of East Baltimore along with increasing tensions from the result of these unfair policies and practices. There was little opportunity for democratic or participatory community building.

In the midst of this isolation, in 1947, East Baltimore residents started the area's first political club, with the leadership of Clarence "Du" Burns (1918–2002), who later became Baltimore's first African American city council president and mayor. Along with other community leaders, they organized residents to challenge the changing plans and broken promises to build houses for local residents in the 1950s Broadway Redevelopment Project.

By the early 1960s, the Congress of Racial Equality (CORE) was a strong voice in East Baltimore, addressing improvement in several areas through ameliorating housing conditions. It met with city officials, urging public campaigns aimed at improving housing conditions, resulting in increased housing code enforcement in some areas of East Baltimore.

In the late 1960s, some of the same houses residents were forced to move into less than 15 years earlier—during the Broadway Redevelopment Project—were targeted for another rebuilding project—Gay Street I Urban Renewal Project, or the Gay Street Area. In fact, at the time of relocation during the Broadway Redevelopment Project, the Housing Authority of Baltimore City had already designated this an area for revitalization. This time, an organized group of residents from the Gay Street Area formed a coalition called Citizens for Fair Housing (CFFH). The introduction to the coalition's 1967 brochure stated: "We are convinced that improving neighborhoods in the Black Community is a must. It is our aim to build a strong community organization through which our people together can affect positive changes. We are therefore, committed to creating a clean, healthy community that will further the development of pride and self determination within our people" (CFFH brochure; figure 3.1).

The coalition was composed of renters, homeowners, ministers, and community leaders. It worked directly with the city's Urban Renewal and Housing Agency— BURHA (today called Department of Housing and Community Development). The CFFH became the Planning Advisory Committee for the revitalization of the Gay Street Area, directly influencing the planning and implementation of revitalization and homeownership by and for African Americans of the area.[1] The CFFH worked closely with its predecessors, CORE—who had influenced the inclusion of three additional blocks into the original boundaries of the Gay Street Area project— and the residents in the area, building trust throughout many meetings, discussions, and conferences. The CFFH also provided neighborhood services and programs for children and the elderly, worked with neighborhood schools and hospitals, and encouraged voter political action.

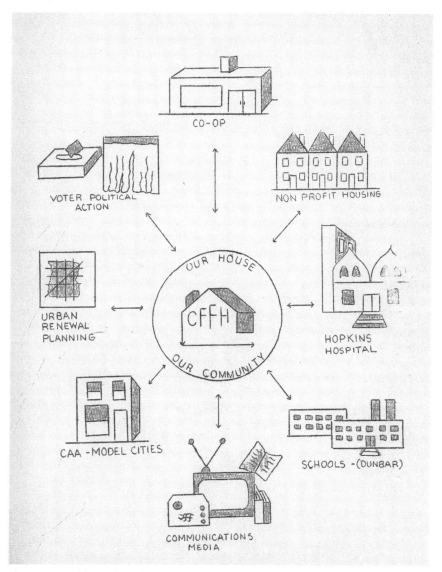

CO-OP

VOTER POLITICAL
ACTION

NON PROFIT HOUSING

URBAN
RENEWAL
PLANNING

OUR HOUSE
CFFH
OUR COMMUNITY

HOPKINS
HOSPITAL

CAA -MODEL CITIES

SCHOOLS -(DUNBAR)

COMMUNICATIONS
MEDIA

Figure 3.1.   Citizens for Fair Housing (CFFH) brochure

The momentum gained by this people-led rebuilding process continued with community organizing efforts to increase resident participation in community up-keep in the Gay Street community and nearby communities, such as Middle East Baltimore. This growing political and community activism in East Baltimore had a gigantic task in attempting to bring city and state resources to this community that had been abandoned for decades. The segregation laws of the past; the continued racist policies and practices in lending, real estate, and employment; and riots of the late 1960s in some areas continued the decline in a majority of East Baltimore neighborhoods. The upkeep that came from having new buildings in one neighborhood of the area did not spread throughout the remaining areas of East Baltimore. Political action groups formed, and representation of East Baltimore in city and state politics evolved onward from the late 1960s. In 1967 the first African American city council person was elected and later credited as a stimulus for increased political and community organizing in East Baltimore and other African American communities: "our entry into the system."[2]

Besides CFFH, many neighborhood associations and groups became active during the mid-1960s and early 1970s in East Baltimore. These included East Baltimore Neighborhood Association, Affiliated Community Organizations Against Crime, Jefferson Street Improvement Association, Madison Square Housing Association, Vocational Educational Advisory Council, and a dozen or so other improvement associations representing a sizable area or only a single block.[3] Several of them shared office space in "Our House"—a community meeting place, community center, office space—on Broadway Street until 1986 when it was demolished for temporary parking for the Johns Hopkins Medical Institutions.

In 1971, the Eastside Democratic Organization emerged from CFFH's leadership and the 1940s political club. Since then, it has served as the training ground for many grassroots community and political leaders from East Baltimore. Several of its original members hold political office in city and state government today.

As currently occurs in East Baltimore today, during the 1960s and early 1970s many area residents received health care through the emergency room at the Johns Hopkins Hospital, without regular and adequate follow-up care. Organized residents were seeking a place where the low-income and working poor neighbors of the area could obtain continued, competent, and affordable care. Members of CFFH and the new Eastside Democratic Organization joined Johns Hopkins Hospital to plan a health clinic that would serve the low-income residents of East Baltimore.[4]

The new clinic—East Baltimore Medical Plan (EBMP)—opened its doors in the mid-1970s, targeting the needs of the local community. Indicative of the overcrowding and poverty of the area, tuberculosis and nutritional deficiencies were regular findings in patients seen in the new clinic. In 1979, the East Baltimore Medical Center was built, enveloping the EBMP.[5]

The East Baltimore Medical Center was formed and initially governed by a board of directors from the community, which later became the nonprofit organization East Baltimore Community Corporation (EBCC).[6] The EBCC worked in the areas of health care, juvenile delinquency, drug abuse, mental health, job training, economic development and housing, child abuse, and family guidance. The EBCC and the Eastside Democratic Organization became the nonprofit and political organizations through which most community leaders and politicians from East Baltimore worked with or were affiliated with the African Americans on the East Side. Both the East Baltimore Medical Center and the EBCC still exist. Currently, the East Baltimore Medical Center is owned and operated by the JHMI. The EBCC continues to offer drug treatment programs, youth programs, and programs targeting juveniles involved with the justice system.

In 1978, members of CFFH organized residents east of Broadway to create a new organization: Middle East Community Organization (MECO). The neighborhood was given its name "Middle East" by the founder of this organization—Lucille Gorham.[7,8] This group became the place where residents could find information about services being offered in the community. It also became the community membership arm of a community development corporation (CDC) that was forming in East Baltimore. The Middle East CDC consisted of some of the same members of CFFH who had successfully organized and effected a community participatory process for the rebuilding of the Gay Street Area. These community organizations, the Eastside Democratic Club, and the East Baltimore Community Corporation were renowned for their political leadership of the African American communities in Baltimore.

For more than 25 years CFFH and MECO were the base for community residents to find out what was happening in their community and to get information about resources outside their community. During these times they had the ear of the residents and the political leadership, and for this reason they were powerful in addressing the needs of the community.

OTHER ORGANIZATIONAL BASES IN
EAST BALTIMORE SINCE THE EARLY 1900S:
FAITH-BASED AND SOCIAL CLUBS

The faith-based community played a major role in bringing residents together in East Baltimore. While the African American churches have always been a source of inspiration and activities in Baltimore and East Baltimore, they also maintained great leadership in addressing the causes and effects of poverty through the years. In addition to offering a place for residents to seek regular support and communion with each other, many of them offered physical space and supportive resources to the different community organizations in East Baltimore.

Coalitions of churches had also been organized to address the concerns of Baltimore and East Baltimore communities over the past 50 years. Two that stand out in East Baltimore's history are the Interdenominational Ministerial Alliance (IMA) and Clergy United for the Renewal of East Baltimore (CURE). The IMA consisted of more than 40 Baltimore area churches and supported resident participation in community rebuilding in East Baltimore. CURE was formed in 1999 by several East Baltimore congregations to address the health, spiritual, and social needs of the area. It partnered with the JHMI to address specific health conditions endemic in the community by providing a conduit for resources and research in East Baltimore.

It continues to exist today, providing back to the community some of the health information the JHMI gathers in the community through programs in churches in the area.

Sweet Prospect Baptist Church on North Durham Street—whose name came from the Sweet Prospect African Methodist Episcopal Church in Woodard, Fairfield County, South Carolina—had served the East Baltimore community since 1962. Its building on North Durham had previously been home to three other churches, the first in 1910. Like the more than 50 churches in the Middle East Baltimore community, older traditional and storefront churches, it was relocated. The John Wesley A.M.E. Zion Church on Ashland Avenue served the East Baltimore community for more than 80 years before it relocated during the current rebuilding plans for Middle East Baltimore.

The only church in Middle East Baltimore not displaced to date is St. Wenceslaus Church, on North Collington Street. Built in 1914, it served a Catholic Bohemian, Polish, and Lithuanian congregation that had roots reaching back to the 1870s. Along with other congregations and churches in East Baltimore, these three congregations and their pastors participated in organizing the Middle East Baltimore community when the plan to rebuild it was announced in 2001.

During the mid-1900s, social clubs were plentiful and offered a place for residents of East Baltimore to meet and learn about their neighbors. Until the late 1960s and early 1970s, manufacturing workers, lawyers, cooks, doctors, homemakers, social workers, teachers, and school principals all lived and socialized together in East Baltimore. The bonds formed here extended to the children in the neighborhood, the adults looking after each other's children and grandchildren. These bonds grew the community together and maintained pride and ownership of the area.

In the 1970s, with desegregation and the shift in manufacturing jobs, those who could afford to move in search of more spacious and comfortable houses—and those who were forced to move—did so, leaving a growing number of unemployed residents looking for work. This change also resulted in a community without the benefit and cushion of a diverse economic base of residents living or socializing together. By the later 1980s and early 1990s, the social clubs slowly lost their plentiful presence in the community. The last social club was forced to relocate during the 2001–2010 rebuilding process in Middle East Baltimore.

CHALLENGES TO ORGANIZING IN THE FACE OF CONTINUED PUBLIC DISINVESTMENT AND NEGLECT IN LATE 1900S EAST BALTIMORE

The Baltimore city agencies were continuously challenged in the 1970s through 1990s to keep up with regular housing inspection, collecting tax liens against delinquent property owners, and tracking down the increasing number of absentee landlords.[9] One city official described the major problem in addressing the increasing vacant and abandoned housing in East Baltimore as: "just getting enough money and manpower to do the job."[10] The result was a growing number of vacant and abandoned houses becoming fire hazards, drug havens, and open doors for crime and drug dealing.

Houses continued to be abandoned, speculated upon, and bought and boarded up by local developers.[11,12] Housing code violations continued by absentee landlords and funding for housing inspections continued to decrease.[13] In the 1970s and 1980s other urban renewal areas in the city were targeted for large-area redevelopment, and East Baltimore was on its own to continue its piecemeal rebuilding effort and in the midst of continued disinvestment.[14]

Federal funding programs for small-scale urban rebuilding of the 1970s—Model Cities program, community block grants—came and went with little effect on deteriorating communities such as East Baltimore.[15,16] Evaluation of how these and other urban renewal efforts continued concentrating and segregating poor and low-income African Americans families did not occur. Instead, such families continued to be perceived and labeled as creators of poor neighborhoods while the systematic laws and policies which pioneered and continued disinvestment in schools, housing, health care, transportation, and recreation in these neighborhoods went largely ignored. The 1970s housing, education, and transportation policies and laws continued this systematic disinvestment in urban cities in general and reinforced deterioration of already disinvested neighborhoods like East Baltimore.[17]

Into the 1980s, existing community organizations like MECO found itself trying to serve the needs of a community that was facing greater unemployment, out-migration, abandoned houses, and more and more renters falling prey to slum landlords. The public services continued to be minimal, drug trafficking and use grew, street-corner liquor stores grew, and speculators and businesses continued to buy and board up houses. Those who could afford to move did, and those who could not leave because of money, nearby employment, or family stayed. The base of the community, and effective community participation and organizing, therefore slowly diminished.

As in many similarly challenged communities, finding time to provide the basic necessities of shelter, food, clothing, and health care was all-consuming and time for organizing was a low priority. Renters had become the majority in the community, and only a few of the homeowners who remained would attend meetings. Previous owner occupants became landlords or sold their homes for little to landlords who rented for cheap prices. Middle East Baltimore slowly became a neighborhood of last resort for those unable to find housing in other areas. The homeowners more recently arrived in the community were uninformed about the past decades of organizing in Middle East Baltimore and East Baltimore. All they saw was an increasingly disinvested community becoming more isolated from the larger areas of Baltimore. They in turn became more isolated, keeping to themselves and not connecting to the existing organized networks in East Baltimore.

As active participation of residents decreased, MECO remained the community organization representing Middle East Baltimore residents. It continued to address many of the issues important to maintaining the community such as whether trash was being picked up as scheduled and issues of safety resulting from the increasing drug dealing that occurred in the area. It offered free lunch for children, after-school programs for children and families with children who needed food and clothing support, tracked newly abandoned houses, challenged the city health department to address the lead-painted houses being rented to low-income tenants with little oversight by inspectors, reported negligent trash removal. And it offered community residents information on social service resources such as drug treatment, employment information, GED programs, and senior programs.

Still, the diminishing base of residents and businesses, tax base, and public services surpassed efforts to increase a base of actively organized and participating residents. Grassroots community organizing, churches, and social clubs were no match for decreasing employment and increasing deterioration, drug use, high school dropout rates, and juvenile and adult incarceration. Leaders and activists of the 1940s and 1950s in East Baltimore had moved out of the neighborhood. Many involved themselves more in the governmental offices of the city and state than in community activism.

Housing renovation continued in small sections, insufficient primary care clinics addressed the needs of the poor, and social programs increased. And the area continued to attract low-income and working-poor African Americans and to experience frequent turnover when tenants could not afford their rent. This continued growth of racialized poverty, diminishing resources, drug trading, and a high turnover of its occupants continued to challenge an area that had constantly attempted to pull itself out of poverty and determine its destiny over the previous decades. These conditions were a challenge not only to those living in Middle East Baltimore but also to the local leaders, the city leaders, and the neighborhoods adjacent to the community.

By the later 1990s, those living in the Middle East Baltimore community were tired of asking their city council representatives to advocate for changes in their community. They were tired of calling the police and waiting hours for a response. The older residents of many years in East Baltimore daily saw their community change from a safe place where they could leave their houses unlocked at night, walk at night without feeling unsafe, and not fear what besides rats was hiding in the abandoned house next door. They saw the rats multiply as fast as the abandoned houses, only the drug trading and shootings managing to keep up with their increase.

The change from a community of homeowners to one with so many transient tenants diminished the trust among neighbors. And many residents of East Baltimore had grown to distrust the very people they continued to vote into office to represent their interests. At the same time, there was a feeling that there was no one else to send to the halls of city and state government: "Who else we gonna vote for? . . . I knew ___ when they were children." They had grown tired of the disrespect with which the city and private services—police, sanitation, health care, education, social services—regarded their community and them as people living in these abandoned neighborhoods. And they had grown more distrustful of a large and thriving institution that seemed to grow at a rate equal to the rate of their community's decay.

In 2000, few formal active organizational structures represented residents. While the Historic East Baltimore Community Action Coalition (HEBCAC) had been in existence since the late 1990s, it had failed to establish itself in the community as a place where residents felt they had an authentic voice in determining what could occur in the community. This organization reflects the "program and services" type of community organization. While this type of community organization helps to bridge relations with necessary service organizations and programs outside the community, the creation of the board was heavily advised by individuals at the JHMI and political leaders of East Baltimore and Baltimore in attempt to receive federal dollars for community development.[18]

Even while several neighborhood associations were represented on the board of HEBCAC, residents felt that they would never have real decision-making power or equal participation in an organization that was funded and founded by the JHMI. This continued perception confirmed the long-held view of residents that, while support offered by the JHMI was valuable, an organization like HEBCAC, with such dependency on and support from the institution, could only continue a paternalistic master-child relationship. The master would continue to offer necessary services in the form of funding for programs (drug addiction, individual housing renovation, small housing repairs, social services, etc.) to the needy child while controlling the land on which they lived: "They're like the plantation."

By 2001, MECO had lost its active organizational presence in the community because so few residents were participating in it. Many felt that the continued deterioration in their community was too great for any one organization to change. Residents did not see this historic organization as capable of challenging the Goliath of the JHMI and stopping it from eventually taking over their community.[19] Many of the more recent residents did not know the long history of MECO's role, along with its sister organization CFFH, in ensuring resident participation in city rebuilding in parts of East Baltimore or the history of the challenge MECO had presented to the JHMI to stop its intrusion into the Middle East Baltimore community. Though MECO was not as active as in the past, this history still maintained it as the conduit into the community for a small number of residents.

Also in existence in Middle East Baltimore at this time was Clearing House for a Healthy Community (CHHC). This organization consisted of local organizers and activists, church leaders, and a board whose majority was Middle East Baltimore residents. Its mission was to serve as a clearinghouse for all research being conducted in the community by the JHMI and other research entities.

Working closely with MECO, CHHC advocated having researchers interested in conducting research in Middle East Baltimore actively engage residents in participating in the planning of the research projects: listening directly to residents talk about their needs before writing research grants uninformed by resident input.

It also advocated a consistent process of informing the community of the research results obtained in the community and establishing continued services to address the research findings (when relevant). It had just started an organizing process to increase resident membership when the plan to rebuild the Middle East Baltimore community was announced. While CHHC actively engaged in leadership development and community organizing, at that time it was not positioned to serve the needs of those affected by the acute crisis of relocation of residents and demolition of houses.

Several months after the announcement of the proposed rebuilding of the Middle East Baltimore community in 2001, the majority of the board of CHHC joined the growing number of residents meeting in churches to address the acute crisis of the unknown of where and when the relocation of residents would occur—meetings that eventually led to the formation of a new community organization. MECO's meetings became more irregular and the leadership was displaced from their homes to clear the land for the planned Johns Hopkins BioTech Park.

THE JOHNS HOPKINS COMMUNITY AS A CHALLENGE TO ORGANIZATIONAL STABILITY AND RESISTANCE IN 1900'S EAST BALTIMORE

The JHMI dominated the East Baltimore area as "both landlord and employer to many residents" during the mid- and late 1900s.[20,21,22] The presence of this powerful institution along with short-sighted public policy for housing for the poor and low-income, contributed both to the one-sided rebuilding and the decay of the community. During the mid-1900s, as time drew near for another JHMI expansion or public housing change to accommodate JHMI expansion, leases in targeted blocks were not renewed and tenants were forced to move. After residents were displaced to nearby blocks—some two and three times in the course of 10 years—further concentrating and segregating poor and low income African Americans, buildings were left vacant and ultimately demolished, the lots serving as temporary parking until the entire block was vacated and new housing was constructed or JHMI expanded.

As Johns Hopkins continued to expand into the community during the 1970s, MECO challenged it to commit to a limit of its physical development into the Middle East Baltimore community. Johns Hopkins responded publicly that it would not expand north of Madison Avenue. This was the power of the organization during these years, demanding and getting a response from its powerful neighbor. Yet, 25 years later, an affiliate arm of Johns Hopkins, the Kennedy Krieger Institute, did cross that line. And today, the biotech park has fully crossed the line, 88 acres over the Madison Avenue boundary.

In the 1970s and 1980s JHMI was repeatedly fined by the Baltimore City Housing Authority for violation of housing codes: failing to rehabilitate or demolish houses it had acquired over the years and left abandoned as it planned future expansions—land banking.[23] When not in violation of codes one local paper described why several blocks of rental houses could not be rehabbed for current tenants and had to be demolished: "Officials say Hopkins and preceding landlords have kept the buildings in compliance with minimum housing code regulations but did not do major work because of a possibility the housing would be torn down for expansion of the hospital."[24]

The community was challenged by the presence of a world-renowned institution which continued to physically grow into their very homes—the ever present developer of small and large areas. Continuously organizing against this type of developer was difficult and contributed to the demoralization of community resistance. Small tenant organizations formed to challenge continued expansion were soon displaced following planned construction of houses for sale.[25] This continued oppression resulting from this powerful institutional presence, unchallenged by the elected officials some of whom had come from East Baltimore, resulted in lost of hope for residents to truly determine the path of their community. Many residents felt a constant fear that it was just a matter of time before "Hopkins would take over their block" and felt immobilized to challenge these private stakeholders of power with tight relationships with government, individually or collectively.[26] This type of "weathering" effect or cumulative impact of consistent disadvantage and stress has direct negative impact on the mental and physical health of individuals and their optimism and contributes to the hopelessness and isolation over the years. (More discussion on the impact on health is presented in chapter 9.)[27,28,29]

Often, residents in community meetings mentioned the medical institution as part of the cause of abandonment and disinvestment, even while expressing a hopelessness that it did not do more for the community. The continued expansion of the institution, while Middle East Baltimore grew smaller in population and greater in abandonment and decay, set the framework for most interactions between these two neighbors.

The rhetoric of the institution over the years has likely contributed to these expectations by residents. The language used by the Johns Hopkins community has consistently embraced a spirit of "community involvement." In an eloquent plea to the public for financial support for expansion in 1946, the president of the Johns Hopkins University stated, "No one with an assured livelihood can keep his conscience clear and remain indifferent to the welfare of his community," and "Our best personal security, and the security of our children, comes from caring for what goes on about us, in all the neighborhoods that make up America."[30]

And in 2011, after the displacement of another 800 households from Middle East Baltimore for construction of the new "Science at the new Johns Hopkins BioTech Park," the current president of the university said "I think if you look at the magnitude of the problems that the community was and is experiencing—crime, poverty, underemployment, low health outcomes—I actually think it behooves the leadership of the city to respond with an ambitious initiative. I don't think we should say it was too much, too fast. There's a real moral imperative here to help this community become strong and healthy."[31]

The outspoken words these leaders of the powerful JHMI speak in addressing their concern for their poor and abandoned neighbors remain the same over the decades. Their actions in planning and in including and benefiting their neighbors have proved different from their words—just as consistently so. Meanwhile, residents continue to ask, "Who is 'this community'" becoming strong and healthy, Johns Hopkins or existing East Baltimore residents?"

Many members of the JHMI who entered the community to conduct research or provide health services carried perceptions of residents as ignorant in regard to their health, incapable of knowing right from wrong. Most lacked understanding of the legacy of racist real estate practices in creating blighted neighborhoods with disinvested services which contributed to unhealthy communities like East Baltimore. Or they lacked awareness of the persistent fear of continued encroachment on people's physical and mental resistance by the institution they represented. This resulted in interactions in which researchers and service providers spent the majority of their time telling residents what they needed to do individually to be healthy and little time listening to residents' perceptions of the cause of their illnesses or addressing the structural and social determinants of the health of their community and themselves.

Residents felt that the JHMI had a responsibility to contribute more substantially to improving the individual and collective health of their community.[32] Instead they perceived that the institution treated delivery of health care services as secondary to the research interests of the institution and its continued expansion into the community. In addition to mistrust, these perceptions fueled criticism by the residents of any Hopkins-led initiative in the community. One resident summed it up this way: "They give us little services, do research on us, till they ready to take our property . . . don't care, just waiting us out . . . they can, they have the power."

SAVE MIDDLE EAST ACTION COMMITTEE: ORGANIZING AND RESISTING IN 2001

When the plan to rebuild the entire 88 acres of Middle East Baltimore was announced in 2001, it did not mention the effect on the current residents. It spoke of buildings and not of people. It spoke of revitalizing a place but not for the people currently living there. It did not speak of addressing the causes and consequences of poverty or revitalizing a people through a shared dream. It was not a plan for the current residents. As one newspaper article later summarized this plan, "Bulldozing entire neighborhoods to revitalize them seemingly went out of fashion decades ago, after the first mid-20th-century efforts at urban renewal were denounced as failures."[33]

Several days after residents read in the paper that they would have to move to make way for this development of a biotech park and mixed-income housing, members of the Middle East Baltimore community gathered in a small neighborhood church in January 2001. At this meeting, fear, anger, and frustration came together. And residents came together. They began to break through the isolation and mistrust of their neighbors that had grown with the abandonment of their community. Now, as residents directly affected by this planned redevelopment found themselves together in the path of the bulldozer, they stood up and together said that enough was enough. It had been almost 50 years since this type of fear and anger came together to birth an organized movement. Residents had a common purpose, an immediate need, they were all affected and one by one they were hearing themselves speak with one voice. The cause of their suffering was clear, their fear of where they would live was urgent. They would not lie down and let others tell them what to do anymore. The "others" were named repeatedly: the JHMI and the city and state officials who supported that powerful institution's plans. Solidarity and purpose came together and was aimed at the "others".

After several meetings, a new community organization, the Save Middle East Action Committee, Inc. (SMEAC), was formed. Community organizers and advocates who did not live in the community but were familiar with the history of redevelopment of East Baltimore also attended these meetings. The formation of SMEAC occurred quickly, with the legal and financial affairs supported and advised by non-Middle East Baltimore participants.

It was clear that SMEAC was to be a community-owned, -led, and -operated organization. Middle East Baltimore residents would be the majority of the members of the board, and leadership development would happen from its inception and continuously throughout the life of the organization. This organization would be a place where residents could participate; their voices would be listened to, and acted upon when appropriate; and democratic processes would ensure transparency internally and externally in the running of the organization. There would be accountability to residents on all activities through a working board communicating back to its general membership. At last there was an organization in East Baltimore where community participation was being practiced wholeheartedly and members were motivated to regularly attend. People needed answers and SMEAC was the only place they felt they would not be lied to or treated with disrespect.

Out of the chaos had come the birth of an organization that would represent the voices of community residents. The driving energy in its formation was people uniting on issues urgently affecting them. Their common goal, justice in this already-decided rebuilding plan, was at the forefront of their work, producing a powerful community force. An individual and collective transformation had occurred in these historic residents, and they were resisting the long-standing disinvestment, disrespect, and discrimination reflected in this attempt to rebuild their community without their participation. This was the glue that bonded individuals into a collective, setting a course that would force the powerful stakeholders to include the community in the rebuilding plans.

SMEAC developed organically into a forum where residents freely expressed their concerns. Over a period of weeks, they raised many issues (box 3.1).

Their questions and comments began to identify the strategies and objectives for SMEAC. During these early times of SMEAC, the only named expectation of the

**Box 3.1. Some Questions and Comments that Began to
Identify SMEAC's Strategies and Objectives**

- When would we have to move?
- Why do we have to move?
- What will happen to my house?
- How can they do this to us?
- How can we stop them?
- Who sold us out?
- What if I am a renter?
- What if I am an owner?
- Will it happen before Christmas?
- Should I not fix the roof?
- Should I get a new heater?
- Where are we going?
- What if I have a mortgage?
- Who will pay for us to move?
- What if I can't afford to own somewhere else?
- How do we find a community that will appreciate us?
- What about my health?
- Will they give us money for our houses?
- Will they give us money for the depreciated value of our houses or the value that
  the land will have after the redevelopment?
- What about our loss of community?
- Does anyone care?
- We have been fighting crime for 20 years and now we just get told to go.
- They intentionally neglected our neighborhood so they could come and take it
  from us.
- What about the loss of our history?
- They have neglected basic services like police and trash services.
- If we move how do we get transportation back to work?
- We want a "square foot for a square foot in a stable community."
- Why can't they renovate some houses in the neighborhood so we can all move
  there and stay in our community?
- Will they reimburse me for the renovations I did to my house?
- If we move can we move anywhere we like?
- If we want to come back can we do that?
- Hopkins finally got what they wanted.

group was a promise that it would seek answers to the questions and report back
to the residents. Residents felt that they stood together with others like them, who
had some similar and some different concerns, and that together they had enough
strength to address them all as an organized force. And, most importantly, the organization was owned by residents and not a puppet organization of Johns Hopkins,
political leaders, or foundations.

These were times of rebuilding trust in the community, among residents who had isolated themselves from each other, a time of forming new bonds or renewing old ones. There was a sense that finally others were listening and a process was in place to search for answers. Residents, church leaders, and business owners were standing together, speaking with separate voices but finding that they cared about the same basic things: the safety of shelter and the right to determine where to live. Previous differences were temporarily discounted and the similarities loomed large, birthing a renewed hope in the strength of community.

While its big institutional neighbor, its city and state government, its elected officials, and foundations all wrote off this community, perceiving it as powerless, a powerful base was forming. In the midst of a grand plan, challenging the likes of these powerful stakeholders was a tall order for a new organization, formed not from a planning process but as a reaction to an acute event. SMEAC was a movement in the making.

What SMEAC Would Do Differently

Resident participation was the principle that SMEAC was founded on. With this as the foundation, the methods and skills to address the questions and directions of residents slowly came together. The next step was to establish the organization with guidelines and standards that ensured a democratic process representative of the resident membership which could affect community participation. Residents were committed to acting differently from the way the planning of their community had occurred: behind closed doors, with hand-chosen stakeholders who would nod in unchallenged agreement, and with disrespect and disregard to the most vulnerable.

The stated purpose as written in the bylaws at the time of incorporation was: "To represent and advocate for the citizens and communities of East Baltimore who will be directly and indirectly impacted by the establishment of a biotech park and to empower those citizens and communities by all legitimate means to negotiate fairly with East Baltimore Development, Inc., Johns Hopkins and our City government. . . . The goal of those negotiations must be to achieve a stable and livable environment in the surviving communities, to lessen the negative impact of the proposed expansion, to preserve the economic, social and civil rights of our citizens, to lessen neighborhood tensions, and to combat community deterioration."

Early steps taken to accomplish this mission included small fundraising initiatives to pay for incorporating the organization. Others were holding regular meetings at the same location, creating processes for reminding membership of meetings, and printing meeting notes for distribution. And a board was formed, with residents in the majority and three board members who did not live in the community and brought experience in organizational development, community organizing, advocacy, and the history of East Baltimore.

And so it was that, in May 2001, SMEAC became the movement to bring community voice to a process of community rebuilding in the form of urban renewal of the mid-1900s—seeking to continue the displacement or ethnic cleansing of communities of color.[34,35] Its mission was bold, driven by a demand for truth and justice: to engage residents to participate in all aspects of the decisions of this rebuilding project.

From the very beginning, transparent internal communication was key to ensuring that SMEAC fulfilled its purpose. No decision was made without board input. When an action was to be undertaken, a phone tree was used to contact all board members, inform them, and listen to their views. In reporting back to the general membership at the monthly meetings, results of meetings with city officials and others involved in the rebuilding process were presented. Members were updated on any new information SMEAC board members became aware of. And different entities involved in planning the rebuilding process were invited to present their information to the general membership.

The president and vice president of the board were community residents directly affected by displacement; they became the voices of the residents in private and public meetings. Outside board members and non-community membership members remained in the background while offering technical assistance and organizational and leadership development opportunities during the course of the organizational work.

SMEAC became known as the community organization in Middle East Baltimore representing the people affected by the rebuilding process. It gained this reputation because it actively sought out the voices of community members of Middle East Baltimore and intentionally attempted to inform every member of the area affected by the rebuilding project.

SMEAC's Goals

It became clear early in its formation that SMEAC could not stop the planned redevelopment. No one talked about a court challenge to eminent domain. Political leaders were nodding approval of the process and did not suggest an alternative. Legal advice was not yet available to this newly formed organization. It quickly became the vehicle to help residents define what was the greatest justice to community members, given a paternalistic plan to displace them from their community with no opportunity to return—one that was conceived by no members of the community dictating what would be best for them and Middle East Baltimore.

SMEAC's working goals during the first years can be summarized as follows: organize impacted residents, churches, and businesses to ensure communication about the relocation timeline; negotiate a fair benefits package; maintain an institutional vehicle for the community to speak with one voice; and ensure community participation in decision making throughout the rebuilding process.

The strategies used to accomplish these goals would allow residents to define what it meant to make them whole and ensure that it happened before and after their community was torn apart.

Community Participation: The Core Value

Community participation was the driving force of SMEAC, its core value. SMEAC attempted to practice this fully within its home, showing the value of resident input in advising how the organization would function internally and externally. This was the major characteristic it presented in all interactions with organizations and institutions outside the community.

In approaching EBDI, SMEAC insisted on having residents participate in all aspects of planning the relocation and rebuilding process. This included residents being involved in the committees that were meeting to set policy for how relocation and rebuilding would occur: how much compensation for houses, how much funding for relocation, how much money toward new houses, the timeline for moving, safety during the relocation period, sanitation during the relocation process, safe demolition practices, planning for the new community, financing the return of residents to the rebuilt community, financial affordability of the new and rehabbed housing in the rebuilt community, economic inclusion guidelines for minority- and women-owned businesses, choosing developers, etc.

SMEAC insisted not only that residents have a place in the process, but also that their opinions be sought and listened to—and acted upon when appropriate. Because community members did not have access to the decision-making body of the EBDI board, they required communication regarding how issues discussed at public meetings were followed up on. They insisted on a process of transparency and requested more sharing of information in a regular format from the powerful stakeholders running the rebuilding process.

This came up repeatedly, as any progress residents made disappeared whenever they or their representatives were not physically present at a discussion. When residents did not attend a meeting, their needs were not primary to the planning process and questions they had raised previously remained unaddressed. A pattern of inconsistency between what was said when a resident or SMEAC member was present at a meeting and the follow-up in their absence was the status quo. And when a white person or person who was not a historic resident was present with residents and advocating their cause, the powerful stakeholders listened a little more. When these advocates were absent, the level of disrespect toward historic residents continued in ignoring residents' questions or speaking in demeaning tones.

This inconsistency of spoken words and actions did not help to build trust in these new bridging relationships with EBDI or governmental agencies involved directly in the planning, relocation, demolition, and construction processes. SMEAC learned early in the process that physical presence was key in ensuring that resident participation was a constant and acknowledged.

Still, it did not ensure an effect on final decisions. And even when residents won concessions, sometimes EBDI and its partners revised history, claiming credit and co-opting resident suggestions.

Skillful Means: Organizing, Advocating, Leadership Development

SMEAC's strategies for ensuring community representation and participation in all rebuilding processes were organizing, advocating, and leadership development. If everyone believed and adapted these strategies, the goals of the organization would be met through full community participation. This meant a consistent effort to involve as many members of the community as possible was needed to carry out its mission for residents to be "made whole" through a community participatory process.

Organizing

To ensure that residents were present at every opportunity to engage with the powerful stakeholders making the decisions so they could offer their opinions on what defined "made whole," and to build the power to ensure that they ultimately got that, SMEAC focused on building and maintaining a strong organizing presence in the neighborhood (box 3.2).

Advocating Change

Advocating was also a key strategy of the organization; it required a physical presence at every meeting pertaining to the rebuilding process. That the rebuilding

---

Box 3.2.   Nuts and Bolts of SMEAC's Organizing

- General membership meetings held monthly at the same convenient time and place that would accommodate the majority of residents' schedules
- Distribution of minutes at each meeting to update those who had missed a previous meeting
- Regular invitation for general members to become more actively involved through subcommittees of the board
- Follow-up by phone when a regularly attending member was missing from meetings
- A continuous door-knocking and listening project to initiate discussion of community needs and provide information
- Meet-and-greets to bring together residents identified through door knocking to unite around their needs
- Various standing and issue-specific subcommittees of the board, including block-captain, media, and ally-building committees
- Participation in policy meetings of EBDI to present community concerns
- Rallies
- Participation at meetings involving all aspects of the rebuilding process (demolition, relocation, school, parks, transportation, health)
- Regular and timely distribution of announcements for general and special meetings
- Phone call reminders of upcoming meetings
- Brochures and newsletters to inform residents and others of the accomplishments of their organization

plans began with no input from the area targeted for redevelopment had sent the clear message that the opinions and ideas of community residents, churches, and businesses were not valued in the rebuilding process. Advocating community input was therefore necessary not only to include participation in general, but to promote recognition of the value of community participation in advising the rebuilding process. Both outside and community stakeholders had to be assured that community members had valuable input, worthy of respect similar to that offered to the powerful decision makers. In addition, once an idea was put forth, consistently advancing and reinforcing the demands made on the powerful stakeholders in the rebuilding process was a continuous challenge.

Because EBDI and its partners had no connection with the community, when anything took place without a community representative from SMEAC present, information about what took place would not make it back to the community. Throughout the first 10 years of this rebuilding process, spoken intentions by EBDI and partners did not result in continuous transparency and information sharing back to the members of the community. Furthermore, the minutes of the public meetings would sometimes selectively reflect comments made by residents and other stakeholders. They were therefore not always a reliable way to learn what took place in one's absence. (More will be said about this in chapter 5.)

SMEAC used several different advocacy methods (box 3.3). The media remained a key tool in broadcasting the needs of the residents to maintain pressure on the decision-making stakeholders, adding this indirect pressure to the continued direct, face-to-face pressure in various meetings. Because the organization was run and owned by residents, SMEAC maintained continuous input about their perceptions.

Community Leadership Development

Development of community leadership was another key strategy in accomplishing SMEAC's mission. Residents involved in leadership roles in SMEAC got their

---

Box 3.3.   Advocacy Methods Used by SMEAC

- Advocating through the media
- Planned events to invite outside organizations to learn more about SMEAC
- Requests to meet with advocacy and community organizations involved in community building and with various city, state, and federal officials concerned with any of these:
  - Planning
  - Development
  - Health
  - Housing
  - Key philanthropic organizations directly and indirectly involved in the EBDI rebuilding process

training on the job. Outside members of the board actively facilitated leadership development through an ethic and a way of doing organizing and advocacy as well as through formal training of SMEAC board members. Consultants expert in grassroots community organizing and antiracism-anti-oppression training participated in bringing leadership and organizational development methods and skills to the entire board.

This on-the-job training included carrying out the functions of the organization as well as developing and administering its infrastructure. The board leaders were elected by a democratic voting process at the monthly general membership meeting. After the initial 6 months of SMEAC's formation, at no time were there more than 2 non-community members (out of 9 to 11 total) on the board. Rules and regulations set out the standard practices and procedures for all new board members.

These included a board-membership training process defining the responsibilities of being a board member, the ethical and legal requirements to become a board member and remain in good standing on the board, and conflicts that would inhibit a general member from being on the board (box 3.4).

The responsibility of the board in supervising the executive director and the financial checks and balances between the executive director and the board treasurer were all aspects of a training process in which each new board member participated. If a board member could not sign off on the ethical standards or adhere to the training process, he or she could not remain a board member.

The bylaws of SMEAC also clearly defined terms for board membership and specific officers, roles and responsibilities of committees of the board, and procedures for committees reporting back to the board and the general membership. This rigid system of accountability set the framework for how SMEAC would function in Middle East and offered an open, transparent process.

It was especially important for SMEAC to define itself in this transparent way, with checks and balances and with accountability to each member. It was a time when residents felt betrayed by their elected officials and their neighbors, felt there were no rules or laws that supported them, and saw the evidence that decisions about

---

Box 3.4.   Areas Included in Board Training

- Legal accountability
- Financial accountability and transparency
- Conflicts of interest
- Transparency among the board members
- Board direction of and participation in daily activities of the organization
- Procedures of the board and of its committees
- Board and staff supervisory responsibilities
- Organizing and leading meetings
- Supporting adherence to the personnel manual

their lives were being made behind closed doors with no opportunity for input. SMEAC offered a different model of how to operate with integrity and transparency—with residents in control.

This model showed that there were rules to be followed, the reason the rules were in place, and how the rules offered a process and procedure to accomplish the work and allow flexibility and feedback. It also showed that the rules and regulations worked to the extent that they were enforced by the officers of the board, the leadership, and the staff. When everyone followed the processes and procedures and held each other accountable in a respectful way, the system maintained its integrity. This integrity allowed it to function as it was intended and produce results.

It was easy to see the practical way this worked in SMEAC, an organization of 9 to 11 board members and a general membership of more than 200, with attendance at monthly meetings of approximately 70 individuals: all representing the more than 800 households affected by the rebuilding process. For example, if someone who attended an outside meeting did not write a summary of it, that made it difficult to provide information from this meeting back to the general membership. Therefore, meetings had to be attended by at least two SMEAC members, and one was responsible for documenting the outcomes within a defined amount of time. These were then reported to the general membership.

This understanding of how organizations formed and functioned effectively offered SMEAC's membership insight into how similarly other organizations functioned. For example, when the past and present CEO of EBDI consistently acted in ways that were disrespectful and paternalistic to the community—advising them that this was the best plan for residents in light of residents stating it is not their choice and that it would harm them, holding an attitude of superiority with residents, raising voices to residents, telling them how their meetings should be run—SMEAC members knew that a way to address this was to deal directly with the board of EBDI, their supervisor. In one instance, residents voted to send a letter requesting the CEO's resignation after he spoke rudely and with an attitude of superiority to a resident who was not agreeing with what he was saying. And from an understanding of SMEAC's funding process, members came to understand that funders have expectations that their grantees will act in a way they deem appropriate. When they did not, a grantor did "scold" the grantee as occurred on several occasions with SMEAC's board and staff.

These examples of organizational processes and development show how SMEAC served as a classroom where its leaders and membership studied how to organize a group, establish processes and procedures, and hold each other accountable through transparency and open communication. It also modeled values it hoped EBDI and its partners would adopt: integrity and transparency.

The need to ensure financial stability was also part of leadership training and development. Board members and general members learned quickly that an organization can only exist if it has sufficient and consistent financial resources to pay for brochures and other organizing tools and for people to organize, advocate, and eventually direct and manage the organization.

SMEAC had to raise funds, and it was a challenge to find funding sources willing to fund community organizations whose main purpose is to organize. Community organizing often may not result in a "product" that can be written about in a funding proposal. Foundations are more likely to fund community organizations organizing a block party, planning a "clean your neighborhood" day, or providing counseling services to 20 or 30 individuals in a month. SMEAC members learned that com-

---

Box 3.5.   Sources of Support for SMEAC

In-kind support
SMEAC received in-kind support in the form of technical assistance from these sources:

- Morgan State University Urban Research Institute
- University of Baltimore Community Development Clinic
- Wide Angle Media
- Neighborhood Design Center

Personal effort
Many individuals—residents and those outside the immediate community—gave of their time to do the following:

- Make phone calls
- Pass out flyers
- Help design flyers and mailings
- Offer historical perspectives and advice regarding past and present organizing efforts and urban rebuilding in poor and African American communities

Financial support
SMEAC did the following to raise funds:

- Collected dues from its resident and guest membership
- Held several dinner events
- Sold a video documentary and book produced in collaboration with Wide Angle Media, "Voices from within: a displaced community speaks out."

These are among the local foundations and organizations that provided financial assistance

- The Annie E. Casey Foundation
- Baltimore Community Foundation
- The Neighborhood Design Center

These are among the national foundations and organizations funding SMEAC

- The Unitarian Universalist Foundation
- Catholic Campaign for Human Development
- 21st Century Foundation
- Marianist Sharing Fund
- Sociological Initiatives Foundation

---

munity organizing work—knocking on doors and listening to residents talk about their needs and what motivates them to get involved—is hard to quantify. This is especially true when none of the doors you knocked on that week resulted in new membership at the general meeting. Telling a potential funder that a seed was planted that may blossom in the next month or two does not offer a quantitative product or a number for the funder to document.

Nevertheless, SMEAC managed to maintain an executive director and a community organizer continuously, on an annual budget of less than $150,000. Sources of support were varied, consistent and often at risk due to the organization's actions of holding the powerful stakeholders accountable to their verbal and written promises, inconsistent words and actions and misrepresentation of facts (box 3.5).

SMEAC members became quickly aware of the challenge to find funders willing to support organizing that insisted on challenging institutions such as the JHMI and city and state governments. Finding support for this type of "politically unpopular, messy" organizing often is difficult. SMEAC was clear in its proposals to funders what the reason for its formation was and what strategies it would use to accomplish its mission. The establishment—those with power to maintain and change systems—sees organizing people for nonviolent protest outside the JHMI on graduation day or rallying outside Baltimore City Hall when legislation affecting the rebuilding plans as politically messy and unnecessarily highlighting inconsistencies in words and actions by EBDI and its powerful partners. These and other strategies are seen as "controversial" and "likely to hurt our donors' sensibilities" (figure 3.2).

Figure 3.2.   SMEAC rallies in front of the Johns Hopkins Hospital for affordable home ownership in the rebuilt area of Middle East Baltimore

While SMEAC maintained its independence in speaking out on behalf of residents in Middle East Baltimore, its funders challenged it to speak carefully. On several occasions, SMEAC's leadership was invited to meet with a funder after challenging the way this local funder was hesitant in addressing the injustices of several initiatives regarding relocation and affordable housing and demolition during the rebuilding process. They were asked to think about being "less noisy and dirty" so as not to disturb potential donors interested in contributing financially to the rebuilding of Middle East Baltimore. The leadership of SMEAC was clear when it decided to publicly challenge this funder; it was willing to risk a major funding source to represent what it perceived as the best course of action for residents. This risk of losing funding for speaking the truth of their lives was a continuous challenge for the SMEAC board of directors and executive directors.

The three-pronged approach of organizing, advocacy, and leadership development describes the tools and skills that SMEAC used to ensure that resident participation was continuous, both in the organization and in all aspects of planning the rebuilding process in Middle East Baltimore. This was the process of SMEAC's work in bringing resident participation to the rebuilding of Middle East Baltimore (figure 3.3, SMEAC logos).

ORGANIZED RESISTANCE EFFECTS CHANGE

An organized community base of social networks was deteriorated and fragmented, like the entire community, when the 2001 plan was announced. Like the physical result of disinvestment and abandonment of the place, residents had succumbed to the isolation resulting from this fragmentation, this separated and unequal faith of racist and classist policies and laws. What made residents leave their isolation and collectively organize as one voice?

SMEAC was formed in reaction to a trauma, an acute event felt by all those affected. When community members first learned of the plans to demolish their community, the residents of Middle East Baltimore didn't know what would happen to them. This trauma affected one of the basic human needs, shelter, necessary for all humans to exist.

Community residents responded to the trauma of loss of shelter by joining together, creating a network of support to learn how they could address their basic needs. Indeed, this is a normal response to trauma: reaching out for social support through communication and connection.

Coming together around this primary issue of shelter, common to all, led to the process of organizing. Organizing opened up communication and bonding among residents. In turn, this organized body began seeking connections and bridges with outside organizations, listened to and were listened to by others who also supported their mission. Such support affirmed the injustice of their forced

A house for a house in a stable community

SAVE MIDDLE EAST ACTION COMMITTEE
2002 A house for a house in a stable community

Save
 Middle
  East
   Action
    Committee, Inc.

"Giving the Middle East Community the power to organize, control, plan and create the direction in which it grows."

2003 Save Middle East Action Committee, Inc.

2007 Make our community whole

Figure 3.3. SMEAC logos

displacement for gentrification, building greater energy for learning ways to address this injustice.

The organized force they grew into, one not present in Middle East Baltimore for more than 50 years, became a power to be reckoned with by the stakeholders entering to rebuild the community. SMEAC, the product of a transformed base, became the vehicle for a political will that had not been present during the initial planning for rebuilding.

When community members organized for justice in 2001 in the rebuilding of Middle East Baltimore, they immediately challenged the legitimacy of the announced plan. They also challenged the legitimacy of the previous plans that had been carried out in East Baltimore and the history of JHMI in contributing to the deterioration and disinvestment. It challenged the public-private relationships that had allowed these previous rebuilding processes which furthered segregation by race and class in similarly disinvested neighborhoods of East Baltimore.

It stood on the shoulders of previous residents and organizations which had done the same in previous years: MECO, CHHC, CFFH, CORE, the churches and social clubs. It ignited the resistance to displacement in new and old residents, businesses, and churches. It brought back memories of previous displacements and stories from elders and children of those passed who had lived at the whim of the powerful JHMI expansion, neglectful city and state representatives, and segregationist policies.

SMEAC slowly gained a reputation for being willing to challenge powerful institutions by speaking the inconvenient truth of their continued race and class segregationist tactics which maintained inequity between the white and wealthy powerful stakeholders and the poor and low-income African American communities: expanding the inequality of power and place.

Of great importance is that the process of organizing in Middle East Baltimore resulted from a transformation beginning with the base: the people. It did not begin with the developers or the funders or community activists and organizers from outside the community telling the community that it should organize and let its voice be heard. It was the residents, standing together and acknowledging that they were tired of "business as usual" in East Baltimore.

This force then became a yardstick by which to measure how much the intended rebuilding process was open to change—changes the initiators of this plan never anticipated. And how could they anticipate such a force to be reckoned with? This had been lacking for almost half a century in Middle East Baltimore.

The next chapter will go more in depth into specific successes and challenges of community residents participating in the rebuilding of Middle East Baltimore. This process reveals the steps taken by the powerful stakeholders in carrying out their planned displacement and demolition of Middle East Baltimore and how residents defended themselves and their community from these actions.

NOTES

1. Baltimore Urban Renewal and Housing Agency. 1967. "The Residents: Their characteristics, houses, needs, attitudes. Gay Street I."

2. *Baltimore Sun*. October 8, 1973. "We live here."

3. *Baltimore Sun*. October 8, 1973.

4. *News American*. September 2, 1973. "EBMP offers adequate care despite strife."

5. *News American*. August 15, 1981. "Striking health workers want wage hike."

6. *Afro-American*. May 15, 1982. "East Baltimore Community Corp. make things happen on the Eastside."

7. *Baltimore Sun*. December 15, 1968. "Urban renewal with a difference."

8. *Baltimore Sun*. October 8, 1973.

9. *Baltimore Sun*. April 26, 1998. "Homeowners angered by Hopkins bids."

10. *Baltimore Sun*. October 17, 1968. "Area to east of Green Mount like a graveyard for buildings."

11. Harvey D. (2000). "Spaces of hope." U California Press. CA.

12. *Baltimore Sun*. October 17, 1968.

13. *Baltimore Sun*. August 9, 1992. "City's blight outpaces housing inspectors."

14. *Baltimore Sun*. October 26, 1969. "Whatever happened to model cities?"

15. *Baltimore Sun*. October 8, 1973.

16. *Baltimore Sun*. October 17, 1978. "City plans for 1979 outlined."

17. Harvey D. (2000). "Spaces of hope."

18. *Baltimore City Paper*. May 31, 2000. "Testing ground."

19. Gomez MB, Muntaner C. (2005) "Urban redevelopment and neighborhood health in East Baltimore, Maryland: The role of institutional and communitarian social capital." *J Critical Public Health*. 15:83.

20. *Baltimore Sun*. October 8, 1973.

21. *Baltimore Sun*. August 15, 1982. "She gave the Middle East neighborhood a name and a dream."

22. Gomez MB, Muntaner C. (2005) "Urban redevelopment and neighborhood health in East Baltimore, Maryland."

23. *Baltimore Sun*. August 15, 1982.

24. *Baltimore Sun*. December 22, 1982. Resident groups tif.

25. *Baltimore Sun*. December 22, 1982.

26. Gomez MB, Muntaner C. (2005) "Urban redevelopment and neighborhood health in East Baltimore, Maryland."

27. Geronimus AT. (2001) "Understanding and eliminating racial inequalities in women's health in the United States: the role of the weathering conceptual framework." *J Am Med Womens Assoc*. 56:133–36, 149.

28. Keene DA, Geronimus AT. (2011) "Weathering" HOPE VI: The importance of evaluating the population health impact of public housing demolition and displacement. *J Urban Health* 88:417.

29. Cutrona CE, Wallace G, Wessner KA. (2006). "Neighborhood characteristics and depression: An examination of stress processes." *Curr Dir Psychol Sci*. 15:188.

30. *Baltimore Sun*. June 11, 1946. "Your debt to the Hopkins."

31. *Daily Record.* February 3, 2011. "The education solution."

32. Gomez MB, Muntaner C. (2005) "Urban redevelopment and neighborhood health in East Baltimore, Maryland."

33. *New York Times.* August 6, 2008. "Building a biotechnology park in Baltimore by rehabilitating a neighborhood."

34. Wallace R, Fullilove MT. (2008) *Collective consciousness and its discontents: Institutional distributed cognition, racial policy and public health in the United States.* Springer, NY.

35. Fullilove MT. (2004) *Root Shock: how tearing up city neighborhoods hurts America, and what we can do about it.* Random House, NY.

II

RACE, CLASS, POWER, AND ORGANIZING IN PRESENT-DAY EAST BALTIMORE

4

The First 10 Years of Rebuilding Middle East Baltimore: The Struggle for Inclusion and Justice for All

"... this [rebuilding Middle East Baltimore] was ethnic cleansing ... had not been for SMEAC it would have been a slaughter." —East Baltimore resident

"Rise up with me against the organization of misery." —Pablo Neruda

A community participatory rebuilding process began in Middle East Baltimore when residents organized and demanded that they be included in planning the rebuilding of their community. This chapter will describe the process of organized residents discovering and challenging the exclusionary way rebuilding of Middle East was planned and continued through the first 10 years. The different activities pertinent to rebuilding of a community are described from a perspective of residents' attempts to participate and assure equity and justice in them.

THE CONTINUOUS STRUGGLE FOR INCLUSION

While it is unjust to enter a person's home without permission and taking their property—illegal according to the U.S. Constitution—we do not consider the same actions on a larger scale illegal. One can liken the powerful stakeholders who devised a plan to displace residents from their homes and businesses without their input with the intent of destroying it and turning the land over for someone else to benefit to "entering and taking of property of value." On this larger scale the taking of something that is not yours, sanctioned by the powers held by the takers, is however supported by American law (figure 4.1).

In 2001, in Baltimore, Maryland, powerful interests saw it as normal to behave this way in a low-income African American community—taking of possessions. And

93

Figure 4.1. "Taking of property" from an individual and community has different outcomes

this attitude pervaded the process of rebuilding Middle East Baltimore for the first 10 years.

The continuous struggle by residents for inclusion in the rebuilding of their community and a process to be "made whole" challenged this attitude of superiority and paternalism held by the powerful stakeholders. This attitude which fueled perceptions of "knowing" what was better for the community residents and "knowing" that continued segregation was better for residents supported a mechanism to remove low-income and African Americans from the vicinity of JHMI and prepare the land for a different group of residents.

Residents challenged this pervading attitude by demanding to be treated fairly through just compensation for their homes, churches, and businesses and involvement in determining what was to happen to their persons and their homes, as renters and owners, ministerial leaders in their churches, and owners of their businesses, and to their community. In this context of stating their rights for justice, the mayor (now governor of Maryland) referred to residents in a public meeting as "ambulance chasers."

This type of response by the powerful outside stakeholders continued to affirm their attitude and perceptions and contributed to the lack of transparency and respect for residents of the Middle East Baltimore community that characterized this process. This race and class discrimination, the belief that African American and low-income people are unable to make healthy decisions in regard to rebuilding their community—healing their lives—shaped the planning and rebuilding of Middle East Baltimore. It presented the context for the struggle by residents demanding equity and justice. And it set up an oppositional and confrontational environment for all interactions involving residents' demands for self-determination.

THE PLANS: 1994, 2000, 2001, 2002

In May 2000, a feasibility study regarding a biotech park in the Middle East Baltimore community was performed for the Johns Hopkins School of Medicine. The group overseeing this planning process included the mayor's office, city and state representatives, the Abell and Open Society Foundations, and Johns Hopkins faculty and administration. Community representatives were not involved.[1]

In September 2000, the mayor put forth a bill to the city council for condemnation or acquisition of 196 houses in a 2-square-block area adjacent to JHMI northern boundary. The land would allow further expansion by JHMI and a park. The council passed the bill with many of the houses removed from the original proposal leaving approximately 1-square-block area for JHMI's expansion.[2]

In the fall of 2000, plans for major demolition and displacement of residents using eminent domain powers were already being considered by HEBCAC's board.[3] The chair of this board—an elected state representative of East Baltimore—and city government and JHMI board members were anxious to move forward with changing the neighborhood secondary to the failure of the 1994 HEBCAC plan for rebuilding of East Baltimore (chapter 2). The mayor supported such new strategies. "I think people are ready for a new approach. . . . We want to do something major."[4]

In January of 2001 the mayor put forth a new plan for rebuilding the entire Middle East Baltimore community, using the power of eminent domain to acquire the properties in this 88-acre area.[5] It merged the revised 1994 HEBCAC plan with the recommendations of the 2000 feasibility study for a Johns Hopkins biotech park—an 8-square-block biotech park and new and renovated houses in approximately 88 acres, or 20 square blocks. This new plan called for major demolition of more than 3000 properties in the area, occupied and unoccupied. It made no mention of community participation in the rebuilding process affecting the approximately 800 households who would be forced to move, of processes to ensure their return, or of the option of staying.

One local paper described the plan, announced publicly in January 2001, as follows: "The plan, which is in the development phase, reflects [the mayor's] strategy of building on the city's strengths—in this case, Johns Hopkins—to boost troubled neighborhoods. . . . Though the plan calls for an expansion of Hopkins, the city is taking the lead on the project. Hopkins spokeswoman . . . said she had no comment about the project because it's still in the development stage."[6]

Responding to this new plan for rebuilding Middle East Baltimore by the mayor and Johns Hopkins, one state senator for this jurisdiction tempered his support for the project by urging Hopkins to include the community and elected officials in the planning. He further emphasized this point, stating, "They essentially have put the cart before the horse," reinforcing his point that Hopkins has not included area residents in forming the development plan. "We're absolutely going to slow the process down until all the players, and I'm talking about the community and the elected officials, are part of the process. . . . We don't want to stop the train. We want to slow it down and get on board."

This was the plan residents first learned of through a newspaper article. There were no community members involved in the design or discussion of this new plan. Sentiments of area residents were summed up in this newspaper article:

> Several community leaders, who met with city officials and consultants at Hopkins late Tuesday to discuss neighborhood redevelopment, complained yesterday that they were not being kept informed of plans for East Baltimore. Those leaders said they were not notified at all or were given varying times for their meeting and were not told of the idea for a bio-tech park . . . "We were really upset that a lot of us didn't know about it and had no idea what was going on . . . Here's a big plan coming down and the people don't have a clue what's going on" . . . "They didn't tell us anything . . . we don't know what the business [of the city] is."[7]

In February 2001, the mayor appointed a committee to review the newly merged and now public plan. It included city officials, community leaders, local nonprofit organizations, and Johns Hopkins officials. It was called the Area North of Hopkins Steering Committee.

It was reported that this plan was an update of a plan HEBCAC had suggested several years earlier. Unfortunately, the majority of residents in Middle East Baltimore were unaware of the previous plan. Those who had heard of a "plan" assumed it was "just another plan of the Johns Hopkins Medical Institution expanding into the Middle East Baltimore community." Residents felt that the JHMI always had a plan to, bit by bit, redevelop or rebuild the Middle East Baltimore community in its image. It was "just a matter of time."

This previous HEBCAC plan, first presented in 1994, suggested that "substantial demolition" might be needed to eliminate blight in East Baltimore.[8] But it made no mention of demolishing all the more than 3,000 existing structures in the entire 88 acres of Middle East Baltimore, nor did it state that displacement of all residents was necessary to remove this blight. It suggested that the Madison Street corridor facing the JHMI be adapted through renovation of the houses into retail or office space, to attempt to soften this "wall" that was present between the JHMI and the Middle East Baltimore community.[9] Demolition was suggested only in blocks where there were consecutive abandoned houses. This was the extent of its recommendations regarding construction of new businesses, demolition, and renovation of row houses north of the JHMI.

One resident who participated in the design of the HEBCAC plans of the mid-1990s remembered being hopeful that residents would be part of the renovated areas being described in the HEBCAC plan: "That one wasn't a Hopkins plan because we participated and we would stay and be part of the renovation." A local paper reported that other residents supported this view in regard to the HEBCAC plans: "We were really pissed about that, . . . [We] wasted four years of our time looking at something that we wanted, only to find out that there is another plan on the table, and it wasn't about the people who lived there all those years, dealing with the drugs, dealing with the crime, dealing with poor services. And now you want us to leave and put something there that we wanted in the first place?"[10]

While some community residents were aware and participated in the 1994 HEBCAC plan for all of East Baltimore, the majority of residents in Middle East Baltimore were unaware of this plan. HEBCAC (described in chapters 2 and 3) did no community organizing, such as door knocking or other types of direct outreach, to include resident participation in the 1994 plan. It worked through the established community organizations and smaller neighborhood groups which were fragmented and often represented small numbers of residents of any one area. The unhealthy disorganized and poor social networks which had resulted from years of disinvestment and abandonment assured that without rigorous community organizing, the majority of residents remained uninformed.

SMEAC was formed several months after the announcement of the merged plan in January 2001. Its membership spoke to the residents, media, city council officials, and church leaders, rallying for community participation. The message was clear: a demand for participation in the planning of the rebuilding of the community, housing development before relocation, justice in any necessary relocation, and first right of return to the community.

Several months after the formation of SMEAC and its demand for inclusion in the process of rebuilding, city officials organized a series of public planning meetings to gather input from Middle East Baltimore residents. It was made clear in these meetings that the plan for a biotech park was moving forward and there would be no change based on community needs. This planning process was to develop a final master plan, building on the plan announced in January 2001.

Community input was solicited regarding the physical layout of the planned housing development, green space, transportation routes, and parks within this designated area of approximately 88 acres. There were no discussions regarding a change in the geographic area or the demolition of existing buildings and relocation of the occupants.

After these meetings, a master plan depicting the proposed physical layout of the approximately 88 acres was drafted; it was made public in December 2001. This master plan accommodated 2 million square feet of biotech space to be located north of the Hopkins East Baltimore campus over 7 to 10 years. Housing 30 to 50 companies, it was projected to provide up to 8,000 jobs. These jobs were designated as follows: one third for high school graduates, one third for college graduates, and one third for those with advanced degrees.[11]

The physical plan included a parking garage for 7,000 cars. There was no description of accommodating the increased traffic that would follow from a parking garage and a biotech park. This master plan stated: "By coordinating the development of such a facility with new residential and community development, the goals of both the community and the biotech facility can be mutually supportive. The community needs new jobs and a new image. The biotech complex needs a stable, secure environment and would benefit from immediately adjacent housing and retail uses."[12]

There was no evidence or mention of a planning process engaging residents to learn what they felt would benefit them. The founders of this plan took the paternalistic view and attitude that they "knew" what the community wanted, without asking. Community engagement came only after the first phase of the plan had been established and announced. This input was sought only on the physical layout of an already existing plan and only after much chaos and challenge from affected community members.

SMEAC STRUGGLES FOR A DECISION-MAKING VOICE ON THE GOVERNING BOARD

It was in late 2001 that East Baltimore Development Inc. was established. EBDI was formed as a public-private partnership organization—quasi-private nonprofit—to oversee and implement the master plan to rebuild Middle East Baltimore. The board of directors represented the range of interests in the rebuilding of Middle East Baltimore, except for the most affected: the JHMI; philanthropic organizations; development, banking, real estate, biotech, and manufacturing businesses; city and state departments; elected officials. There were no residents representing the community on its board.

SMEAC spoke out loudly and consistently about the right of residents to participate in every aspect of the rebuilding of their community, especially with respect to this board governing the entire rebuilding process. This advocacy included repeated lobbying and meeting with city council representatives and the powerful stakeholders on the EBDI board and gaining media exposure regarding the lack of fair community participation in the board.[13] More than 1 year after the formation of this board, two positions on it were identified for community representatives.[14] The persons to fill these positions were chosen by the city council representatives for Middle East Baltimore, and they did not live or work in the affected area.

It took 4 years from the initial formation of EBDI for a resident from Middle East Baltimore to be accepted as the community representative. Currently the board includes one local community member residing in the greater East Baltimore area and a representative living outside the community. The community representatives continue to be nominated by city council officials.

SMEAC RESPONDS TO THE MASTER PLAN

SMEAC presented the proposed master plan to its general membership, offering residents the opportunity to review it and ask questions that had not been asked or answered at the planning sessions. SMEAC and a coalition of supporters requested and attended meetings with the deputy mayor and other stakeholders and city council officials—the ad hoc team that was organizing the infrastructure for implementation of the new master plan (Area North of Hopkins Steering Committee). SMEAC's supporters were from the University of Maryland School of Social Work, Progressive Maryland, Historic Preservationists, Smart Growth advocates, 1000 Friends of Maryland, Citizen Planning and Housing Association, Environmental Defense Fund, and community activists interested in revising different aspects of this plan.

Some of the questions asked at these meetings pertained to the physical aspects of the plan: preservation of historic buildings, seamless transition into the adjacent communities, location of the biotech park and parking garage, and public transportation to accommodate the anticipated increase in population. Other questions were about housing development before relocation, relocation assistance, options to stay, and options to return. The inability to respond to these questions confirmed that there had been little consideration or planning for residents to remain in rehabbed or newly constructed houses, the welfare of residents during the relocation process, or the return of residents to the redeveloped area.

The public hearing before the city council, seeking approval of the demolition of the more than 3,000 structures in the approximately 88 acres, had not yet occurred. Still holding hope that the complete demolition of Middle East Baltimore could be prevented, many community members looked to the city council hearing as an opportunity to slow down the process and negotiate construction before relocation and demolition of their community.

SMEAC and its broader membership consistently requested that houses that could be rehabilitated be renovated first, so that residents forced to relocate from blocks planned for demolition could stay in their community. Neither city council officials nor the members of the Area North of Hopkins Steering Committee were open to these suggestions.

The master plan was presented for public comment in a city council hearing in April 2002. SMEAC organized residents to testify on their own behalf, regarding their choice to stay or leave, at the public hearing. Community members testified in front of their city council officials, requesting the rehabilitation of houses able to be preserved, so that residents could remain in their community. Residents living on a previously rehabilitated block of Washington Street rallied for removal of their homes from the demolition plan. Some of these residents had been relocated twice in 10 years in previous redevelopment efforts.[15]

Other than the two blocks on Washington Street that had been rehabbed within the previous 10 years, all structures in Middle East Baltimore were approved for demolition.[16] None of the city council representatives, EBDI, mayor-appointed committee addressed the concern of residents to remain in their community. Everyone would be relocated according to the powerful stakeholders in 2002.

The nonparticipatory planning for rebuilding Middle East Baltimore continued in this haphazard way. From the perspective of the community members, the "cart was before the horse" in all aspects of the process. And residents were constantly attempting to get on board a train that had long ago pulled out of the station with a destination not open for change.

Community members wanted to participate in the planning before there was a final plan. Their request was for a plan to include "housing before relocation." The originators of the 2001 plan had no intention of building or rehabbing houses for residents in the first approximately 30 acres just north of the medical campus. The Middle East Baltimore community was not the intended recipient of the redevelopment of the area bordering the prestigious medical complex. From the perspective of Johns Hopkins, EBDI, government officials, and the foundations, the horse was strategically placed in front of the cart, dragging community members away from the campus in preparation for a more suitable neighbor.

Because there was no transparency, and responses from EBDI consistently ignored the option of constructing sufficient houses before acquisition in the approximately 88 acres, it became clear that this plan was for the benefit of Johns Hopkins and the new community for whom it was being developed. EBDI made no attempts to involve residents in adapting the plan to minimize relocation of residents, which created even more distrust.

For residents involved in organizing their neighbors, living with this haphazard process and lack of transparency was like having a time bomb ticking away, not knowing when it would explode and take their homes with it. The stress and fear were palpable.

The master plan as adapted in 2002 did not address any preservation of historic houses within the approximately 88 acres, new school construction, or grocery or other local business ownership opportunities or participation. In regard to community participation, city officials declared that the master plan was not the context in which to describe the involvement of community in co-owning the process of rebuilding. At this time, there were no other processes in place in which any type of community participation could occur.

COMMUNITY PARTICIPATION AND STRUGGLE FOR JUSTICE IN RELOCATION

In the fall of 2001, the mayor appointed a Relocation Advisory Committee—later named the Housing and Relocation Committee—to address the relocation aspect of the master plan. Co-chaired by the city housing commissioner and the state delegate for the Middle East Baltimore area, this committee included no residents living in the community. SMEAC challenged this committee for its absence of community representation.

In December 2001, the Relocation Advisory Committee presented the first draft of a relocation policy advising the relocation process and how renters, owners, churches, and businesses in Middle East Baltimore affected by the master plan would be compensated.

The introductory text of the policy proposed by the Relocation Advisory Committee stated, "With the goal of creating a healthy Middle East community, and securing the edges of the communities surrounding Middle East," a previous master plan that had been "adopted by the Historic East Baltimore Community Action Coalition (HEBCAC)" had been built upon to include "a Biotech Center close to the Johns Hopkins Medical School and a large mixed-income, mixed new construction—rehabilitation housing and commercial development neighborhood to the north of the Biotech Center." Of note, this policy also stated, "These developments will be complemented by residential redevelopment of several nearby neighborhoods." (We will return to the extent of the peripheral redevelopment in chapter 7.)

The process and planning for this relocation policy draft were not informed by community residents or elected community representatives. There was no community participatory process, no input from residents, no negotiation as to what was justice in relocating residents against their will. At this time, there was no invitation or process for residents to attend or have a voice in meetings of the Relocation Advisory Committee. Residents were being told what their housing needs would be in the future by outside professionals—and some who had no expertise in the matter—who had shown little or no respect toward them and did not take the time to get to know the history, the people, or the needs of the community directly.

This first draft policy stated that compensation for owners who would be forced to relocate would be based on the current fair market value of their houses plus a relocation benefit (consistent with the federal Uniform Relocation Assistance [URA] Act: "All homeowners and tenants will receive the appropriate relocations and benefits consistent with the Uniform Relocation Assistance Act of 1970 and Section 104 (d) of the Housing and Community Development Act of 1974, as amended.") of up to $22,500.[17,18] This combined amount was to allow purchase of another home that was comparable in size or equity.

In 2001, the average value of a home in Middle East Baltimore was between $20,000 and $30,000. This current fair market value plus the $22,500 relocation benefit meant that residents would have an average of $44,500 to $54,500 with which to purchase a home elsewhere. The fair market value did not account for the value the land would gain after the redevelopment process was completed. During the city council hearing of the master plan to amend the existing urban renewal plan for Middle East Baltimore, SMEAC members and other residents and activists testified that a more fair value for their homes would reflect the anticipated value following redevelopment.

SMEAC and its supporters met several times with city council officials and other stakeholders, requesting a change in the fair market value that was being used to determine the benefit package for community members forced to relocate. The purchaser of residents' property was the city government, using federal dollars to purchase private houses under the state law granting eminent domain to the city. They argued that the law was allowing the city to take private property "for the public good." But exactly who was the "public" who would benefit if residents were being forced to relocate with no plan for how they could return to benefit from this good?

Those who would benefit were the Johns Hopkins community and the developers constructing a biotech park and housing—with subsidized loans, grants, and tax incentives from the government. Because the area was considered disinvested, subsidies to attract developers would allow them to build and increase their assets once construction was complete and property was sold or leased.

Middle East Baltimore residents, who had lived and worked through the abandonment of their community, were now forced to move and offer up their property for the benefit of others, some of whom had contributed to the cycle of decay and abandonment. The sting of this injustice was deep, hard, and continuous. For residents, it seemed that the only justice left was a relocation benefit package that was fair and a similar package to allow return to the rebuilt area for those who chose to return.

The first two pivotal documents, the initial plan to rebuild Middle East Baltimore and the relocation policy, presented the most important steps in the initial planning of rebuilding, sealing the intention of the projection. They both lacked a community participatory process. Unlike the Gay Street I Urban Renewal Project in the 1960s, the second major redevelopment in East Baltimore, this was not initiated, developed, or maintained as a resident-owned or resident-participatory rebuilding process. Instead, much like the first major redevelopment in East Baltimore, the Broadway Redevelopment Project of the 1950s, the Middle East Baltimore rebuilding project had patterned itself to repeat this unfair and disrespectful history of "Negro removal, or Negro clearance" of the urban renewal processes of the 1960s.[19,20] The stage had been set: there was no community participatory process in place and there was much work for SMEAC to do.

SMEAC organized more residents, making them aware of the injustices of these two important plans. The documented proof sparked community members to speak out more loudly and without fear. Many residents felt, "What else do we have to lose? They're taking our homes." At the same time, SMEAC continued to reach out to outside organizations to bridge relationships that would nurture a more collective force against gigantic odds: powerful stakeholders entrenched in racist and classist attitudes, determined to rebuild communities to hide urban poverty while continuing its growth.

With the help of the American Civil Liberties Union (ACLU) of Maryland, SMEAC reviewed, interpreted, and distributed this first relocation policy to the residents of Middle East Baltimore in various ways. One was to rewrite the text of the policy in more conversational language and distribute that—along with the original text—to community residents. Residents were encouraged to take these documents home, share them with friends and family, and return with unanswered questions. SMEAC also produced a skit, acting out the proposed process of relocation and using the language of the relocation policy.

Residents had many concerns about the fairness of this document (box 4.1). These concerns were documented and presented to the Relocation Advisory Committee.

SMEAC continued to agitate, increase its membership, formalize its practices of ethical leadership development, and encourage residents to speak from their hearts.

In late 2002, the Relocation Advisory Committee became a standing committee of the EBDI board, "charged with further detailing the design and implementation of an equitable relocation plan." Now called the Housing and Relocation Committee, this new committee of the board would "incorporate meaningful community participation into its deliberations and decision-making."[21] There was no description of who

---

Box 4.1.   Residents' Concerns About Initial Relocation Policy

Residents had many concerns about the fairness of the initial relocation policy documents:

- The $22,500 was based on a 1974 law and had not been adjusted to the current year.
- It forced segregation again by making a loan available only to residents who relocated within East Baltimore (in an area similar in all the social and economic indicators to the neighborhood they were being forced to move out of).
- They were being asked to take on a mortgage to get into a house that was comparable in size to homes in Middle East Baltimore.
- They were afraid of being shackled to the city through a loan.
- It was not clear what would happen to the loan if the owner died.
- It was not clear whether the loan would ever be forgiven.

would decide what was "meaningful," and this language sent feelings through the community that they were dealing with the same paternalistic attitudes held by these outsiders of past redevelopment projects. Reminiscent of East Baltimore residents' protests to urban renewal policies in the 1960s, these powerful outside stakeholders continued to decide what was best for low-income African Americans.[22]

Residents described EBDI and its committees as "parents telling you what to do," and many feared to speak up directly in meetings where outsiders were present. When residents requested advance notice of times and places of meetings, they received inconsistent information and last-minute notice of changes. Most meetings were held during the day. This kept many residents from attending, because they worked during the day. The outside stakeholders directing the rebuilding effort showed no knowledge or skills in practical ways to involve community residents. This was the beginning of rebuilding Middle East Baltimore and continued to dictate the exclusionary tone of the entire process.

After challenging the times meetings were scheduled meeting times were changed and the Housing and Relocation Committee began meeting monthly, in the evening, throughout the first 10 years of the rebuilding process. These meetings became the battlefield where residents and EBDI and its powerful partners struggled. Here is where challenges to unfair policies—relocation, demolition, housing, employment, economic inclusion—occurred and while the only way residents could participate, these meetings were dreaded by residents and their representatives. These meetings provoked anxiety and stress for residents while some of the powerful stakeholders attending these meetings referred to them as a game. For residents, it was not a game, not fun and continued to increase the burden of stress already present from living in unhealthy communities and the unknown of where one would live next. The power imbalance in these meetings were clear and the paternalism by the leadership of EBDI was consistent. Still, community residents and others interested in the relocation and housing planning for Middle East Baltimore residents regularly attended. It was not a decision-making body, but it acted to deliver suggestions from this public meeting to help inform the EBDI board on issues affecting relocation, economic inclusion, and housing.

RELOCATION POLICY CHANGES AS COMMUNITY RESIST SEGREGATION, AGAIN

SMEAC reviewed each subsequent draft of the relocation plan, interpreted it to the general membership, and challenged it for more equitable processes. SMEAC received questions from the general membership, directly or indirectly, and presented them at the monthly Housing and Relocation Committee meetings.

If new answers were offered at the Housing and Relocation Committee meeting, these were taken back to the general membership in meetings, flyers, or door-knocking outreach.

Box 4.2.   Residents' Questions About Relocation Policy

These were the major questions posed by residents regarding relocation during 2002 and 2003:

- When do we have to move? How? Where?
- Will it be this year? Before Christmas?
- Will I have to remove my child from school?
- How do I find a new school if I don't know where I will live?
- How will I get to work?
- Who will watch my kids if Ms. Smith is not around the corner anymore?
- What if my son and his family live with me?
- What if the house was given to me by my uncle with no papers?
- Can we move into a one-story house?
- My kids live with me now, where will they live afterwards?

This process of engaging residents in shaping the relocation plan, through questions and answers, helped to reduce some of the stress on residents anxiously waiting to learn about their fate. It was a significant step in bringing control back into the hands of the community. This engagement process also informed the writing of the final relocation policy, so that it was substantially improved by community participation. It could not have been completed in its final form without the input of residents (box 4.2).

After the first draft of the relocation policy was challenged for its clear injustice to community members, another draft offered the current fair market value (FMV) of a house, plus the original $22,500 of the URA Act benefit, plus an additional amount up to $40,000 toward the purchase of a new home (FMV + $22,500 + up to $40,000).[23]

The $40,000 plus the original $22,500 was the total benefit calculated to account for inflation since the 1976 URA Act was enacted. However, to be eligible for the additional $40,000, the newly purchased house had to be in the larger historic East Baltimore area. In addition, this $40,000 was a loan by the city to the owner, which would incur no interest or monthly payments if the owner did not sell, refinance, rent, or lease, and occupied the house as his or her primary residence.

In effect, the additional $40,000 was a lien—a loan secured against the property—eventually repayable to the city if the stated conditions were no longer being met. Residents who moved outside the historic East Baltimore area but remained within the city limits could receive up to $27,500 of the $40,000 toward purchase of their new homes. If residents moved outside the city limits, they could not receive any of the additional $40,000. The language in the policy stated: "To be eligible for supplemental benefits through EBDI you must relocate in the City of Baltimore."[24]

Residents responded with shock to the restrictions tied to the additional $40,000, feeling the proposal was reminiscent of the history of overt racial segregation in housing for African Americans. Many conditions in the four areas within the historic East Baltimore footprint were similar to those in Middle East Baltimore. This was the reason they were part of the original areas HEBCAC determined to be in need of redevelopment. In fact, they were all registered in city records as urban renewal areas.[25] Reminiscent of the 1950s Broadway Redevelopment Project, and smaller projects since, this plan attempted to force residents to congregate in similarly disinvested areas, away from the Johns Hopkins campus. Instead of addressing the causes and effects of past racist housing and redevelopment practices, this plan was ensuring that race and class segregation continued well into the twenty-first century: Negro removal in the twenty-first century.[26]

For residents who were renters, those who qualified would be offered Section 8 vouchers and the ability to move where they chose, in or outside of the city of Baltimore. Renters who preferred and qualified for public housing would be assisted by the Housing Authority of Baltimore City. Residents who were currently renters and able to move into homeownership would be offered Section 8 vouchers to assist in the purchase of a home.

In this draft of the relocation policy, no mention was made of the up to 5-year supplemental cash benefits afforded to renters under the URA Act to help pay for potential increased monthly housing costs due to relocation. Also not mentioned were the long-term consequences, once it expired, for renters who might receive this 5-year supplemental cash benefit. It was likely that some renters would have to relocate yet again after this benefit expired—and likely into neighborhoods with similar conditions as the one they were being forced to move, or become homeless.[27]

Moving expenses up to $1,050 would be covered for all relocating households, regardless of where they moved. These included moving expenses, security deposits, and other associated costs.

Business owners would be compensated according to the URA Act, in amounts that would vary from business to business. This policy was to be monitored for its "professional and compassionate" implementation by the Relocation Advisory Committee.

With the help of protests by residents and the continued demands in local meetings—in person and in writing—and media exposure regarding the unfair proposals, this second draft policy underwent revisions. Released in fall 2002, the third draft stated that instead of the previous $22,500 benefit toward purchasing a home of comparable value and space, the amount was adjusted to $70,000 to accommodate the 30-year period since the law was passed. The "loan" of up to $40,000 was removed from the proposal and restrictions on where residents could relocate were lifted. Now owners would receive the fair market value for their current homes and up to $70,000 toward the purchase of a home matching the equity in their previous home in Middle East Baltimore (FMV + up to $70,000). This policy stated that renters had access to a 5-year supplemental cash benefit. No mention was made of the risk of homelessness or relocation into another abandoned community after the 5-year supplement expired.

Over the 20 months that followed the fall 2002 revision, this policy was further revised with language detailing the process of relocation. These revisions included phases of relocation (which changed from three to two phases in 2002, during the plan's development), anticipated dates for relocation, process of housing assessment and selling of homes, finding a new home, financial counseling on purchasing or renting new homes, moving assistance, and other social services when necessary.

Social services offered in the final relocation plan included support for finding schools in the new neighborhoods, referrals for drug or substance abuse treatment, credit improvement counseling, employment readiness services, and other case management services. Besides policy guiding acquisition, purchase, relocation, and follow-up, this final relocation plan included a broad scope of services intended to individually and together support a less chaotic transition for relocation of a family.

In this plan there was no mention of relocation back into the community. The revised relocation plan was accepted by the city council in October 2003 after a public hearing and subsequently accepted as the final draft by the EBDI board. The plan continued to be updated with amendments into fall 2004.[28]

Relocation was set up to occur in two phases (see figure 1.2). Phase 1 would address approximately 1000 properties, including approximately 400 buildings occupied by owners and renters, in a contiguous geographic area of 10 blocks, or approximately 30 acres.

Figure 4.2a. Middle East Baltimore project with cleared land sits after displacement and demolition while plans change 2008-2011

The first notices informing residents that their homes would be acquired by the City of Baltimore reached residents in Middle East Baltimore in February 2004, 3 years after the initial announcement of relocation.[29] This started the series of steps that would result in residents leaving their homes in the community, the uprooting of a historic African American community.

EBDI contractors offered financial advice regarding the purchase of new homes and use of Section 8 vouchers or supplemental benefits for rental housing. Families were offered three sites to look at before choosing. When residents reported to SMEAC that they felt their counselors were showing them houses only in certain areas, SMEAC challenged EBDI to address these issues. These requests were made in writing, with an expectation that a response would be made in writing, detailing how the issue would be addressed.

When residents reported that the appraisers who were looking at their homes were not making appointments and were showing up uninvited or were not entering the houses to make appraisals, SMEAC engaged in a letter-writing campaign to change the company doing the appraisals. Over 500 people signed letters. This pressure by the organized residents resulted in replacement of the contractors doing the appraisals.

When residents reported that they felt they were being spoken to disrespectfully during their counseling sessions or that their relocation counselors swayed them into looking in certain neighborhoods, SMEAC volunteered to be present during these sessions, with signed permission of the resident.

SMEAC remained an active observer and participant in many aspects of advocacy and organizing, helping residents ensure that their voices were being listened to. It was committed to minimizing the stress of the oppressive action of the uprooting of a culture and the resultant toll on the spiritual, mental, and physical well-being of each person in Middle East Baltimore. The detail of each action in the process of relocation could begin the healing or continue the fragmentation. One of SMEAC's logos read, "Making our community whole." This motto evolved from discussions of the wholeness that would come from addressing the spirit, the mind, and the body in the rebuilding of the community of Middle East Baltimore (box 4.3).

**Box 4.3.   SMEAC Defined Being 'Made Whole' as
Assuring Equity and Justice in the Rebuilding Process**

This Included:

- houses to be built before acquisition and relocation began
- resident participation and decision making in all processes
- a house for a house, square foot for square foot, in a stable community
- fair relocation packages
- right of return
- affordable houses to return to
- fair relocation packages to afford returning back into the community

By the end of 2006, 396 households and more than 1000 families had been relocated out of the Phase 1 area just north of the Johns Hopkins campus. Though there were no limits on where residents could relocate, the majority of families in Phase 1 relocated primarily to two areas of the city: East Baltimore and Northwest Baltimore. Renters relocated primarily to adjacent areas of the Middle East Baltimore community, communities not so different from the areas they had been relocated from.

During the detailed door-knocking and listening project SMEAC conducted from 2002 through 2005, residents ranked the neighborhoods they would prefer to move into.[30] These neighborhoods included, in order of preference: East Baltimore, Falls Road near Hampden, Canton, Federal Hill, Pikesville, Roland Park, Mt. Washington, Belair-Edison, Seton Hill, Reservoir Hill, and Randallstown. The neighborhoods that residents were regularly shown as available for relocation included fewer than half of these choices. The majority of residents moved into areas they were shown by EBDI staff.

A major organizing motto of SMEAC, based on resident feedback, was that fair relocation meant the equity in their new homes should equal the equity in their old homes and they should be in a community more stable than the one they were being relocated out of: "square foot for square foot, in a stable community." Chapter 7 will discuss how the relocation into unstable communities affects residents and the communities into which they relocate.

PHASE 2: MORE CHANGES IN RELOCATION AND MASTER PLAN

In 2006 after almost all the households in Phase 1 had been relocated, demolition of houses continued, and rats ruled the day and night in the increasingly abandoned Middle East Baltimore. This was when EBDI announced that the continued relocation of residents in Phase 2, occupying the additional approximately 58 acres to the north of Phase 1, was being placed on hold due to reported challenges in financing.

This report regarding financial challenges came at a time when: "The pay and benefits at the nonprofit [EBDI] increased by 46 percent, from $2.6 million in 2005–2006 to $5.6 million in 2008–2009, when eight employees made more than $100,000 a year. During that time the staff expanded from 43 to 72, according to . . . EBDI's chief financial officer."[31] The benefit to EBDI's leadership and staff was clear and financially supported and remained unclear in regards to residents.

What was very clear was the continued stress and anxiety residents in Phase 2 experienced when they were again placed in a state of the unknown and flux. They expressed panic and fear about what would happen to them. Some residents had delayed much-needed repairs to their homes—fixing leaking roofs, replacing inadequate heaters—after being advised by EBDI leadership and staff that they would be relocated before these hazards became dangerous.[32] Now, it was unclear when relocation would happen. And some residents were left living in even more isolated blocks after their neighbors in the first phase had been relocated.

Another public planning process was convened in June 2006, to engage residents in revising the plan affecting the second phase. These meetings resulted in a revised master plan, now including a school on 7 acres of land, a widening of the area on the northeast boundary, and a new time frame for the process of relocation for residents in Phase 2.[33]

The initial plan had called for complete relocation of all residents—in both phases—by 2007. This new plan was unclear as to when relocation would begin for residents in Phase 2 and even less able to ensure when relocation would be completed.

During this time of change in 2006, a subcommittee of the Housing and Relocation Committee, called the Policy Subcommittee, was formed to discuss alternatives for development of housing options specific to land in Phase 2. Phase 1 was not up for discussion, only Phase 2. Discussion of the feasibility of rehabilitating and preserving some blocks within the approximately 58 acres, to allow residents to remain in their community, was now on the table.

This had been ignored during the first 5 years of rebuilding and was not an option in Phase 1. Discussing it now was a complete turnaround from previous decisions made by the EBDI board in 2001–2006. In fact, this was what residents demanded in 2001, after first learning about the plan to relocate all residents and demolish the entire area. Now, in 2006, EBDI and its stakeholders were entertaining and supporting preservation of blocks—within Phase 2.

In the fall of 2006, SMEAC began negotiating for grants that would enable residents to rehabilitate houses in Phase 2 blocks and stay in their community. Almost 2 years later, after consistent organizing and rallying by SMEAC and allies and residents in Phase 2, much media publicity, and continued documentation and challenging of conflicting oral promises made by EBDI and stakeholders, a revised housing plan was adopted.[34]

During this struggle for rehabbed housing in Phase 2 SMEAC was again called in by its primary funder and cautioned about speaking to the media. The CEO of EBDI attempted to persuade SMEAC's executive director, in private, to not publicly attack EBDI and its powerful partners and to settle things privately. SMEAC used the tools it could access in its struggle for inclusion and justice against these powerful stakeholders. The use of media was always a tactic to inform the public about the inconsistency of verbal and written promises and actions by these powerful people outside of public spaces. And the public embarrassment of unfair practices occurring during this "urban renewal" rebuilding process was an important tactic in assuring that EBDI and partners followed through on their promises. This struggle for housing was one such example.

This revised housing plan offered residents the opportunity to stay in the neighborhood and move into a new or rehabilitated house or to relocate outside the neighborhood as their neighbors in Phase 1 had done. If residents chose to move outside the neighborhood or into a newly constructed house in the neighborhood, they were eligible to received relocation benefits consistent with the updated Maryland legislation of 2007 which differed from previous benefits provided to residents in Phase 1 (an additional $5,000 compensation for a replacement home).[35]

If a resident chose to move into a rehabilitated house in the Phase 2 area, he or she was eligible for a grant to cover the rehabilitation cost, if the fair market value of his or her house did not cover the cost of the repairs. This was called the House for a House program.

In late 2007, relocation of residents in Phase 2 began. By 2011, 10 years after the announcement of displacement from their community, still all residents from Phase 2 had not been relocated. Of the more than 50 households remaining, 39 of the almost 340 households in Phase 2 have chosen to stay and participate in the House for a House program or remain in their original homes (after they undergo preservation through historic preservation grant subsidies). The remaining households chose to relocate out of the Middle East Baltimore community.

Like the stalled rebuilding effort in the 1950s Broadway Redevelopment Project, when the plans changed after residents were displaced and building demolished, the current rebuilding of Middle East Baltimore suffered the same fate. After residents were displaced from the land necessary for Johns Hopkins expansion the remaining land sat vacant as plans changed (figure 4.2a, 4.2b).

Figure 4.2b.   Middle East Baltimore boarded houses sit while plans change 2008-2011

THE NEW SCHOOL

Also in 2006, EBDI and partners put forth a plan for the construction of a new pre-K through grade 8 school. It is unclear when this new aspect of the rebuilding plan was actually decided on, because no community engagement or input was sought from community members, directly or through SMEAC. It was made known to the community in mid-2006, when a shift in the first master plan was announced. What was clear was that to attract higher-income residents to the rebuilt area, which would be affiliated directly or indirectly with the Johns Hopkins Medical campus, a "suitable school" for the children of these individuals was necessary.

While plans for a new school was already decided and known by EBDI and its partners, community residents learned much later. This was evidenced by the Johns Hopkins University courting of their choice for a new president during this announcement. He was then the president of the University of Pennsylvania. In Philadelphia, he had been instrumental in establishing a charter school in a similarly disinvested and abandoned community near the university, secondary to its expansion into the community. This expansion of the University of Pennsylvania was also directed by the current director of EBDI. The rebuilding of Middle East Baltimore continued to be directed by the JHMI and affiliates, through EBDI and its powerful partners, while the community continued to struggle for transparency and inclusion in the rebuilding of their community.[36]

The plan for a new school resulted in an additional two square blocks being targeted for acquisition and demolition, expanding the boundaries farther east than had originally been proposed (see figure 1.1 in chapter 1). The new school, to be built on 7 acres, would be a public charter school. It would enroll students from the surrounding area; children of residents forced to relocate; and children of employees, students, and affiliates of the JHMI. Some in the community noted that residents were not the primary target for the school and questioned how displaced children would have access to the new school.

SMEAC requested, orally and in writing, that community participation be sought and maintained throughout the planning and implementation of this new school. Community residents engaged in the original planning meetings for the school toured model schools in other cities, and rallied for children of relocated residents as well as those in several of the communities peripheral to Middle East Baltimore to attend this new school.

The new school opened in its temporary site in 2009, with classes for first and fifth graders. Its permanent site is planned for completion by 2013.[37]

At the end of its first academic year, residents reported that the children were "off the hook" in disorderly behavior and wondered how this environment was supportive of learning. Because it is a new school and the majority of its enrollment is from East Baltimore, it is not surprising that the students failed to achieve passing scores on state standardized tests after one academic year. After all, the current students are the same ones who have been living in abandoned communities with under-resourced services in education. But because of the greater resources secured for this school, and its role as a magnet for the higher-income community EBDI and partners are targeting, it is anticipated that the scores will show continuous improvement in the coming years. If EBDI and partners see no signs of improvement, changes will likely occur, as recently happened with the firing of the first principal.[38]

The JHMI is deeply involved in all aspects of the planning, design, and hiring of staff and providing input on the learning model of this new public school in East Baltimore.[39] While there are two other public schools in the area, this school has the benefit of the substantial resources of local foundations—Annie E. Casey Foundation, Atlantic Philanthropies, Weinberg Foundation—in addition to the resources of human and social capital of the JHMI. EBDI has also solicited financial assistance from the Baltimore City Public School System, which has been unable to provide appropriate support to the two existing public schools in the area, and tax subsidies.

THE STRUGGLE TO REQUIRE SAFETY PROCEDURES FOR DEMOLITION

Starting in 2001, SMEAC requested in writing that safety procedures be used during the demolition and construction phases of the rebuilding process. In 2003, studies showed that the dust produced during demolition of buildings in previous rebuilding projects in Middle East Baltimore contained lead levels 6-fold to 81-fold higher than the level the U.S. Environmental Protection Agency regarded as safe.[40] The studies reported that the houses adjacent to the ones being demolished could likely be contaminated by the dust spread due to the force of the debris and wind direction.

In 2003, the demolition practices approved by the city did not address these issues specific to houses with lead-based paint. In addition, community members and contractors reported poor enforcement of minimal safety requirements in previous and current demolition in other parts of East Baltimore.[41] Armed with these and other data supporting the need for a demolition protocol that would protect the residents near the demolition sites, SMEAC partnered with Morgan State University and other community organizations in organizing a campaign for safe demolition.

Beginning in 2004, EBDI directed demolition to begin in the Phase 1 area. Before beginning demolition, it did little preparation regarding safety procedures. As a result, nearby residents who left their windows open before going to work returned home in the evening to find dust layered throughout the houses. Without proper protection around the demolition sites, neighborhood children were playing in the dust that settled outside buildings being demolished. Houses were being hosed down inconsistently during demolition, and residents called in daily to SMEAC offices reporting these unsafe procedures.

These were some of the issues that SMEAC and its partners raised in pointing out that the demolition of houses was being performed haphazardly and without concern for the safety of residents. SMEAC coordinated a Rally for Safe and Healthy

Box 4.4. Letter requesting that EBDI assume greater responsibility for a safer demolition protocol

Save Middle East Action Committee, Inc.
(S.M.E.A.C.)
2100 E. Madison Street, 3rd Floor
Baltimore, MD 21205

May 26, 2004

Mr. xxxxx xxxxxx
East Baltimore Development, Inc.
1731 E. Chase Street
Baltimore, MD 21213-3133

Dear Mr. xxxxx:

Attached please find a letter to SMEAC from Dr. xxxxx xxxxx, Director of the Institute for Urban Research, Morgan State University. This letter is in response to your request of May 14, 2004 to Dr. xxxxx to provide information and examples of safe demolition practices involving lead abatement in the United States.

Enclosed is the response that Dr. xxxx provided to us. We are pleased to forward this response to you.

Having done so, I must also state that *the primary responsibility for gathering this type of information and ensuring that the public health risks that current demolition practices pose to residents and other stakeholders working in the community, as detailed in the report by Dr. xxxx xxxxx, belongs to EBDI and to the contractor(s) hired to implement demolition efforts – not to SMEAC and not to those providing technical assistance to SMEAC in these matters.*

The burden of keeping the community safe from this health risk should not be placed on the backs of those being directly affected by the demolitions and community displacement; those who are most at risk and who will currently derive little to no benefit from the revitalization of the community since there is no plan in place for their right to return to the newly gentrified community.

The information that you requested is provided in good faith and in a spirit of moving the process forward to help protect the health of those who live here and whose health is therefore at risk. We fully expect, though, that EBDI – as the implementation arm of ensuring the success of this effort -- will assume their rightful responsibility in researching additional models and concentrating on solutions that eliminate the health risks instead of protocol that leaves the responsibility of mitigating those risks squarely on the shoulders of residents.

Sincerely,
xxxxx xxxxxx
Chair, SMEAC Board

Cc: xxxxx xxxxx.
       Director, Institute for Urban Research
       Morgan State University

xxxxxx xxxxxxxx
Morgan State University

Demolition, which resulted in substantial media exposure. The rally called for cessation of the current demolition, a new and safer demolition protocol for all sites, and relocation of all residents in the Phase 1 area before demolition was restarted.

EBDI's protocol advised residents to wash their windows, floors, and carpets each day during demolition of houses nearby. It placed the burden to remain safe and prevent harm on the residents and provided for minimal prevention practices by the demolition workers and little supervision to ensure safety (box 4.4).

Changing the protocol to ensure safer demolition practices would cost the project more than it had originally budgeted for demolition and change the timeline for demolition of houses. This timeline was set to deliver the cleared land for construction of the first biotech building occupied by JHMI. In setting this timeline, EBDI had anticipated demolishing blocks of houses currently vacant before houses in adjacent blocks were vacated. Slowing down demolition would slow down preparation and delivery of the land. This was not about the convenience and safety of residents, it was about the convenience by all means necessary for the construction of a biotech park.[42]

The campaign for safe demolition processes continued. SMEAC and partners wrote letters to the mayor and 20 other stakeholders in 2004 and 2005, challenging the unsafe practices that were being undertaken are letters to the mayor and foundations regarding the campaign for safe demolition (box 4.5 and box 4.6).

Demolition was halted temporarily and the protocol was revised to ensure that proper procedures were used to minimize the risk from demolition of houses painted with lead-based paint. In September 2004, EBDI presented a revised proposal reflecting an effort to improve on the protocol it had initially used for demolition.

In early 2005, an expert panel was engaged to review the effects of demolition on dust spreading during and after demolition, test samples acquired from different points at various distances from the demolition sites, and offer recommendations regarding the revised protocol. The panel presented its findings periodically during the initial period of demolition, with community residents in attendance. This panel of experts subsequently judged this protocol to be safe, and it was adapted for continued demolition practices in Middle East Baltimore.[43,44]

Similar to the process of community participation in revising the relocation policy, this process of community engagement clearly was a necessity for challenging the way EBDI had engaged contractors to perform demolition. EBDI and its partners ultimately funded the additional processes for the safety of residents. But until SMEAC challenged their methods, EBDI and its partners saw no need to stop performing demolitions without a clear perimeter, consistent hosing down, and adequate notice to nearby residents; without providing cleaning supplies to rid nearby homes of the dust from the demolition in a preventive and timely manner; and without maintaining a radius of vacant houses to minimize unnecessary exposure and risk. They did not see it as necessary to change, and they resisted stopping the demolition that had begun or looking into the initial protocol. Scrutiny by the public, after the rally and letters to various media outlets, brought a different set of eyes to this aspect of the process that was occurring in rebuilding Middle East Baltimore.

Box 4.5. Letter requesting a safer demolition protocol

November 18, 2004

Dear Mayor   ,

I am writing to you in regard to the current redevelopment project that is underway in the Middle East Baltimore Neighborhood, north of the Johns Hopkins Medical Institutions. As Director of the Institute for Urban Research and Professor at Morgan State University,   Dr.   of the Public Health Program here and I, have served as technical advisors for residents in the area concerned about their safety during the proposed demolition. The Save Middle East Action Committee, Inc. (SMEAC) represents residents who currently live or do business in this area. They have requested that we provide technical assistance in regard to planned demolition practices and the lack of transparency in these matters; it is within this role that this communication is provided.

We are extremely concerned about the proposed demolition that has been proposed by the East Baltimore Development Incorporation (EBDI). Research has consistently shown that the homes have excessive amounts of lead due to the year in which they were constructed as well as an excessive amount of lead-poisoned children in these zip codes. In addition, researchers at the Johns Hopkins School of Public Health have shown that during and following demolition of houses in this area, there exists excessive amounts of lead and other particulate matter in the air which pose a risk of lead poisoning and exacerbation of respiratory and cardiovascular illness in residents in adjoining houses as well as workers and pedestrians within the area. Of particular concern, is the potential risk of new and additional exposure of lead in children and women of childbearing age, and acute respiratory and cardiovascular illnesses in the elderly and others with chronic illnesses. These reports state that it is currently unknown how far this toxic air may travel and the degree to which a safety threat is borne by nearby residents, workers, and pedestrians.

We have requested that relocation of residents before demolition is initiated in the entire Phase 1 area occur. This is the only way to assure that residents and nearby individuals are not at risk of exposure to these toxic levels of lead and other particulate matter in the air. Any other process would in effect be a 'research protocol' to determine how much exposure occurs during and after the proposed demolition, while placing individuals at unnecessary risk. And in fact serves as an intentional act of injustice against a targeted group of people, not unlike the Tuskegee Syphilis Study promulgated against African Americans between the 1930's and 1970's.

Our most recent request for 'relocation before demolition' was sent to EBDI on October 7, 2004. We are still awaiting a response and the access to the planning and decision-making process of whether relocation before demolition will occur; to date these processes have remained non-transparent. Lastly, we have been informed that rather than seeking safer ways to reduce potential harm to the health of residents during demolition, EBDI has instead been primarily focused on blocking potential injunction processes. This is negotiating in bad faith and clearly shows only secondary regard for the safety of Baltimoreans living in this neighborhood.

We bring this to your attention and seek the expertise of your staff in informing the redevelopment process in a way that will maintain the safest circumstances for all at risk of exposure to this tremendous health hazard. For your information, please find attached a copy of the last letter sent to EBDI and a summary copy of a Health Impact Assessment of the proposed demolition process.

Sincerely,

Morgan State University
1700 East Cold Spring Lane
Baltimore MD 21251

CC:

In 2010, this protocol was presented to the Maryland legislature as the safest way to perform demolition and subsequently adopted as law governing demolition practices in Maryland. EBDI and partners took full credit for developing a safer protocol for urban demolition. They forgot about the struggle by impacted residents who were exposed to lead and hazardous conditions, who raised their voices and demanded safety for themselves and their community. This forgetting, of the residents who sat through the years of disinvestment and unhealthy neighborhood conditions and who initiated changes in the "Master's plan" through struggle and resistance, has been consistent during the first 10 years of rebuilding Middle East Baltimore. The fact is that it took community organizing, advocacy, and leadership development to ensure that the powerful stakeholders acted with integrity in regard to the health and safety of community members.

THE STRUGGLE FOR CONSTRUCTION
OF AFFORDABLE HOUSING

SMEAC consistently advocated construction of affordable houses, the right of return for displaced residents, and local ownership of business ventures and economic development opportunities in the rebuilt community. Results of its door knocking and community organizing during 2002 through 2005 made clear that 66 percent of households wanted to move back into the redeveloped area, and 67 percent percent wanted to participate in the redesign of the planned redevelopment if the opportunity was provided.

Box 4.6. Letter requesting participation in demolition protocol development

Save Middle East Action Committee, Inc.
(SMEAC)
2111 Ashland Ave. (mailing address)
Baltimore, MD 21205
410-522-3360
smeacbaltimore@verizon.net

Executive Director   Board Chair

March 25, 2005

President
The Annie E. Casey Foundation
701 St. Paul Street
Baltimore, MD 21206

Dear xxxx,

While we are glad to learn of the potential input of the health experts, invited in by Casey and EBDI to assess the health impact of demolition in Phase I, we are disappointed that community participation continues to be absent from the process. SMEAC has requested twice that we have an opportunity to meet with them; both times you confirmed that this would be the appropriate thing to do. However, at the March 24, 2005 Housing and Relocation meeting, no invitation to SMEAC or other community residents was extended when the 'potential' meeting with these experts was announced.

SMEAC is officially requesting that we be involved in this process so as to accurately present the view of the residents. Your summary of the community perspective was not fully accurate in your presentation at the above mentioned meeting and evidence of the need for a real community presence and voice in issues that directly or indirectly impact residents. In addition, HUD requirements and local law governing the Redevelopment Project in East Baltimore states that community participation is required in all processes concerned with this project.

We look forward to working with you and other stakeholders to maintain accountability and transparency in all processes pertaining to this Redevelopment Project. We are confident that you are supportive of changing the historic and intentional minimization of true community participation in 'decision-making' that affect the safety and health of their lives.

Sincerely,

xxxx
Executive Director

cc.

SMEAC used this information to further organize residents to advocate on behalf of the larger community for more low-income housing in the proposed housing plan. With the assistance of the Community Development Clinic at the University of Baltimore School of Law, SMEAC insisted that written policy govern the types of housing being constructed in the rebuilt community. Its campaign included more than 500 signatures from residents requesting that construction of new houses include one third each of low-income, moderate-rate or median-income, and market-rate housing.

As a result of this campaign and other organizing for affordable housing in the rebuilt community and support by local elected officials, the following was agreed upon by EBDI and partners: one third each of low-income, median-income, and market-rate housing, to be intermixed and not separated according to cost. Each income category would have an equal number of homeownership and rental opportunities. This became the housing plan for EBDI and partners for rebuilding Middle East Baltimore in 2005 and echoed publicly in 2006: "EBDI's plans call for a third of the 1,500 to 1,800 units of new housing to be priced for lower-income residents and another third for what EBDI President and CEO . . . calls 'work-force housing for medium-income people, like firefighters, police, nurses, teachers.' The remaining units will be set at 'market rate.'"[45]

SMEAC advocated to city council representatives to enact this in law, as well as language assuring community participation. In 2005 the Middle East Baltimore Urban Renewal Plan was amended to include the income level of houses to be constructed:

> Ensure that significant housing resources are made available to households of varying income levels, specifically, low income (50 percent or less of the median income applicable to Baltimore City as published and annually updated by the United States Department of Housing and Urban Development), moderate income (making more than 50 percent of median income applicable to Baltimore City but less than 100 percent of median income using a combination of price adjustment and buyer financing assistance programs, sponsored by the state of Maryland and other sources), and market rate without regard to income"; resident participation in the planning of the community: "Substantial Community Involvement" means: Community participation that is consistent with the required approval of the "Planned Unit Developments"; and a comprehensive development plan: "comprehensive plan of development that is approved through a process that has substantial community involvement."[46]

The negotiation around the types of housing to be constructed in the rebuilt community reflected why resident participation was crucial in all aspects of the planning and implementation phases. Suggestions put forth by EBDI partners included trying to pass off low-income housing for Johns Hopkins students as fulfilling the low-income housing opportunities, building residences for Johns Hopkins students before houses for residents forced to move, and building the biotech park area before housing for historic residents and those moving from other communities of East

---

Box 4.7.   Housing Units Completed in the Phase 1 Area, 2010

- 78 low-income rental units for seniors (Ashland Commons, completed 2008)
- 74 workforce (moderate-rate) rental units (Park View, completed 2008)
- 63 moderate and market-rate rental units (Chapel Green, completed 2009)
- 5 market-rate ownership units (Townes at Eager, completed 2010)

Baltimore. There were many negotiations, many revisions, and review for loopholes by SMEAC's attorneys before the final language was agreed upon. To address the attempt to include JHMI graduate student housing as low-income housing the 2005 Urban Renewal Plan legislation specifically stated: "Ensure that the Development Project Area provides (excluding student housing) one-third low income housing, one-third moderate income housing, and one third market rate housing."[47]

The terms used to describe the types of housing have changed since EBDI agreed on the numbers and types of housing. For example, in some documents, workforce housing is used in place of moderate-rate housing and rental assistance has replaced low-income lists total housing units completed by 2010 (box 4.7).

MASTER PLAN CHANGES AGAIN
BUT EXCLUSION OF RESIDENTS DO NOT

With the economic downturn after the housing market peaked in 2008, 2009 found EBDI's housing and biotech business plans challenged. Its intention to build 50 units of market-rate housing, "The Townes at Eager," was not received with much interest from consumers and resulted in only 5 units being completed. The first biotech building opened in 2008. New or existing companies slowly moved in and 3 years later it remains not fully leased. Engaging retailers in leasing the ground-floor space remains a challenge. Prices have been lowered to entice businesses to occupy the spaces, now vacant for over 3 years.

There was no process to engage community residents in learning about potential occupants or offering their opinions on preferred occupants. No training or workshops to engage residents of the area in entrepreneurship, shared-equity business ownership, or co-owning businesses have occurred. Wealth development through entrepreneurship and other aspects of increasing assets, a concrete way to address movement out of poverty, has been lacking in the overall rebuilding process. Instead, EBDI and its powerful stakeholders determined who would lease retail space in the biotech building, making decisions about what were appropriate shops to benefit the new community.

SMEAC suggested that low-income homes for owner-occupants be constructed before or along with homes for median or market-rate ownership, to ensure that the residential atmosphere of the rebuilt area would reflect the culture of the historic community—not a completely new and gentrified community. EBDI and its representatives confirmed that they would be. But this did not occur: the first ownership opportunities were for moderate- and market-rate owners and as of this writing no low-income housing has been constructed in Phase 1.

Ground breaking for the previously planned 586-unit graduate-student housing occurred in 2010. Also in 2010, the Maryland Institute College of Art (MICA) renovated a school acquired by EBDI from St. Wenceslaus to use for its community arts and social design programs and 14 units of student housing.[48] MICA's proposal process was a surprise to community residents, who were not informed about it until well after EBDI had been negotiating with MICA representatives. After learning about the negotiations, residents requested details of how the space would be used and whether it would be accessible to local residents. As a result, MICA representatives agreed that the space would be open and welcoming to community residents and provide meeting space for community functions. The center opened in the fall of 2010, but resident gathering in the renovated space has yet to occur.

In the fall of 2010, with approximately 50 households in Phase 2 still not relocated, the physical plan continued to change. Construction of a 1,500-space parking garage and a new building to house the state health department was now on the agenda. EBDI and partners made no more mention of 3 to 5 biotech buildings.[49] Instead, new consultants began planning for a revised master plan in 2010; there was no community participation invited for this planning process for a third master plan.

Approximately 1 year later, in 2011, EBDI and partners attempted to present this third master plan to residents through a slide show, without copies of the revised plan for individual review. The developer presenting the plan was not allowed to continue, as residents requested that they be included in the planning of rebuilding their community.[50] The 2005 Urban Renewal Amendment legislated that residents be included in all planning and yet EBDI and partners ignored the law and did not invite residents to plan their community.

A revised housing plan was included in this new master plan and suggested more market-rate housing be constructed.[51] No mention of low- or moderate-rate housing construction was made. Again, the 2005 Urban Renewal Amendment which clearly stated the types of housing that were to be constructed in the 88 acres was ignored. To date, housing constructed or rehabbed in the project area are affordable to low-income Middle East residents only because of the relocation benefits accorded by URA Act.[52] No other low-income person would be able to afford to purchase these homes without substantial subsidies.

Residents demanded a community participatory process and requested to see the results of the surveys given to the Johns Hopkins community and selective neighborhoods of similar income, which helped the consultants to formulate the new plan for housing, businesses, and retail space. One resident had this to say about not being included: "I asked the developer why we weren't included. He said that they didn't survey residents because residents have a preformed opinion, therefore the results would be meaningless." The clear intention and bias in selecting communities with specific income levels to survey in regard to what they wanted in a community confirms the class of residents EBDI and partners were seeking to attract to the rebuilt community. This was the same strategy used by JHMI and developers in the 1950s Broadway Project, after displacement of more than 1000 families.

EBDI's executive director acknowledged that the plan had not engaged residents but was now seeking residents to review it. Again, just as had occurred a decade earlier, the majority of residents were informed of the new master plan through word of mouth and newspaper announcements, after the fact.

THE STRUGGLE TO PREVENT GENTRIFICATION: AFFORDING THE NEW TAXES AND PARTICIPATION IN A BENEFITS DISTRICT

The change in the tax burden on residents of the Middle East Baltimore community was a primary concern to SMEAC in 2001. It declared that the increased tax burden on low-income residents could result in loss of their homes. The challenge for residents moving into higher-priced homes was clearly a risk. So was the increased tax on new and rehabbed houses in the rebuilt community. Middle East Baltimore residents could be taxed out of their homes in the rebuilt community, resulting in its gentrification. This has been the pattern for many similar rebuilding projects in the United States.[53,54] Similarly, they could be taxed out of the communities into which they relocated. While renters moving into higher-rent units do not face an increased tax burden, they face increased rents, which also results in their moving out of the rebuilt area. As a result of their displacement, they could also be forced to move out of the higher-rental units they were moved into.

SMEAC met with Middle East Baltimore city council representatives and requested legislation to hold EBDI accountable for tracking the tax burden of residents forced to relocate out of their community, as well as the housing outcomes for renters. This did not occur. With the assistance of the University of Baltimore Community Law Clinic, SMEAC also challenged EBDI to pay the amount of the increase in taxes, at 100 percent for the first year, then at 50 percent for 3 years after. This would apply whether residents remained, were relocated out and remained out, or returned. It was hoped that over this time, residents would be able to adjust to the increased tax burden through different city and state tax programs. EBDI amended its relocation policy in September 2004 to state that 100 percent of the tax differential (cost difference between previous tax bill and new bill) would be paid the first year after relocation and 50 percent the second year to help prevent foreclosure for those unable to pay their increased tax bills.

As predicted, displaced residents continue to be faced with increased tax bills, sometimes $1,000–$2,000 more than in Middle East Baltimore. Some homeowners have faced foreclosure due to the greater tax burden and higher mortgages in the relocated communities. Many report that they were not provided sufficient information about the sharp increase in tax burden that accompanied the increased value of the houses they relocated into. While the value of the house increased, there was no parallel increase in income to match the increased cost of living in and maintaining these houses. Many relocated households report that they fear future default on taxes.

In 2009, a community benefits district was proposed for the rebuilt Middle East Baltimore. A community benefits district is a legal mechanism that allows increased taxes on property within a geographic area to supplement public safety and maintenance services in that area. This increased tax, proposed to be fully phased in by 2010, would support greater sanitation and security for the area. Current resident homeowners present before the start of the rebuilding process would not be expected to pay these increased taxes if they remained the primary occupants of their new or rehabilitated homes.

In addition, these same historic Middle East residents would not have a vote in decisions affecting the benefits district. Residents challenged EBDI and partners to remove this restriction on their participation in decisions affecting their neighborhood, but EBDI remained unchanged in its original proposal. Continuing in the tradition of paternalism and oppression of other urban renewal projects, EBDI and partners—through city and state representatives for East Baltimore—introduced this into legislation. The bill proposing this legislation currently sits awaiting a hearing and a vote in the Baltimore City Council after being approved in the state legislature following introduction by the East Baltimore's representative and denied by EBDI's executive director that such legislation had been presented.[55]

WHY THE SAME EXPERIMENT AGAIN?

This detailed report of the rebuilding process during the first 10 years provides evidence of an exclusionary process: from inception in the late 1990s to 2011. It documents the struggle by an organized community and the results gained from their vigilance and diligence. But why must residents be forced to struggle for inclusion, justice and transparency at every step of the way? Why must they live with a constant fear of missing a meeting for fear of losing an opportunity to stay informed or challenge some unfair plan? This exclusionary way of rebuilding abandoned communities in America is not new today: in Baltimore or America. The terms "Negro removal" and "gentrification" came into being because they branded the methods and results of urban renewal processes of the past and today.[56] And such processes succeeded because of the legacy of race and class segregation building power and growing the distance between those with and those without. When those with power—like JHMI—decide to expand they have the power to negotiate the terms to their benefit. They have strong bonds with public sources to assure that they accomplish their goals and benefit, whether those without power benefit or not.[57]

The current rebuilding of Middle East repeats this history once again in East Baltimore. Surprisingly the details of the 1950s urban renewal strategy in East Baltimore mimic those of the current rebuilding process. Then the Hopkins-driven 1950s Broadway Redevelopment Project changed several times during the almost 10-year process of completion. The first was when the city's planning department reported that there had been a change in the available funding for construction of houses for the historic African American residents of the area. Then JHMI stepped in and took over the development of the land, conveniently cleared of their low-income African American neighbors. The same occurred in this current rebuilding process. After the land was cleared in the first phase, a second and third master plan was designed, a new school appeared on the agenda, a park, housing for the middle and market rate earners, and JHMI became more visibly involved in the planning of Middle East Baltimore.

Another explanation offered in the 1950s for the changing plans was that the redevelopment was a "guinea pig" and therefore had to proceed by "trial and error."

Almost 60 years later, EBDI and partners described the current rebuilding of Middle East Baltimore as "an experiment".[58] EBDI's leadership stated that in these type of projects "there will need to be changes along the way".[59] Interesting is that the changes are acceptable because those with power are the ones making the changes. The disenfranchised and impacted residents must be happy with these changes and accept the nature of the experiment, each time being informed after changes are decided and struggle again for inclusion and transparency.

As there was in the rebuilding process of the 1950s and 1960s, there is a basic assumption that if things do not go according to plan, or that if the plans do have to change and inconvenience people, this group of people is less likely than others to challenge or question their changes. Likewise in this rebuilding process in Middle East Baltimore, a master plan now in its third revision, twice without community input, is acceptable to this "experiment" in Middle East Baltimore. And whether or not those affected by these changing plans challenge them, they will have to accept the changes inherent in "experiments." This legacy of experimenting with the most vulnerable populations—the poor, people of color—in and outside the United States is not new to the privileged and powerful classes in public health, medicine, and community development.[60,61,62,63,64,65] (See chapter 1 for discussion of this.) Likewise the history of lack of gaining consent or input or nontransparency of plans and outcomes of experimentation.

Similarly the struggle for inclusion and justice in the face of powerful entities like JHMI, mayors, city departments and wealthy foundations, and business interests is not new to East Baltimore (chapter 2).

This history of community rebuilding in East Baltimore suggests that the populations that planners, developers, business interests, and philanthropic organizations feel are okay to "experiment" with are low-income and people of color: the most vulnerable of our populations, the least powerful. These types of "experiments" would not be initiated in primarily white and middle class communities. The lack of power in low-income and people of color communities, disinvested of material and political assets, allows many to "try out new ideas." Even when the intention may not be to harm, taking these risks of causing harm in these disempowered communities is negligent and would not be taken in white and higher-income communities with more power and privilege.

In Middle East Baltimore residents were forced to organize and demand justice from these powerful stakeholders "experimenting" with their version of "Negro removal" in the twenty-first century: "organized misery." The same stakeholders through disinvestment, public-private partnerships, and land banking had participated in causing the decay of their community directly and indirectly. Their power came from their collective voice, their partnerships with other organizations, and using the media to publicly reveal the injustice and inconsistency of this urban renewal project. Each struggle toward equity, health and safety, and affordability to return to their community through necessary changes in plans for relocation, demolition, and housing was initiated and maintained by organized residents.

The next chapter will describe the stakeholders and their roles in supporting and challenging the successful outcomes of residents' struggles for inclusion and justice in the rebuilding of Middle East Baltimore.

NOTES

1. Urban Design Associates. "East Baltimore Study." May 2001.
2. Urban Renewal Plan, Middle East Baltimore, Amendment 6. 2000.
3. *Baltimore Sun*. October 15, 2000. "Eastside looses ground in effort to stem blight."
4. *Baltimore Sun*. October 15, 2000.
5. MD. Real Property Code Ann. § 12–101. General provisions.
6. *Baltimore Sun*. January 11, 2001. "City, Hopkins weight plan for east-side development."
7. *Baltimore Sun*. January 11, 2001.
8. Historic East Baltimore Community Action Coalition. (HEBCAC) Baltimore, MD. "Community Revitalization Plan." May 1994.
9. Historic East Baltimore Community Action Coalition. 1994.
10. *Baltimore City Paper*. February 22, 2006. "Moved and shaken."
11. Urban Design Associates. "East Baltimore Study." December 2001.
12. Urban Design Associates. 2001.
13. *Baltimore Sun*. July 26, 2001. "Hopkins neighbors react to its recent struggles."
14. *Baltimore Business Journal*. 2002. "City names Hopkins Biotech Park board." www.bizjournals.com/baltimore/stories/2002/09/16/daily42.html. Accessed January 2011.
15. *Voices from Within: A displaced community speaks out*. Wide Angle Video. 2004.
16. Urban Renewal Plan, Middle East Baltimore, Amendment 7. 2002.
17. MD. Real Property Code Ann. § 12–102. Relocation and assistance.
18. EBDI. (2001) Draft of Historical East Baltimore Community Relocation Policy and Benefits. November 2001.

19. Valparaiso (1969) *Judicial Review of Displacee Relocation in Federal Urban Renewal Projects: A New Approach?* 3. *Vol. U. L. Rev.* 258. Available at: scholar.valpo.edu/vulr/vol3/iss2/7. Accessed November 2010.

20. Massey D, Denton NJ. (1993) *American apartheid: Segregation and the making of the underclass.* Harvard University Press, Boston.

21. EBDI (2002) Statement . . . of the EBDI Special Committee on Relocation.

22. *Baltimore Sun.* December 15, 1968. "Urban renewal with a difference."

23. EBDI (2002) Homeowner Acquisition / Relocation Process Guide.

24. EBDI (2002) Homeowner Acquisition / Relocation Process Guide.

25. Urban Renewal Plan, East Baltimore, Amendment 3. 1994.

26. Valparaiso (1969) *Judicial Review of Displacee Relocation in Federal Urban Renewal Projects: A New Approach?*

27. Keene DA, Geronimus AT. (2011) "Weathering" HOPE VI: The importance of evaluating the population health impact of public housing demolition and displacement. *J Urban Health.* 88:417.

28. EBDI (2004) Relocation Policy.

29. *Baltimore Sun.* February 17, 2004. "Official notices of move are met with resignation."

30. Gomez M. (2005) *Shelter Force: Demanding a better deal.* November/December, 144.

31. *Daily Record.* February 1, 2011. "The muddled money trail."

32. Gomez M. (2005) *Shelter Force.*

33. Sasaki Associates Inc. (2006) East Baltimore Neighborhood Project.

34. *Baltimore Sun.* August 26, 2007. "Residents back 'House for a House.'"

35. MD. Real Property Code Ann. 2007. § 12-105.1; 12.202; 12.204; 12-205.1. Real Property-Condemnation-Procedures and compensation.

36. *Daily Record.* January 30, 2008. "East Baltimore community school will displace at least 25 homeowners, 47 renters."

37. *Daily Record.* January 30, 2008.

38. *Daily Record.* August 1, 2011. "Miles out as East Baltimore Community School's head."

39. *Baltimore Sun.* August 26, 2011. "Hopkins, Morgan take the reins in Eastside school."

40. Farfel MR, Orlova AO, Lees PS, Rohde C, Ashley PJ, Chisolm JJ Jr. (2003) "A study of urban housing demolitions as sources of lead in ambient dust: demolition practices and exterior dust fall." *Environ Health Perspect.* 111:1228.

41. *Baltimore City Paper.* March 16, 2005. "Danger zone."

42. *Baltimore City Paper.* March 16, 2005.

43. Jacobs DE, Mucha A, Stites N, MacRoy P, Evens A, Rafferty P, Phoenix J,Persky. (2007) "Preliminary results of lead particulate deposition from housing demolition." *American Industrial Hygiene Conference and Exposition.* June 2007.

44. East Baltimore Demolition Protocol. (2005)

45. *Baltimore City Paper.* February 22, 2006. "Moved and shaken."

46. Urban Renewal Plan, Middle East Baltimore, Amendment 8. 2005.

47. Urban Renewal Plan, Middle East Baltimore, Amendment 8. 2005

48. *Baltimore Sun.* July 27, 2010. "The art of activism."

49. *Daily Record.* January 31, 2011. "A dream derailed."

50. *Baltimore Sun.* July 29, 2011. "Residents give cool reception for new vision in East Baltimore."

51. *Baltimore Sun.* July 29, 2011.

52. *Baltimore City Paper.* May 2, 2007. "Don't you be my neighbor."

53. Smith N, Caris P, Wyly E. (2001) "The 'Camden Syndrome' and the menace of suburban decline: Residential disinvestment and its discontents in Camden County, New Jersey." *Urban Affairs Review.* 36:497.

54. Kennedy M, Leonard P. (2001) "Dealing with Neighborhood Change: A Primer on Gentrification and Policy Choices" (www.policylink.org/pdfs/BrookingsGentrification.pdf) accessed January 2001.

55. *WBAL News.* October 2010. "East Baltimore Tax District Plan concerns some."

56. Massey D, Denton NJ. (1993) "American apartheid: Segregation and the making of the underclass."

57. Gomez MB, Muntaner C. (2005) "Urban redevelopment and neighborhood health in East Baltimore, Maryland: The role of institutional and communitarian social capital." *J Critical Public Health.* 15:83.

58. *WEAA radio show.* January 2011. Marc Steiner.

59. *Daily Record.* January 31, 2011.

60. Valparaiso (1969) *Judicial Review of Displacee Relocation in Federal Urban Renewal Projects: A New Approach?*

61. *Washington Post.* August 24, 2001. "My kids were used as Guinea pigs." www.gwu.edu/~pad/202/readings/lead-hopkins.htm. Accessed November 2010.

62. U.S. Government Printing Office. Trials of war criminals before the Nuremberg Military Tribunals under Control Council. 1949 Law No. 10, Vol. 2, pp. 181–82. Washington, DC.

63. Centers for Disease Control. U.S. Public Health Service Syphilis Study at Tuskegee. www.cdc.gov/tuskegee/timeline.htm. Accessed March 2011.

64. Bioethical Commission Report on Guatemala Research. 1946–1948 inoculation STD studies in Guatemala. www.bioethics.gov. Accessed September 2011.

65. Skloot R. (2010) *The Immortal Life of Henrietta Lacks.* Random House, NY.

5

Who the Stakeholders Are in Rebuilding Middle East Baltimore

"Whenever I get anything from them [EBDI], I throw it in the thrash." —East Baltimore resident

". . . the War on Poverty is 'noisy, visible, dirty, uncomfortable, and sometimes politically unpopular.'" —S. Shriver

This chapter describes in more detail the different stakeholders involved in rebuilding abandoned communities in general and Middle East Baltimore in particular. Their roles relative to each other and how they shaped the first 10 years of this project are discussed.

THE ROLE AND RESPONSIBILITY OF COMMUNITY

SMEAC's purpose was to hold itself and other stakeholders in the rebuilding of Middle East Baltimore accountable to the area's residents. Through its structure and practice of inclusion and transparency its own accountability to residents was primary and attempted to bring integrity into old ways of doing business in East Baltimore and other disinvested and abandoned communities in America. Though other entities, such as the funders at the table or the development organization, supported a vision that residents' needs should be addressed, their primary agenda, their reason for being at the table, was not to represent the residents. When a SMEAC member was not at the table, residents' needs were often forgotten or ignored. The powerful stakeholders had other priorities and concerns in regard to rebuilding the community. For example, funding for the construction of affordable housing or funding to ensure ease of transition for relocated residents was not always a focus for the developer or the banker. They were more interested in ensuring that a biotech building was constructed on time to meet the demands of their constituents of leasers or investors.

Through SMEAC's community organizing efforts, going door to door asking questions and listening to residents share their desires for change in their community, the voices of residents were brought to the larger table of stakeholders. The process of insisting on accountability included the continuous presence at the table of as many residents as possible, persistent questions about how the process affected residents, and consistently following up to get responses to questions.

Without that consistent follow-up, questions often went unanswered. SMEAC documented the dates when questions were asked so as to remind EBDI that residents were expecting answers. Demanding accountability involved constantly reminding EBDI, city and state government officials, city council officials, funders, and other stakeholders that residents had a right to direct their destiny and not to be treated as children—being told how, when, and where to move. This teaching to the powerful stakeholders was repeated over and over again as many brought their historic views of residents as the cause of decay and disinvestment to the table. They perceived themselves as there to save the community from itself. SMEAC'S actions repeatedly unsubstantiated these perceptions which pervaded the rebuilding process. But with a particular agenda aimed at removing the historic residents and replacing them with a community to the liking of JHMI, these perceptions supported their strategies and mission and were difficult to change.

Residents in leadership roles in SMEAC, and others not directly involved in SMEAC, reviewed the applications for all processes affecting rebuilding: the master developers' proposals, demolition contracts, economic inclusion contract, the school planning documents, and other applications for programs relative to the rebuilding of their community. When EBDI did not make the documents available, SMEAC requested them. Still, EBDI failed to provide many documents pertinent to the rebuilding process at the public meetings, and SMEAC had little opportunity to obtain them.

Residents attended and testified at planning commission meetings, city council meetings, and other governmental meetings pertaining to plans and legislation affecting the rebuilding of Middle East Baltimore. EBDI often failed to give notice of these meetings in its public meetings or announcements which resulted in SMEAC learning about it late and rushing to organize residents to testify. The planned unit development (PUD) hearing at the department of planning for the first phase of the 88 acres in Middle East was a glaring example of EBDI and partners' strategies in locking out resident participation in all aspects of the rebuilding process.

When the powerful stakeholders determined that the working master plan of the first 5 years needed to be changed, residents requested that the planning session include greater community leadership and participation than the planning sessions in 2001. SMEAC submitted written questions and comments after the revised master plan was presented in the planning meeting, requesting a written response by a due date.

Box 5.1.   The Powerful Stakeholders Whose Assets Dwarfed Those of SMEAC

- EBDI—whose executive director's yearly salary alone was more than $250K
- The Annie E. Casey Foundation—whose president's yearly salary alone was more than $250K
- The JHMI—whose president's yearly salary alone was more than $250K
- The city and state government
- Various business and nonprofit interests

It continued in this way throughout the first 7 years of rebuilding Middle East Baltimore, a small community organization, with a yearly budget of less than $120,000, challenging and attempting to hold accountable the powerful and well-resourced stakeholders whose assets dwarfed those of SMEAC (box 5.1).

Clearly there was a David and Goliath relationship at the base of the interactions between, on the one hand, SMEAC and the community it was accountable to and, on the other, EBDI and its powerful stakeholders. Because EBDI was seen as representing the JHMI and governmental interests and not the interests of residents in Middle East Baltimore, and because no acknowledgment and repair had occurred to heal the history of abandonment and expansion, EBDI remained the outsider representing the interests of the powerful race and class elite.

Well into EBDI's fourth year of existence, almost half the residents in the community were still not attending EBDI meetings. Many who attended found the information confusing and sought out SMEAC leadership to interpret it. SMEAC had gained the trust of the community residents even while some individuals in the larger East Baltimore community criticized it for challenging the powerful EBDI and partners.

Some offering this critique feared reprisal in relocation benefits and employment outcomes. Others simply wanted the old, nontransparent process they had come to know in East Baltimore, in which a few self-appointed community leaders served as doors—gatekeepers—into the community. Still others preferred a more hierarchical model of leadership without an opportunity for all members to represent themselves.

This model of disconnected or no social networks or fragmented ways of communication is typical in many communities of low income and African Americans. It results in small groups or numbers of individuals competing with each other as the voice of the entire community. This dynamic was present in East Baltimore as it became more and more disinvested and abandoned and became a community with large numbers of transient residents. Such dynamics were used by JHMI in accessing the "voice of the community" when it needed to publicly announce it had involved residents in some initiative.[1] This same dynamic of attempting to split the community developed between EBDI and its partners and continued throughout the first 10 years of rebuilding Middle East Baltimore.

SMEAC offered a different model of resident engagement and leadership, maintaining a strong commitment to the individual membership and a democratic process of representation: everyone's voice was valuable and had something important to contribute. Like the larger community, the organization's leaders were themselves being forced to relocate and were directly affected by the stress of an unknown future. Most resident leaders were offered the opportunity to relocate early. Most refused, insisting on staying until the majority of residents in the first phase were relocated. This direct connection maintained the tight bonding relationships within the resident base in SMEAC's membership and in the larger community and offered a way of merging previous fragmented voices. The collective voice fortified the power of SMEAC.

SMEAC also offered EBDI and its supporters an organized conduit into the community of Middle East Baltimore. Without this community organization, EBDI had no regular way of accessing the input of residents, because it had no organized communication or process of interacting with the community. Even though it was important for residents to participate in the public meetings about relocation and housing, flyers announcing EBDI's meetings or activities were often late or not sent to all residents. Mailings and occasional flyers remain the ways EBDI attempts to keep the community informed about activities affecting residents' lives. A question of whether this is sufficient and reasonable effort to inform residents and assure community input secondary to the Baltimore City amendment to the Urban Renewal Plan for Middle East Baltimore remains unanswered.[2] Word of mouth became the way residents communicated meeting dates and times after SMEAC disbanded.

Rebuilding a community with participation from all residents required time and energy from the residents. During the first years of the rebuilding process, SMEAC learned that six out of ten residents in the targeted area were renters—people who rented. But the majority of SMEAC's membership from its beginning were owners. Owners felt they had a right to demand justice when the city decided it would take the property they owned. Many renters felt less empowered. They had no ownership or direct investment in the homes they were living in. Many renters felt that their landlords were the ones who could challenge the plan of mass relocation and that they had no say in the matter.

SMEAC tried to organize renters to attend meetings and voice their concerns. But it appeared that many renters were more willing to watch and wait. Some who were newer to the community or saw their presence there as temporary felt little investment in the community. Many of the renters who were regularly involved with SMEAC had been living in the community for more than 5 years, some more than 15.

Low-income renters who live in disinvested communities like Middle East Baltimore, where landlords are often deemed "slumlords," may do so from necessity. And often they have little leverage for demanding that their landlords comply with the laws, to attend to necessary housing repairs or remove lead-based paint from the houses. If these renters could, they would live in a different neighborhood. Such a renter often has little investment in the physical house and may find it challenging to have any investment in the physical and social upkeep of the neighborhood.

Additionally, in a working-poor, single-mother household like those of some of the neighborhood's renters, becoming involved with organizing against gentrification may not be a priority.

In most redevelopment projects of low-income housing and publicly assisted housing, renters have historically had little opportunity to address what changes will occur. They often feel disempowered in the process of community change and rebuilding. Many are repeatedly relocated and are lost to follow-up efforts to assess whether relocation was beneficial and they can afford living in their new communities. For those who have been followed, the economic, social and health outcomes for displaced renters remain mixed with no overall improvement in these areas (chapters 8, 9).[3,4,5,6]

SMEAC advocated strongly and consistently for EBDI and partners and the city council to set into policy and legislate for long-term follow-up with relocated residents, particularly renters. This will be discussed further in chapters 7 and 9.

Still, throughout SMEAC's existence, when there were rumors going around the community about a change in rebuilding plans, renters would show up at a general membership meeting, or call the organization, to ask whether the rumor was true. Though they did not regularly attend or participate in SMEAC activities, the organization was a resource they trusted and felt they could turn to.

COMMUNITY CHALLENGING THE DYNAMICS OF PATERNALISM AND NON-TRANSPARENCY

Because each stakeholder had its individual responsibility, resident participation was mandatory to ensure that resident needs were consistently on the agenda. This was SMEAC's role and accountability: to keep the issue of residents' concern on the table, on the top of the list, right there next to the concern about the developer's timeline to deliver a graduate student housing building or a biotech building to the Johns Hopkins complex. Each stakeholder had a role, and for each stakeholder's needs to be remembered at each meeting, a representative had to be present to ensure that they were not forgotten.

Throughout the rebuilding process, if at any moment representatives of the historic community were not at the table, in that moment they became less valued stakeholders. SMEAC existed to ensure that these moments occurred as rarely as possible and that the voice of one or two residents at the table reflected the voices of many who were not present. SMEAC was a vehicle negotiating the adversarial, and at times highly charged, interactions that are inevitable when those holding resources are challenged to listen to demands for justice. Meeting residents' demands would mean redistributing resources differently than was initially planned for use in the rebuilding of Middle East Baltimore. It would change the way benefit was determined and how benefit would be equitably distributed between the stakeholders and their constituents. The planned outcome was for continued benefit inequality, gentrification, as had occurred in past rebuilding processes in East Baltimore and similar disinvested and abandoned communities in America.[7,8]

At times EBDI and its partners perceived the demands for justice as excessive requests on behalf of residents. And when EBDI made changes in line with residents' demands, it expected gratitude from residents. This paternalistic attitude, as if it were giving a gift to a child, persisted throughout the many negotiations around residents' demands. It supported the roles of "us" and "them" throughout the first 10 years of rebuilding. The opposing groups stayed in their corners of the "rebuilding ring," EBDI and its stakeholders against community residents forced to relocate.

The majority of residents perceived EBDI and its partners as the "puppet" for the ever-present giant of the JHMI, carrying out its wishes to keep it in Baltimore. Whether this meant displacing the people and demolishing the place of an entire community did not seem to factor into the planning and actions of EBDI and partners. Because there had been a lack of trust before the announced plan to rebuild, and there had been no structured process to acknowledge this mistrust and the disrespect with which the initial planning occurred, this remained the ground on which all interactions between residents and their supporters and EBDI and its supporters rested.

This adversarial relationship continued, conceived by some as the Middle East Baltimore community residents the antagonists and EBDI and its powerful partners—Johns Hopkins, government, private funders, and private business developers—saving the community from its past. There is still no indication that any deeper understanding has taken root in the minds or hearts of the powerful stakeholders of this experiment of rebuilding Middle East Baltimore. Neither has there been much change in the perceptions of the majority of historic residents of Middle East Baltimore.

What did change was the language EBDI and its partners used. With time, they began to speak of "rebuilding Middle East for the residents" and its being "a community participatory process." The executive director began using words like social justice in describing EBDI's rebuilding efforts.

This slow co-opting of residents' words evolved over time. The years of community struggle for a place at the decision-making table vanished as that place at the table became the "original intention" of EBDI and partners. They became the "responsible rebuilders," the experimenters in the social engineering of a "new Eastside of Baltimore." The changes advocated for through persistent demands from SMEAC and supporters, in the form of rallies, protests, letter-writing campaigns, meeting attendance, consistent questions, and media attention, were slowly co-opted until they were being presented as "original intentions" of EBDI and partners.

In 2008, one of the powerful stakeholders publicly described the previous 7 years of struggle by residents this way: "And, while skepticism and fear for the future remain strong, these meetings are now more about collaboration and co-management than they are about confrontation."[9] Co-optation meant there was a lot of talk about collaboration and co-management while decision making remained in the hands of the outsiders with power. These outside stakeholders were unable to know the experience of the resident base from which these demands originated. Their parroting of the words of the community's movement was not informed by experience; it attempted to cover up the separation that existed between the needs of the community and the intentions of the powerful outsiders.

The transparency of these intentions remained under the radar, covered by the elaborate words of collaboration. Reports published by the major foundation partner of EBDI of the relocation policy, demolition protocol, and economic inclusion process described transparency as a key factor in these processes. The years of struggle and stress and the unknown impact on residents' health is ignored and misleads the reader of the true process which occurred to assure fair relocation, safe demolition and economic inclusion. Meanwhile, EBDI continues to refuse public disclosure of its financial audits, claiming its status as a quasi-public-private entity as reason for non-transparency.[10]

In ignoring the history of Middle East Baltimore residents, EBDI and partners trampled on the past. They insisted that residents come to remember the past and know the present through an outsider's lens. This lens shows an image of a rebuilt community without them in it. Today they continue to insist that residents fully embrace a plan that ignores and demeans the collective experience of this African American community. The Middle East community had maintained a community in the midst of the deterioration. The rooting out or cleansing of this history were the unspoken words. The relocation of the community to make room for a more gentrified class of people was the overt action, the "noble social experiment." Still the community maintained its responsibility in representing the experience of residents by voicing their needs and demanding a place at the table to be heard.

WHO WERE THESE OUTSIDE STAKEHOLDERS AND WHAT WERE THEIR INTERESTS?

The powerful stakeholders of the rebuilding of Middle East Baltimore included EBDI and its partners. Besides the Johns Hopkins Institutions, there were the private investors that fund the foundations, the city and state elected representatives, local leadership from the past, the city and state governmental offices affecting community planning and development, and local nonprofit organizations.

Foundations

Foundations were consistently involved in the rebuilding of Middle East Baltimore throughout its first 10 years.

The Abell Foundation provided initial funding to assess the feasibility of a biotech park in East Baltimore, and it maintained a direct and indirect role in advising the financial and housing processes in planning the redevelopment of the community.

The Annie E. Casey Foundation maintained a vigorous presence from the beginning, through its membership on EBDI's board of directors and several committees of the board, and through providing technical assistance in implementing and assessing the social supports in the process of relocation of residents. When the foundation decided to contribute funding for the changed relocation benefits package, it became a major stakeholder in the rebuilding process. With this increased financial buy-in, the foundation appointed itself the new national authority in defining the most equitable relocation processes in the redevelopment of urban communities. It took on greater responsibilities in planning for affordable housing models when the master plan changed for the second phase of redevelopment in 2006, offering substantial technical support as well as leveraging its assets to ensure additional financial support from other foundations and businesses. Because of its philanthropic stature in the United States, it was able to leverage its resources to guarantee loans that otherwise might not have been afforded to the rebuilding of Middle East Baltimore. Its direct financial input has exceeded $50 million as of this writing.

The foundations on a whole have direct accountability to the funders who place their assets in the foundation. Each foundation provides grants to organizations and projects that fit its goals and meet its criteria.

The Annie E. Casey Foundation extended its accountability when it took responsibility for directing the rebuilding of Middle East Baltimore. The contribution of its assets and the leverage of its status brought it the power to take on this directing role. Its accountability then extended more directly to its board of trustees and the EBDI board because of the greater resources it brought to the rebuilding effort and its direct role in planning and rebuilding.

This foundation has consistently guarded its reputation since partnering with the JHMI and the city government in this urban gentrification project. It did not want to be perceived as participating in a rebuilding effort that was simply another gentrification process driven by the same old racist and classist actions.

Other philanthropic organizations include the Morris Goldseker Foundation of Maryland, Inc., and the Harry and Jeanette Weinberg Foundation, Inc., each of which has contributed more than $25 million. And several other foundations have contributed, directly and indirectly, to different aspects of the rebuilding of Middle East Baltimore.

The role of foundations in urban renewal and other aspects of community development is not new. What is new here is the leadership role the powerful Annie E. Casey Foundation took on. In 2010, the president of the foundation retired and shifted from the role of EBDI board member to EBDI board president. The foundation continues its permanent role in directing this rebuilding process with the current president as an EBDI board member and continued presence of staff and technical support to committees of the board and functions of the the organization.

Johns Hopkins Medical Institutions (JHMI)

The JHMI's direct financial contribution totals more than $20 million currently. In addition to this monetary contribution, it has been the driving force behind the rebuilding of Middle East Baltimore. Without it, there would have been no incentive to develop a biotech park. Additionally, its intention and practice to surround itself with a more gentrified community remain both spoken and unspoken intentions in rebuilding Middle East Baltimore. There are two official positions for JHMI on the EBDI board as well as additional board members who serve and have served on boards of the hospital and university. The president of the university has been a constant presence on the EBDI board. JHMI is accountable to the boards of the various institutions that make up JHMI (university, hospital).

How accountable it is to its East Baltimore neighbors depends entirely on the community's ability to hold it accountable. To heal the past and present gentrification actions and ensure that the future does not repeat this pattern are parts of its responsibility to the community outside its walls and to the community it represents. The animosity that continues today will begin to heal only when the institution has acknowledged and repaired this past, setting an example for similar histories of dispossession, displacement, demolition and maintenance of unhealthy, segregated, and deteriorated communities throughout the United States and the world.[11]

City Government

The various city government sectors, particularly the mayor's office, Economic and Community Development, Housing and Community Development, and Planning, acted with little transparency throughout the first 10 years of rebuilding Middle East Baltimore.

During the year preceding the 2001 announcement of the plan to rebuild Middle East Baltimore, the mayor's office offered very little opportunity for dialogue or direct communication regarding the upcoming plan. After the public announcement, when the office did respond to requests for meetings with residents, answers were few and plans remained nontransparent.

Even though the Deputy Mayor of Economic and Community Development directed EBDI during the first years of rebuilding, the departments generally appeared publicly unaware of what EBDI was doing. The Baltimore City Department of Housing and Community Development consistently ignored questions from the community about low-income replacement housing. At this writing, no accounting of one-for-one replacement for all the low-income housing that was and is being demolished was in the public documents. And no disclosure from the office has been forthcoming, even though it is required for development projects receiving loans and grants from the U.S. Department of Housing and Urban Development—which this project received. The Baltimore Housing Commissioner maintains an ex-officio position on the EBDI board.

The city's Department of Planning responded to a request from SMEAC for information regarding planned unit development (PUD) during the first few years of the process, and it responded in a timely manner to requests by residents for schedules

and testimony at public hearings. But it took no initiative in offering a planning opportunity with residents before, during, or after the publicly announced plan.

These departments appeared to be onlookers to the mayor's and the JHMI's plan
to rebuild Middle East Baltimore. The word puppet was often used in describing the
role of the city departments involved in planning and community development in
regard to rebuilding Middle East Baltimore. While governmental offices are meant
to be accountable to the people, it is abundantly clear that these departments were
not so throughout the first 10 years.

The city's department of health and social services were not directly involved in
any of the rebuilding processes. During the challenge to the demolition protocol,
the health department was consulted. SMEAC requested that a health impact assessment be completed at the beginning of the project but received no response to this
request. The department of transportation did not request meeting with residents
or SMEAC.

Elected Officials

The elected city, state, and federal officials representing Middle East Baltimore
and the larger East Baltimore area remained supportive of this bold new plan
through the first 10 years, orally and in writing. City officials initially worked
with SMEAC and residents to gain resident representation on the EBDI and East
Baltimore Incubator (EBI) boards, establish the Community Advisory Committee
(no longer standing), affect the relocation benefits and process, and support desig-
nating a percentage of affordable housing for low-income residents in the rebuilt
community. Most state officials responded directly to SMEAC's request for meetings but seldom responded with public support to any of the organization's public
challenges—relocation benefits, demolition safety, affordable housing in the rebuilt
community. Federal officials also responded to SMEAC's request for meetings. Like
their state counterparts they did not publicly support any of SMEAC's campaigns
when their support was sought.

No elected officials were willing to support SMEAC's challenge to change the
way the rebuilding process initially was set to begin into a process of rehabilitation
and construction of new houses first to allow residents to remain in the community.
During much of the adversarial campaigning involving EBDI, most of the elected
officials remained quiet on the issues.

What all elected representatives directly and indirectly supported throughout the
first 10 years of rebuilding Middle East Baltimore, and requested proof of, was the
inclusion of minority businesses and economic benefit to such businesses. Legislation was proposed in the city council, in 2006 and 2008, for EBDI and its partners
to report on the progress of the rebuilding of Middle East Baltimore "to provide
information on the level of MBE/WBE goal participation of the major contractors,
sub-contractors, developers, and other business entities that are part of the revitalization effort; to report on efforts to address the housing and other social needs of the

residents displaced by the re-development process; and to assess efforts of all participants and stakeholders to reach the EBDI goal to work to recapture the essence of East Baltimore, and restore the community's vibrancy and productivity" (2006, adopted) and to report "the status of their current projects, their use of minority businesses in current development projects, and their current procurement and hiring practices (2009, hearing)."

Following a 5-part investigational series by The Daily Record in 2011, city officials held a public hearing requiring EBDI to provide greater transparency in regard to its accomplishments and financial accountability during the first 10 years.[12,13,14,15,16]

East Baltimore Development Inc. (EBDI)

Established in 2001, EBDI is a quasi-private-private organization managed by a board of directors. The board of directors consisted of: JHMI; philanthropic organizations; development, banking, real estate, biotech, and manufacturing businesses; city and state departments; elected officials; community representatives (only after a challenge by SMEAC after the first board was formed without community representatives).

The board did not share a common understanding of "for whom" the rebuilding of Middle East was intended. And it did not always make its intentions clear to the leadership of the functional unit implementing the day-to-day activities of rebuilding Middle East Baltimore. EBDI, the functional organization, became the center in Middle East Baltimore where meetings and all business pertaining to the rebuilding of the community occurred. From a series of offices in Middle East Baltimore, the staff managed and implemented the processes of fundraising, acquisition, demolition, relocation, developer selection, follow-up, and school start-up and support—and, later, development of rehabbed houses and workforce development.

The relocation services it offered directly, and indirectly through subcontractors, included diverse family support services: access to workforce training; substance abuse and mental health counseling; credit counseling; utilities assistance; legal services; literacy and education programs; health services; and after school, childcare, and mentoring programs. In time EBDI focused on "workforce development, employment, and asset building," its primary initiative in an effort to prepare residents of the larger East Baltimore community and other areas of the city for construction opportunities and later biotech opportunities.

This reinforced effort aimed to address the initial plan's promise, still unfulfilled, of 8,000 permanent new jobs. To date, more than 2,000 employment opportunities have been created over the first 10 years. The majority of these have been temporary construction positions that lasted several months and provided no apprenticeship opportunities for future employment. The subcontractors were not held accountable for hiring a percentage of local residents. This resulted in them bringing in their own crew—many from outside Baltimore and Maryland—for constructing buildings in a community which had the highest rate of unemployment in the city and which was promised jobs as a benefit from this bold new redevelopment. In total, approximately 400 permanent jobs have been documented.[17]

While EBDI provided services to try to ensure that residents affected by the rebuilding of Middle East Baltimore were relocated according to the relocation policy, sometimes the policy did not accommodate or reflect the actual circumstances of a household. Sometimes individuals on the staff of EBDI found ways to address these situations. Other times, when the conditions were not favorable, these needs were not addressed.

It is not unique to this organization that real life does not always follow a plan or a policy directive. But it is predictable that policies informed by the individuals they affect will be more in line with real life. And policies that lack community input and review will more likely be at odds with the actual, day-to-day lives of the people they are intended to help. The input from residents in regard to the real-life issues of being forced to leave your homes and the stress this presented was never addressed by EBDI and staff. Because it was not acknowledged, the resources and remedies to address them was not included in the policies and procedures aimed at displacing residents.

In 2009 EBDI continued to assure the public that its previous plan for three to five biotech buildings inclusive of two million square feet was still on target, though late and more costly than originally described. By 2011, a revised master plan—now the third—described no construction of additional biotech buildings. Instead a park, a school, a grocery store, and retail businesses had become the "economic engine" for revitalizing and building on the 88 acres of historic Middle East Baltimore.[18]

"What happened to the Biotech Park?" was the question being asked by all. In 2001, when the plans for a three-to-five-building biotech park were announced, a biotech incubator board was formed. This board's responsibility was to develop a focused business plan during the first 7 years of the project. A member of this board reports that this board did not convene and no meetings ever occurred.

Because the board did not convene, no experienced experts in the field of biotechnology—executives, investors, manufacturers, or researchers—were focused on the development and implementation of a business plan during the preconstruction phase of the first biotech building. Such expertise would have helped to ensure that potential clients were being approached and invited to invest in the biotech park and drive construction of the necessary buildings.[19]

After the original plan describing the potential 1,300 companies that would be interviewed for the 30 to 50 companies that would occupy the three to five biotech buildings, no tangible action was taken to accomplish this goal. There was no functional board and therefore no functional organization to create or implement a business plan. Because of the lack of this organizational capacity to develop a biotech park, it is therefore not surprising that the master plan has yet again been revised—without community input. What remains unclear is why such measures were not developed by a $1.8 billion redevelopment project, whose major partner directing the process is a world-renowned research university. Some residents feel there was never any intention for a biotech park: "they just wanted to move us out of there so the city helped get us out."

Now, 10 years and one 300,000-square-foot biotech building later, this single building still is not fully populated, and it provides approximately 400 jobs. The majority of these positions were transferred from other locations and are not new employment for East Baltimore residents. Now EBDI is seeking an additional $300,000 in state general obligation bonds to entice an institution to occupy the only biotech building.[20] The money would be a loan to the institution to guarantee its hiring of 60 employees in East Baltimore for 3 years.

It remains unclear who EBDI is accountable to. The board of directors, whose chair is appointed by the mayor, is supposedly accountable to the mayor. However, due to the public-private status of the organization—supported by private investment—their records are not open for accountability to the public which leaves it to the discretion of the board of directors to reveal its finances and decision-making processes. In regard to the citizens directly affected by the rebuilding of Middle East Baltimore, none of the three mayors who have served during the first 10 years of this project have been accountable and responsive to the requests of the majority of residents.

FINANCIAL ACCOUNTABILITY AND WHY IT MATTERS

The projected overall cost of the rebuilding of Middle East Baltimore was $600 million in 2001; by 2010 it was $1.8 billion. The money actually committed as of 2010 totaled approximately $565 million, divided as follows: public investment from city, state, and federal funds represented more than one third (38 percent), from private developers another one third (38 percent). The remaining one third was provided by federal tax credits (8 percent) and foundations (16 percent). To date, $64 million of the projected total $1.8 billion was set aside for contracts with minority-owned and women-owned businesses.

Besides the two public hearings requested by the city council, one in 2006 and the other in 2009, little was done to hold EBDI accountable to the public in regard to its promises based on the master plans or in regard to overall spending. In the first 10 years, elected officials at the city, state, and federal levels did little to bring accountability to this process, financially or socially.

The public-private status of EBDI allowed it discretion in accounting to the public on its financial matters, even while a major portion of its financial support came from public sources and a federal law granting it permission to take private land for "public benefit." In addition, this status has resulted in local and state government accommodating EBDI's continued need for financial sustainability through additional bond sales and payments in the midst of challenging financial times to the city and state.[21,22]

In early 2011, this changed. After a week-long investigational series by one of the local newspapers showed that the financial accountability of EBDI was lacking, with no transparency to city officials regarding spending of more than $200 million public dollars during its first 10 years of operation, a hearing was scheduled.[23] The city council hearing required EBDI to report on the spending of its funds and to account for the accomplishment of tasks for which it had secured these funds.[24] Still, there was no accounting for the inaccuracies discovered during this investigation: inconsistencies in EBDI and the city department documentation of spending on infrastructure and projected and actual private investment. The private investment since 2008 had been eliminated completely from reports revealed by EBDI.[25]

During the first 10 years, it was the empowered residents, with the technical assistance and voice amplification SMEAC provided, who pushed the powerful stakeholders to be accountable to the residents they were displacing. Without this force, it is unlikely that the relocation benefits or the demolition protocol would have changed, and the agreement to construct 1/3 low-income homeownership house or renovated existing houses (House for a House Program/Home Rehab programs) would have occurred. When EBDI finally agreed to renovate homes in the second phase, its slow process and ineffective engagement of potential homeowners from the second phase resulted in many residents who had wanted to stay instead relocating out of the community. They had grown tired of waiting for the houses to be rehabbed, and fearful of living on increasingly isolated blocks.

The powerful stakeholders have responded poorly to concrete plans to ensure that residents stay or return to the rebuilt community. Their response has been more positive in ensuring that residents relocated safely out of the community. This will be discussed further in chapter 7.

It is clear that many of SMEAC's challenges and campaigns to keep the rebuilding of Middle East Baltimore focused on the residents would not have successfully accomplished their aims without the financial support of the governmental and private entities involved. The private and governmental resources these entities directly and indirectly leveraged afforded the increased cost of the relocation benefits package, improvement in the safety and health conditions in the demolition process, increased funding to secure loans and bonds for other services offered during the relocation of residents, and increased assets to guarantee bank loans to offset housing costs for community residents to remain and new residents—Hopkins students and staff—to enter.

Why would some of these foundations support the changes demanded by an organization that was challenging the process of how Middle East Baltimore was being rebuilt? In response to the demand for more low-income houses, subsidies were offered to low-income residents so they could afford moderate- or market-rate houses. To secure grants for rehabbing houses in the subsequent phase, loans were guaranteed on assets of the powerful stakeholders.

Many philanthropic foundations provide direct and indirect resources to organizations and individuals involved in "improving their lives and their communities." SMEAC clearly demonstrated that it was doing this, even while it also challenged the role of these very foundations in minimizing, marginalizing, or co-opting the voices of residents. The foundations have a reputation for "supporting community-based initiatives" and would be challenged to not support the effort of SMEAC. It was the only organized community voice in Middle East Baltimore.

Additionally, the Annie E. Casey Foundation is headquartered in Baltimore and had just began to implement one of its nationwide initiatives in East Baltimore when the plan to rebuild Middle East Baltimore was announced. It not only quickly got onto the "rebuilding train" after this announcement was made, canceling its newly formed initiative, it also took the reins in the rebuilding process and set out to redefine the role of foundations in "urban renewal" efforts.

Why would the JHMI financially support the rebuilding of Middle East Baltimore? The involvement of major foundations in the rebuilding of Middle East Baltimore was dependent on this powerful neighbor's role in leveraging resources. They anticipated that it would bring resources not just by having a reputation and attracting tenants to the biotech park, but also by providing direct funding in all aspects of rebuilding Middle East Baltimore. While past rebuilding efforts did not demand this type of direct monetary support from the JHMI, this one did. This one also has had more involvement of philanthropic organizations, leveraged by the presence of the Annie E. Casey Foundation.

The JHMI would support residents' demands for safe relocation because it would facilitate their moving out of the area, allowing the acquisition and demolition processes that were necessary for eventual construction efforts to continue. The JHMI stands to gain enormously and disproportionately from the rebuilding of Middle East Baltimore.

In fact, one could say that rebuilding Middle East Baltimore is really an expansion of the JHMI community. Its members would like to walk to work and live in a thriving and energetic community near downtown—as reported by surveys of the JHMI and larger areas of Baltimore. In light of the revised plans for the more than 88 acres—a park, marketing to a moderate- and market-rate housing market, retail and restaurants that cater to a moderate- and market-rate population, a new school with the leadership of JHMI—there is clear evidence that the rebuilding of Middle East Baltimore targets the JHMI community.

Why should these powerful stakeholders be accountable to residents and support a rebuilding effort that makes them whole? They should do so because it was the historic residents who lived through and waited for a change in their community and an opportunity to participate in this change. They should do so because it is their land that is being taken to rebuild the community. They should do so because the historic and current racist lending practices of the banking industry, federal grant programs, and governmental real estate agencies resulted in the making of segregated communities like East Baltimore prone to exploitation by powerful institutions like JHMI.

In Maryland and other states of the United States, private lenders, real estate agents, and entrepreneurs capitalized on these housing practices and grew powerful on the backs of low-income and people of color communities. One could not grow larger and more powerful without the other growing smaller and more disenfranchised. These assets of land, income, and social status accumulated and expanded over the generations—for the privileged white population. And they have been redistributed within the white and powerful establishments of universities, hospitals, foundations, real estate developers, banks, and other powerful institutions: the legacy of wealth accumulation in the United States. An intentional redistribution, directed back into these economically and socially disinvested communities—replenishing and not displacing—may begin to address this legacy of economic and social injustices and transform them into healthy neighborhoods to live, work and play.

The stakeholders involved in rebuilding Middle East Baltimore can assure that benefit from this project is equitably distributed. To date, the will to do so by the powerful stakeholders has not been present. The changes for more equitable relocation, demolition, and affordable housing processes were initiated by organized residents and supported to differing degrees by the other stakeholders. This struggle for justice took its toll on residents, before, during and after displacement. The next chapter will describe the challenges faced by SMEAC during its struggle for inclusion and its eventual disbanding after the majority of its membership was displaced.

NOTES

1. Gomez MB, Muntaner C. (2005). "Urban redevelopment and neighborhood health in East Baltimore, Maryland: The role of Institutional and communitarian social capital." *J Critical Public Health*. 15:83.

2. Urban Renewal Plan, Middle East Baltimore, Amendment 8. 2005.

3. Levy D, Kaye D. (2004) *How are HOPE VI families faring? Income and employment*. Washington, DC: Urban Institute.

4. Fullilove M. (2001) "Root Shock: the consequences of African American dispossession." *J Urban Health*. 78:72.

5. Keene DA, Geronimus AT. (2011) "Weathering" HOPE VI: The importance of evaluating the population health impact of public housing demolition and displacement. *J Urban Health*. 88:417.

6. Manjarrez C, Popkin S, Guernsey E. (2007) "Poor health: Adding Insult to Injury for HOPE VI Families." Washington, DC: The Urban Institute Press: 5.

7. Perez G. (2002) "The other 'real world': gentrification and the social construction of place." *Urban Antropology*. 31:37.

8. Wallace R, Fullilove MT. (2008) *Collective consciousness and its discontents: Institutional distributed cognition, racial policy and public health in the United States*. Springer, NY.

9. Nelson DW. *Simply Put: Selected speeches of Douglas W. Nelson, the Annie E. Casey foundation president & CEO, 1990–2010*, (2010). www.aecf.org/-/media/Pubs/Other/S/SimplyPut SelectedSpeechesofDouglasWNelson/Nelson_simply_put.pdf. Accessed March 2010.

10. *Daily Record*. February 1, 2011. "The muddled money trail."

11. Wallace R, Fullilove MT. (2008) Collective consciousness and its discontents: Institutional distributed cognition, racial policy and public health in the United States. Springer, NY.

12. *Daily Record*. February 1, 2011.

13. *Daily Record.* January 31, 2011. "A dream derailed."

14. *Daily Record.* February 2, 2011. "Seeking a new vision."

15. *Daily Record.* February 3, 2011. "The education solution."

16. *Daily Record.* February 4, 2011. "An uncertain future."

17. *Baltimore Sun.* July 29, 2011. "Residents give cool reception for new vision in East Baltimore."

18. EBDI (2011) Revised Master Plan. July 28, 2011.

19. *Baltimore Sun.* May 22, 2002. "A business plan for biotech park."

20. *Daily Record.* August 10, 2011. "Board of Public Works sell bonds for state health lab."

21. *Daily Record.* February 1, 2011.

22. *Daily Record.* September 18, 2011. "Baltimore finds funds for EBDI TIF."

23. *Daily Record.* February 7, 2011. "Resolution on New East Baltimore hearings pass unanimously."

24. *WBAL News.* March 30, 2011. "EBD-Ire—Residents of Middle East (an E. Balto. neighborhood) attack quasi-public corporation renovating their community, at City Council hearing."

25. *Daily Record.* February 1, 2011.

6

Displacement and Disbanding of a Movement for Community Participation: Why, How, and Afterward

"It's been 6 years now, who's gonna wanna move again after 6 years? . . . They waiting us out." —displaced East Baltimore resident

"I am not going to die, I'm going home like a shooting star." —Sojourner Truth

This chapter will focus on the internal and external challenges faced by SMEAC over the 9 years of its existence. From its inception, SMEAC was at the same time building a membership base and addressing a process that had already taken off. The first years of SMEAC's work focused internally on building trust within the community and at the same time representing this newly bonded community's voice to the outside stakeholders. As more and more residents were displaced out of Phase 1, it was increasingly difficult to maintain an organized resident base within which authentic leadership development could continue to occur. SMEAC disbanded in 2009 even while the powerful stakeholders continued their nontransparency and exclusionary behaviors. Without an organized resident base they remained unchallenged.

GROWING DISPLACEMENT OF THE BASE?

The majority on the first board of directors of SMEAC was residents from Phase 1. Residents from this phase felt the most urgent need to understand and redefine a plan that would most acutely affect them, though redefining this plan would benefit not only them, but also all residents in the following phases.

While all residents of the entire 88 acres were encouraged to seek greater leadership roles in directing the organization, participation was consistently greatest among those in Phase 1. For example, no residents of Phase 2 served directly in the leadership of SMEAC during the first 3 years of the organization, though residents from the entire Middle East and larger East Baltimore communities attended monthly general membership meetings. Toward the end of its third year, SMEAC recruited more residents from what at the time were the subsequent phases (later to become simply Phase 2) to become more active in the organization. Slowly, the board began reflecting an equal representation of residents from the entire affected area.

Relocation of residents in Phase 1 began in 2004; by mid-2006, almost 400 households in Phase 1 had been relocated out of the Middle East Baltimore community. The strong membership base actively represented during the first 5 years of the organization changed as the almost 400 households from the first phase were slowly relocated out of the community. Only those residents who were directly involved in the organizational processes of SMEAC returned from their new communities to attend the committee meetings of SMEAC's board and the monthly membership meetings. While some continued to return to their historic community for almost 5 years, over time, fewer residents returned to general monthly meetings.

This out-migration of resident membership in the group and involvement in the rebuilding process was reflected in the 2006 planning session to revise the master plan. SMEAC advocated greater participation of community and guaranteed input from residents in this planning process. With almost all of the Phase 1 residents relocated out, the planning meeting to change the previous master plan was attended primarily by residents living in Phase 2 and some of the peripheral communities. By 2007, the more than 700 households that formed the base of the organization at its inception in 2001—the ones actively represented—were diminished by half. With this shrinking, the challenges of maintaining a strong and cohesive organization became more acute.

"Just when we thought the plan was clear, they changing it again . . . I'm fed up and tired" was a typical sentiment in 2006, when EBDI announced it was unclear when relocation would occur for residents in Phase 2. Accompanying this was "They trying to wear us down and wait us out . . . they know they can." There was a long history of "waiting for us to get out their way so they can do what they want." When EBDI and its powerful partners made a statement, it was unclear whether that was part of the truth, all of the truth, or temporary truth just for that moment. What was clear, the consistent truth, was "We know we got to go . . . the Massa want the land."

The bright spots also were clear. The organization had paved the way for residents in Phase 2 to have a better opportunity at a fair relocation process, safer demolition practices, and continued input regarding affordable return to or remaining in the rebuilt community. New negotiations began between SMEAC and EBDI and partners in regard to options for residents from Phase 2 to stay in the community. Concrete discussion began in regard the renovation of houses in the Phase 2 area for residents to relocate into and preservation of some houses. Later, these became the House for a House program and Home Repair program.

During door knocking and other organizing efforts in 2007, many residents remaining in Phase 2 expressed greater concern for their safety because of the increased number of vacant properties, the increased problems of rodents, and their frustration with the uncertainty of when they would be relocated. SMEAC renewed efforts to ensure residents' safety through increased block meetings and door knocking, encouraging greater community leadership to address these matters.

SMEAC's leadership was consistent in maintaining communication with the membership, but at times it had nothing new to report because nothing was happening. The chronically changing plans—not informed by residents—maintained the absence of any trust, transparency, or inclusiveness that shaped the rebuilding of Middle East Baltimore. And they continued to drain the energy of collective fight from the organized community stakeholders representing residents. This was 2007.

EBDI continued to offer no certainty about when relocation in the Phase 2 area would begin. It confirmed only that whatever benefits were being offered to residents in Phase 1 would be offered to residents in Phase 2.

Relocation of residents in the second phase began in 2007. By 2008, residents who were promised that they could stay in the community and move into rehabbed houses (House for a House program) saw no rehabbing of houses. They became tired of broken promises and wondered whether the plan was changing on them yet again. The cleared land sat vacant, no new houses were being built or rehabbed, and the process of relocating residents slowed down in the depressed housing market in 2008 and 2009. Throughout 2010–2011, residents from Phase 2 continued to be relocated out of the community.

While some residents waited for their rehabbed houses to be completed in the community, plans continued to change with no engagement of residents. Responses to questions about how many residents remained to be relocated included "some walked away" and "some died." Owner-occupied homes assessed for preservation and estimated for cost through the House for a House and Home Repair programs were later targeted for demolition, with no discussion with the owners. Said one resident, "They [EBDI] sent assessors to figure out how much it would cost to rehab it, then we heard a rumor that they decided to demolish the whole block . . . no one told me . . . why waste our time." The disrespect continued.

INSUFFICIENT BRIDGING RELATIONSHIPS

While specific partnerships with organizations and institutions outside of Middle East Baltimore were developed during the first few years, a systematic campaign to increase bridging relationships outside the Middle East Baltimore community did not begin until late 2004. Building the trust within the membership had been foremost during the first years of SMEAC, to solidify a base that residents could work from and that could receive advice and support from trusted outside sources. After the many years of fragmentation in the community, it took years to reconnect and build trust. However, because of the way the rebuilding had been planned, this growing base of organized residents was simultaneously being displaced, and the entire Middle East Baltimore community would eventually be displaced.

As SMEAC's membership continued to decline, by early 2005 it became urgently clear that the organization needed more bridging relationships with other similarly affected neighborhood groups in the larger East Baltimore community to maintain the energy of the community-driven process that it had initiated and solidified during its first 3 years. Identifying new partners outside of Middle East Baltimore and solidifying existing partnerships became major goals of the organization between 2005 and 2008.

SMEAC's reputation as a true grassroots community group that had risen up to demand, define, and achieve some form of justice was known in other low-income African American communities throughout Baltimore. Using the successes of the first 3 to 4 years as a reference, SMEAC attempted to offer similarly affected neighborhoods insight into more participatory community-building processes. Because the organization insisted on resident leadership, the diminished membership was left to divide itself among the growing number of meetings, all the while coping with the demands of daily life.

During these times, a citywide coalition advocating greater community participation in maintaining and rebuilding communities was also a goal for SMEAC. However, the organization did not have the resources to organize and lead such an effort effectively. Other goals had priority: increasing participation among the diminishing base of residents still in the Middle East Baltimore community, ensuring that residents not yet relocated in Phase 2 were treated fairly, maintaining pressure on EBDI and partners to offer transparency and follow through on promises for affordable housing in the 88 acres, and securing an affordable "right of return" and "right to remain" plan.

Unlike EBDI and its well-resourced partners, which could provide lucrative compensation to those carrying out their efforts in the rebuilding process, SMEAC had the resources of residents, who volunteered, and the paid staff of SMEAC, who did not receive any comparable degree of compensation for their efforts. The budget did not allow for increasing staff to devote more time to expanding the organization's base into neighboring communities of East Baltimore and Southeast Baltimore and into a citywide coalition. In presenting this goal to the organization, the executive directors were not convincing. And the current funding did not support this goal.

TIRED FROM THE STRUGGLE: CHANGING PRIORITIES, CHANGING PLANS

One thing affecting these growing challenges of diminishing membership and insufficient bridging relationships was how the collective energy had diminished with time. In early 2001, in the midst of the initial fear of the unknown and threat of loss of shelter, energies were activated. During the first years, residents from Phase 1 did not know whether they would have to move within the next week, month, or year. Experiencing a fight-or-flight response to this danger, residents chose to focus their energies to "fight." Much of this fear and disbelief activated residents to look deeply into how they could affect their future. SMEAC evolved from a crisis, a reaction to a trauma. After this initial reaction to the trauma of forced displacement, this "root shock," the energy slowly dissipated.[1]

It was replaced with fatigue from the stress of the first 5 to 6 years of a struggle for justice.[2,3] People were tired. They were tired of the struggle, the false promises, the need to consistently monitor for transparency in a process governed by non-transparency, the preparation for "battle" before each meeting with the powerful stakeholders acting in paternalistic ways, and the ongoing changes that continued the uncertainty of the future. This tiredness led to frustration and deep fatigue that affected the mental and physical well-being of many community residents. Some residents reported their blood pressure going up, their doctors telling them their asthma was worst, their difficulty sleeping, their sadness from having to leave. They reported in their own words, the worsening of their health during this intense period of struggle for justice. While there were bright spots in the rebuilding process, there remained unknowns in each step. And every bright spot occurred only after much struggle and the resulting tension that came from them.

For 8 years, SMEAC—three executive directors; five community organizers; three board presidents; and a board of directors, the majority of whom were Middle East Baltimore residents and the minority outside supporters; and its organized membership—stood up to the power of a rebuilding process that had no intention of addressing the needs of residents: a revolution occurred in Middle East Baltimore. This entire process of rebuilding Middle East Baltimore began on the basis of an uninformed plan without transparency or trust. Throughout its lifetime, SMEAC strove to establish residents as equal partners in the rebuilding process—experts in their own right.

The organization made its many accomplishments only by continuously placing pressure on the powerful stakeholders, convincing them of the justice of resident participation and ownership in a plan to move toward the community's "being made whole." It emphasized the history of continued land banking and expansion of JHMI and the racist and classist laws and policies which increased segregation and together fueled their community's demise into an unhealthy place to live, work, and play. It exerted its power directly in public meetings with those stakeholders, and when they ignored the demands for justice for residents, it took its demands to the streets and to the media. Those stakeholders' disrespect for the residents and their allies was continual, sometimes glaring and at other times just below the surface.

For example, in one meeting the executive director of EBDI pointed his finger in the face of the president of SMEAC, insisting that he "listen" to what he was being told (figure 6.1).

Figure 6.1. EBDI's executive director speaking to SMEAC's board chair during a community meeting to address sufficient affordable housing

This was a glaring manifestation of the persistent attitude of paternalism, racism, and classism of the powerful stakeholders that continues to drive this rebuilding process.

Similarly, back in 2006, when a renter refused to accept the houses that she was being shown by the city and EBDI staff, they described her as being "uncooperative." Because she wanted to be relocated into a house that would accommodate furnishings she had in her current city-owned apartment of more than 20 years, she was deemed uncooperative.[4] This more subtle manifestation of power, the expectation that residents should settle for what EBDI decides is adequate, persists today.

SMEAC's foremost task at the beginning of its struggle was to convince residents worn down by the same processes that had so drained their community that they had the right to demand justice. SMEAC insisted that one person's injustice was not an individual issue, but a collective problem. Once residents recognized their collective struggle, the next priority was to convince the powerful stakeholders, who were so sure of their own vision, of the injustice of a rebuilding process without resident participation. Next was to convince them to participate in shaping a more just process of rebuilding, even though doing so would require changing the initial plans and attempting to decrease the risk of Africans Americans being forced out of their community with no hope of returning.

The toll on the organizers and directors of SMEAC was not small, mentally or physically. The giant of EBDI and its powerful supporters had greater resources, and they did not share the history of being on the receiving end of racial and class oppression that the Middle East Baltimore community had endured over time. This "weathering" or accumulation of stressors and their negative health consequences, from living in an unhealthy neighborhood for many years compounded by the new stress of displacement from community, social networks, and home, was a challenge that was not voiced by many and certainly was not on the radar of the powerful stakeholders.[5] This toll is reflected by one resident, after finally accepting the house she was shown, saying, "I've been trying to get as good a deal as I could. I have put in a lot of work. I can't deal with it anymore. I'm tired."[6]

CHANGES WITHIN SMEAC

In 2006, a period of new unknowns as to how relocation would change for residents in Phase 2, SMEAC was undergoing many changes. The membership of the board of directors was shifting from the majority being residents of Phase 1 to more residents from Phase 2, a new president of the board (from Phase 2) was voted in, and a new executive director was hired.

The new executive director was not a person of color; the previous two were. This change in the racial makeup of the leadership represented an important shift from the shared trust and understanding that had been developed with the previous executive directors. A white director now had to build trust with the general membership of SMEAC and the larger base of African American residents in Middle East Baltimore, as well as within SMEAC's organizational structure of board and staff.

He had to quickly come to understand the underlying base of white supremacy that shaped the rebuilding of Middle East Baltimore. And he had to just as quickly understand the privilege he brought into the relationships within and outside of the community. This awareness was key in determining how residents would come to trust his understanding of racism and its effect in shaping communities of low-income and African American like Middle East Baltimore.

Energy had to be shifted to developing this trust—energy that could have been used to deal with the external issues of relocation and the housing issues now facing the residents in Phase 2. Also, the new director's organizing methods differed from those of the previous directors. They worked with a consensus model of organizing and incorporated this in leadership development broadly: everyone had something of value to offer when integrity ruled. Listening to—and recognizing value in—the experiences and wisdom of the community were natural for the previous executive directors, as people of color—the elders in Middle East Baltimore—were not different from their family elders whose wisdom shaped their lives. The new executive director emphasized more hierarchical roles of leadership, took a different view of leadership development, and was not used to having a board of directors involved in all the activities of the organization. These differences would eventually build on existing separation and distrust within the board, race and class struggles within the staff, and resultant separation within the larger membership of the organization.

With new leadership in both staff and board, the organization turned to its internal structure to reaffirm many of the ethical behaviors it had placed at the core of its internal and external interactions. This included using a consensus process for the general membership to elect the board of directors, specific and general training processes for new board members (discussed in chapter 3), and holding each other accountable through transparency and open communication—modeling a way the organization hoped EBDI and its partners would follow.

These changes within the organization took place when it was already challenged by the changing base of residents being relocated out of the community—half the community had already been displaced. As more residents from Phase 2 attended meetings in 2007, less members from Phase 1 were there to pass the history of the first 4 years of their struggle together. The trust that had previously existed within the organization, that solidified its base, slowly changed and diminished. Basic questions regarding a process for accountability, within and outside of the organization, were being raised 6 years into the struggle—challenging the framework, the fundamental core, of SMEAC's existence. The new individuals on the board had no opportunity to develop trust as quickly as the previous Phase 1 board members who were quickly thrust together in the midst of the fear the community was experiencing when SMEAC first formed.

The new members did not know the difficult steps the organization had collectively taken to gain inclusion of residents or the struggle for changes in relocation and demolition practices over the previous years. Because they had not actively participated in the struggle of the first 6 years, they were unaware of this history and this process of negotiation. They were unaware of how this struggle had been a movement that built trust and accountability, the bright spots coming out of the most demanding times.

More residents from Phase 2 also began attending EBDI meetings without knowing the collective process SMEAC had established for successfully negotiating the needs of residents. A growing movement toward more individual negotiations slowly emerged.

As fragmentation increased during 2008, individual community members slowly stepped up to represent only themselves. This led to their negotiating with EBDI on only their own behalf, leaving the collective voice behind. EBDI readily responded to and invited these individual negotiations. In the past, SMEAC was invited into individual negotiations on behalf of a resident and EBDI staff were often offended by their presence. This new way of negotiating was exactly what they preferred. EBDI slowly built a trust with these residents, some of whom continue to speak on behalf of EBDI's positive role in the community. Slowly EBDI helped to assure increased fragmentation within the remaining residents. This fragmentation was representative of the processes that were also taking place internally to SMEAC.

The executive director was involved more in organizing and less in directing, leaving a gap in the organization's continued development of grassroots leadership. With insufficient training of the new members of the board of directors of SMEAC, the processes and procedures of the board became haphazard. And within the board, a line was drawn between the old and the new: the old board members, former residents of Phase 1 who had relocated out of the community, and the new board members, who were residents of Phase 2.

Some felt the principles were too strict and that individual character should be sufficient to ensure trusting relationships. Others, who had been around since SMEAC's formation, demanded continued attention to and implementation of the written bylaws that had guided the organization since its inception and through many difficult times. SMEAC had gained a reputation for being transparent to all its members and accountable to each and every resident. It earned this reputation through rigorous adherence to the bylaws, policies, and procedures agreed upon by the board of directors. Between 2007 and 2009, it became challenging to ensure the implementation of these guiding principles through consensus and majority vote. The trust was gone, tensions were palpable, and communication within the organization was at best irregular.

At a board meeting in October 2009, without any advance notice to the general membership base that this would come up, members of the board moved to close the organization based on a majority vote of those in attendance. Communication had continued to be strained and agreement was not consistent among all members of the board. This was evident when only those in attendance at the decisive board meeting had the opportunity to participate in the vote to close the organization.

The organization's leadership had decided that SMEAC had changed at its core. Instead of existing under the name SMEAC with a different set of values, it would not exist at all. Those choosing to continue with some form of organization could organize a new group and establish their own code of ethics.

With a changing and diminishing membership resulting from continued displacement of residents, new members not informed by the first 6 years of struggle due to displacement of former members, a continuously changing plan as to how Middle East Baltimore would be rebuilt, core challenges of trust of the powerful stakeholders, growing differences of organizational value inside the organization due to the effects of displacement, and the toll of accumulated physical and mental stress of a difficult struggle, SMEAC closed its doors in 2009, officially resigning its nonprofit status in 2010. And so came the end of the most powerful and purposeful organized movement that represented the Middle East Baltimore community's struggle for inclusion and justice in rebuilding its community—in the twenty-first century.

The formation and disbanding of SMEAC reflects the history of previous powerful community organizations in East Baltimore which challenged the powerful JHMI and city and state government. Specifically, Citizens for Fair Housing (CFFH) which formed in the early 1960s to organize and assure resident participation in community development—at that time the Gay Street 1 Project—did so after the tremendous injustice of false promises and blatant disrespect and displacement of residents in the Broadway Redevelopment project (1950–1960) (chapter 2). The insult and pain of forced displacement and demolition of their homes for continued growth of JHMI ignited the fire of resistance and struggle in residents who had just been displaced for the Broadway Project. CFFH organized residents and demanded and participated in rebuilding their community.

Similarly in 2001, when the plan to rebuild Middle East Baltimore announced the same strategy of another 800 households being displaced for the expansion of JHMI, residents responded to this trauma with resistance and solidarity against the clear perpetuator of this insult. As in the 1960s, the enemy and the goal was clear: JHMI was the oppressive developer and community participation to assure their plans did not take over the community yet again was the goal.

CFFH maintained its membership base because the majority of residents were not displaced. The eventual movement of its base out of the community came slowly during the late 1970s and early 1980s and onward—secondary to the change in industrial employment in the 1970s, continued disinvestment by city and state government which did not stem the abandonment of houses or stabilize the infrastructure of the community, and continued slow accumulation and boarding up of property by JHMI which contributed to the decay of East Baltimore.

SMEAC's membership base was displaced during the rebuilding of Middle East Baltimore because this was the intention of the project from its beginning. Any negotiation to construct houses before demolition within the area was neglected by EBDI and partners. The long wait between displacement and eventual rehabbing of houses for residents to return to was 4 to 6 years after residents from the first phase were displaced. Construction of new affordable housing for residents to return did not begin as of 2011 and neither have surveys of what types of houses residents prefer, been conducted. SMEAC's listening projects during the early 2000s documented that some residents preferred single family dwellings and one-story homes due to their age and ability to get around—presented to EBDI and partners. The current master plan has no such houses projected for construction.

INDIVIDUALITY AND LOSS OF HISTORY IN POST-DISPLACEMENT MIDDLE EAST BALTIMORE

In its wake, individual residents from Phase 2 have formed small groups. At any one time, two or three exist, competing for the presence of remaining residents of the area, self-appointing leadership with no formal policy and procedures.

In 2010, there remained fewer than 50 historic households in Middle East Baltimore, confirming the difficulty of SMEAC's continuing—with a diminished community base, increasing fragmentation, and insufficient bridging relationships with neighborhoods outside of the Middle East Baltimore area. Organizing residents who were being relocated out of the community was a challenge in the beginning and remained a challenge in the end. Without a pool of residents from which to draw and build a base of members, there is no resident participation.

And because the plan to rebuild Middle East Baltimore did not conceive or manifest a genuine plan of return for the more than 800 households who would be relocated, many residents left with no real belief that they had an option to return—whether they wanted to or not. Once relocated, they had no need to continue or interest in continuing to participate in an organization in the community they perceived they could not return to. Indeed, as of 2011, there still was no concrete plan for residents who relocated out to return to the area. This plan of "no return" will be discussed further in the next chapter.

Since the end of 2009, there has been no authentic collective representation of the community at EBDI's meetings, only individuals representing their interests in their own home or own relocation package. Individuals have taken to the meetings concerns about the lack of equity in assessed values for their homes, living on an isolated block with a lack of adequate sanitation and security measures, affording the proposed tax-benefit district, and questions of when they would be relocated. Their concerns were taken on an individual basis. They were not looked into as parts of the collective issues that should be systemically addressed by EBDI and its stakeholders. There was no accountability to an organized group and therefore nothing to ensure systemic changes that could affect the collective.

Without an organized force negotiating for collective change it becomes easier for those in power to simply address an individual's need instead of looking into the systemic process that resulted in the problem. Without a SMEAC, EBDI addresses residents' concerns on an individual basis. Individuals raising questions in meetings are asked to save their questions for a discussion with EBDI staff, after the meeting.

This type of deferring of individual concerns occurred infrequently during the organizing activities of SMEAC. When an individual resident brought up questions in a meeting, a SMEAC representative reinforced them as something that should be addressed for all members of the community. Certainly the individual was addressed in regard to his or her concern, but the advocacy from the organization placed pressure on EBDI and its partners to look into how other individuals would be similarly affected. This forced EBDI to investigate and address each individual issue for its systemic root, which could prevent it from occurring again.

In addition, if an individual did or said something that offended EBDI and partners, he or she had the support of an organized group of residents. Residents knew there was an organization holding EBDI and partners accountable to residents, and this supported them to speak out more in meetings. Today, in the rebuilding process in Middle East Baltimore, there is no such organization or united voice of residents to support the individual voice challenging some perceived inequity, leaving his or her benefit at risk.

Because an authentic, collective voice of the remaining community of Middle East Baltimore does not exist, EBDI and partners have had no authentic collaboration with residents since SMEAC disbanded in 2009. There remains no cohesive community participatory process. Meetings to discuss a new name for the rebuilt community are not announced publicly and no opportunity for community participation is made public. When questioned about opportunity for resident input in this issue EBDI claimed no part in it and reported that it was being conducted by the developer and Johns Hopkins representatives.

This remains the reality in early 2011, though several of the non-community stakeholders publicly respond that they are engaged with grassroots community organizations in Middle East and East Baltimore. In truth, none has existed for them to engage with for more than 1 year. What remains is the same small fragmented community groups which had no real power in demanding change in their communities before the 2001 plan was announced. These organizations were unable to unite as a collective whole to organize for justice in community change before SMEAC was formed. Currently, they remain separate, not a trusted support for the remaining residents in Middle East Baltimore and the greater East Baltimore.

In retrospect, had SMEAC attempted to bring these different smaller groups together as part of an Eastside coalition, this fragmentation might not remain today. This initiative would have required more effort from the very beginnings of SMEAC, when a strong resident base of more than 800 households was still intact. It would have been a challenging process to engage residents not directly impacted in the current rebuilding process. As it was, engaging residents who were directly impacted, but not until Phase 2, was a challenge during the first years. Still, building more bridging relationships with neighborhood groups certainly would have been a worthy challenge, to ensure sustained efforts and a larger membership base inclusive of all of East Baltimore after relocation had begun. It would have required a broader vision, greater resources, and a strategic plan that went beyond the scope of the first 10 years of the rebuilding process.

Another important effect of the disbanding of SMEAC is the potential loss of the history of the community organizing process in rebuilding Middle East Baltimore. Because all of the residents of Phase 1, and the majority of residents of Phase 2, are now absent from the tables of negotiation, there is no witnessing and no reference to the substance that went into changes along the rebuilding path. For example, the changed relocation benefits, demolition protocol, and housing development in Phase 2 would not have occurred without the presence of an organized community voice demanding justice.

And as minutes of these first meetings about Phase 2 reflect, it was the insistence of SMEAC in 2006 that initiated formation of the details of the House for a House and Home Repair programs. Yet, later, EBDI's executive director announced that they were "his idea." To bring these two housing programs into existence required almost 2 years of intense demands, confrontations, rallies, and media publicity, in addition to EBDI's participation and adequate funding (box 6.1, box 6.2).

Such co-optation of the community's ideas included the revision of the demolition protocol. During an interview of a staff member of one of the foundations in 2006, they stated that it was their plan to change the first demolition protocol. This co-optation of the work of SMEAC continued into 2011.

Box 6.1. Letter from SMEAC to EBDI's executive director regarding changes in EBDI's housing plans in Phase 2

July 16, 2008

xxxx xxxx
President/Chief Executive Officer
East Baltimore Development Inc.
1731 East Chase Street
Baltimore, Maryland 21213

Dear xxxx:

Following your meeting with SMEAC and residents within the so-called Preservation Block area on June 23rd we have had time to reflect on the implications of this new EBDI plan.

At SMEAC's General Membership Meeting on July 14th residents noted that this plan represents a vast change in policy for EBDI. Previous to the change -the policy supported Preservation Block homeowners' right to stay in Middle East. Now-the policy assures that most homeowners will have to relocate.

SMEAC and the residents find this policy change unacceptable.

Under the new EBDI policy, it seems that the Housing Code will be used as a club to effectively drive most homeowners from the community. The Housing Code is barely enforced throughout the city. And those areas of the city where the code is strictly followed are carefully chosen. The Housing Code is a public policy tool that is conveniently utilized in a selective manner.

Therefore, we must ask the obvious question. What interpretation of the Housing Code will be applied by EBDI in Middle East Baltimore? Most certainly, what will be employed is "to the letter" approach to the housing code.

In fact, SMEAC thinks that this new EBDI policy represents a violation of the spirit of our joint EBDI/SMEAC House for a House efforts. The House for a House program has been designed to keep Middle East Baltimore homeowners within the EBDI project area. The new Preservation Block policy takes EBDI in an entirely opposite direction.

As a result of this policy change - there will be fewer low-income people of color in EBDI's New East Side. Many residents are asking why EBDI would do that.

EBDI must change its priorities. The policy for the Preservation Blocks must be redesigned to reflect the priority of keeping current Middle East Baltimore home-owners within the EBDI project area.

SMEAC has been accused of unnecessarily scaring the residents about EBDI's intentions. But this is a misperception. Rathe, it is EBDI's drastic change in policy that is truly frightening to Middle East Baltimore homeowners.

SMEAC and the residents must hear from you, xxxx as EBDI's leader as to what *standards of enforcement will be used to vet Middle East Baltimore residents' right to stay in their homes.* stay in their homes. We do not want respected Middle East Baltimore homeowners driven out with the club of a selectively enforced Housing Code.

xxxx, the residents have some additional concerns that we have outlined in the accompanying document.

Please reply in writing to these concerns about the Housing Code matter and the other topics that we have introduced.

Sincerely,

yyyy yyyy, President
Save Middle East Action Committee, Inc.

zzzz zzzz, Executive Director
Save Middle East Action Committee, Inc.

EBDI and its powerful partners, the foundations and the JHMI, involved in lever-aging millions of dollars in the rebuilding process, could claim, as they do, that they were ultimately responsible for the change in these aspects of rebuilding. After all, the changes in the relocation benefit package could not have occurred without the funding necessary to secure the increased cost. Neither could the more costly demolition protocol or the funding schemes that allowed forgivable loans for rehabbing houses.

But without the community residents organizing and standing up for fair and just relocation, demolition, and housing rehabbing, the changes would not have occurred. The powerful stakeholders plan showed no desire to change, no vision for change, no motivation to change until the organized residents pressed their demands for change.

The Civil Rights Movement in the 1950s and 1960s resulted in laws changing. It was the power of their collective and resistant voices and actions, which sent a

Box 6.2. Letter from SMEAC to the chair of the Housing and relocation committee—chaired by the president of the Annie E. Casey Foundation—addressing transparent, responsible, and timely communication in regard to the housing programs in Phase 2

February 17, 2009

xxxx xxxx
President
Annie E. Casey Foundation

Dear xxxxx xxxxxx,

On February 6th oooo oooo, Chairman of the EBDI Board, sent a letter to yyyy yyyy, SMEAC President. In that letter he said that EBDI's Board would get back to SMEAC in writing by February 16th in response to our December 12th letter to oooo and answer the questions about EBDI's dealings with tttttttttt on the House for a House program.

As of this afternoon, there has been no written response.

As of this point, SMEAC cannot see why we should not use all of the resources at our disposal to make our issues public ones. If these EBDI to SMEAC communications do not work then what choice do we have except to go public.

We have been in touch by phone with zzzz zzzz about this. zzzz said he knew nothing about it. And he referred us to oooo oooo directly. Does the CEO of EBDI have nothing to do anymore with these important policy questions? SMEAC thinks that he does.

Let us know what you think. And let us know when we can expect our reply from the EBDI Board.

With regards,

yyyy yyyy, President
Save Middle East Action Committee, Inc.

pppp pppp, Executive Director
Save Middle East Action Committee, Inc.

forceful message about the moral injustice of racial oppression, which influenced and changed the minds and actions of those in the offices capable of directly affecting these changes. The movement created the conditions for those who had the authority and means to make the laws to do so. The law was a vehicle to implement the change that the movement envisioned and pressed for. Dr. Martin Luther King, well-known leader of the Civil Rights Movement, consistently declared "we shall overcome" in assuring those affected and supporting the efforts of the Civil Rights Movement. President Johnson in speaking to the Congress in 1965 stated "we shall overcome" when signing into law the end of legal segregation in the USA.

The Civil Rights Movement showed how powerful organized presence is a tool necessary to effect change in the face of political, social, and economic establishments either unable or unwilling to stand up for justice. EBDI and its partners declaring their ownership of resultant changes in the rebuilding process can be compared to the president signing into law the Civil Rights Act and declaring it was his doing and not the result of the Civil Rights movement. The disrespect continues.

SMEAC acted on its intention for equity and justice, through organizing for the collective. While other stakeholders may also have desired equity and justice, their perception of what that meant initially looked different, and their priorities going into the rebuilding process were elsewhere.

Today each of these fundamental changes SMEAC organized for and won has largely been co-opted by the powerful stakeholders. They do not mention the process of community organizing against the powerful racist and classist plans or the trauma and stress on the life of the community that led to these changes. Nor do they mention the history of racist and classist public policy and law which created disinvested and abandoned communities like East Baltimore, previous segregationist tactics used by JHMI and the city of Baltimore in East Baltimore and their role in creating unhealthy communities, the unsafe exposure to lead dust from demolition in previous and current rebuilding projects, or the persistent attempt to minimize the number of residents able to remain in their community. Left out of their accounts is the real history of how the now boldly publicized "respectable relocation plan" came to be and why it remains insufficient to assure equity in benefit for displaced residents and the peripheral communities remaining.

SMEAC's disbanding allows this history of a 9-year community movement to be quickly forgotten. Without this collective force, community members remaining must individually challenge the powerful stakeholders for justice. Without any challenge to the blind spots of the powerful stakeholders, without organized community participation, the next 10 years simply cannot address equity.

We do not know our blind spots until they are pointed out to us. When addressed, they have the potential to become bright spots. This was the process of change in the first 10 years: SMEAC pointed out the blind spots and helped negotiate the path to the bright spots.

The next chapter will focus on the question of "who benefits from rebuilding abandoned communities in America?"

NOTES

1. Fullilove M. (2001) "Root Shock: the consequences of African American dispossession." *J Urban Health*. 78:72.

2. Geronimus AT. (2000) "To mitigate, resist, or undo: addressing structural influences on the health of urban populations." *Am J Public Health*. 90:867.

3. Fullilove MT. (2004) *Root Shock: how tearing up city neighborhoods hurts America, and what we can do about it*. Random House, NY.

4. *Baltimore City Paper*. February 22, 2006. "Moved and shaken."

5. Geronimus AT. (2000) *To mitigate, resist, or undo: addressing structural influences on the health of urban populations*.

III

THE FUTURE OF EAST BALTIMORE: RACE, CLASS, POWER AND ORGANIZING AS CAUSES AND CONSEQUENCES IN REBUILDING ABANDONED COMMUNITIES

7

Who Benefits and Suffers From Rebuilding Abandoned Communities?

". . . Hopkins and their friends don't care about residents; residents have to care about residents . . . but people are tired from being lied to . . . it's a lot to know the truth and still have to sit and listen to them say one thing and do another, over and over again . . . they [residents] know this [project] is about Hopkins." —East Baltimore organizer

"The equality proclaimed by our institutions is not—as certain people absurdly seem to think—some illusory equality of education and ability among all concerned, nor is it the equal distribution of property; it merely implies that the law does not distinguish one person from another, leaving this up to nature and fate: it means that the aim of all institutions should be the moral, intellectual and physical improvement of the largest and poorest social class." —D.S. Sarmiento

This chapter addresses the question of benefit—to whom—and how equity in benefit is determined in rebuilding Middle East Baltimore. While previous chapters have discussed how residents directly impacted by displacement suffered as a result of the way rebuilding occurred, this chapter will address the effect on the peripheral communities surrounding the 88 acres. Because the root causes of disinvestment and abandonment have not been addressed, the rebuilding process has simply pushed the symptoms of poverty away from the prestigious neighbor—crime, drug dealing, consciousness of poverty—into similarly disinvested communities nearby; greater wealth inequality is the result.

Understanding the intention behind rebuilding Middle East Baltimore will help in assessing the negative outcomes which have been ignored. Understanding how equity in benefit must be assessed can help future rebuilding of abandoned communities, using public-private partnerships, to strive to authentically rebuild abandoned communities without creating new segregated communities, address the root causes of poverty and racism, produce more equitable "public benefit," and include community participation in all aspects of rebuilding.

To answer the question "For whom are we rebuilding Middle East Baltimore?" requires looking into several factors: the decision makers of the original plan and subsequent master plans, the relocation process—in and out; the use of eminent domain powers and other public-private partnerships, and the effect on the peripheral communities. Lastly we look at how transparency of intent can benefit outcomes of rebuilding processes.

PLANNING AND DECISION-MAKING

The first plan in 2001 suggested "building" on the Historic East Baltimore Action Coalition Plan (HEBCAC).[1] HEBCAC's plan of the mid-1990s included a charrette process for community participation, input, and engagement. The original HEBCAC plan suggested even greater resident engagement to inform a final master plan and rebuilding all of East Baltimore to benefit its historic residents. HEBCAC's plan included no description of the entire Middle East Baltimore neighborhood relocating out of the area.

Indeed, the first public plan to rebuild Middle East Baltimore—announced in 2001—did "build" a great deal on the community-informed HEBCAC plan. The feasibility study for a biotech park, initiated by the Johns Hopkins Medical Institutions (JHMI) in 2000, was not a part of the original HEBCAC plan in 1994 and did not include a community engagement process. Why should it have included community? Because the biotech park was proposed to be built on land the community lived on, it had value to them in the current condition. Meanwhile, the HEBCAC planning process included participation and decision making by JHMI representatives.

The original master plan of December 2001 suggested that the neighborhoods adjacent to the Middle East Baltimore community—making up the greater East Baltimore area (Oliver, Madison East End, Broadway, Gay Street, Collington Square, Milton-Montford)—become the areas where residents displaced from the first 31 acres would be relocated to stabilize the rebuilt community. That same month, the first draft of the relocation policy also stated that loans for purchasing homes would only be provided to residents who relocated to these same areas.

No residents were involved in developing this draft relocation policy. While they did not state it directly, these two documents made it very clear that there was no intention for displaced residents to return to benefit from the rebuilding of the Middle East Baltimore area. Confirming this unwritten intention, the first master plan suggested only market-rate ownership homes for new construction.

The 2006 revised master plan added a 7-acre, new, $50 million public charter school—co-managed by the JHMI. The plan for a school was presented to the community after the decision was made to include it as part of the rebuilding process. When it was made public, a plan for funding was already in place, as were the intended location and a timeline for completion. Residents unaware of a new school being constructed where they currently lived were given short notice to relocate. The area targeted for rebuilding increased with this revised plan.

The most recently announced revised master plan, of 2011 (the third since 2001), involved no community input. Residents were not targeted for the surveys which informed the plan because they had "pre-formed opinions." Their opinions were therefore "meaningless." As one resident said: "This is the Master's plan."

The average income of those surveyed to inform the plan did not match the income of East Baltimore residents; neither did the type of housing they desired. Reflecting this difference, the current plan has no single dwelling units or one-story housing planned for construction.

The meetings of the committees of East Baltimore Development Incorporated's (EBDI's) board were open to the public during the first 10 years. There, residents appeared to have an opportunity to participate, but it was simply input. Decisions were not made in these meetings.[2] As described in EBDI's review of the first relocation process, community members were "advisors".[3] One resident described the process: "We went to the meeting and said we didn't like the plan, they smiled and nodded; we knew it didn't matter . . . it's the same plan . . . why waste our time?" The decision making occurred in private, among key members of the EBDI board. The full EBDI board was a body that mostly heralded and signed off on the already-made decisions of a few key stakeholders.

The JHMI has resisted publicly reporting its major role in decision making directing the rebuilding of Middle East Baltimore since its announcement in 2001. The mayor's office described JHMI as "key investor" and mentioned "close ties".[4] That was then. By 2011, the institution proudly claimed its ties to the biotech park.

> The entire medical campus is expanding: the Johns Hopkins Hospital is now in Phase II of a $950 million construction project to be completed by the spring of 2011; a new education building is opening in the fall of 2009; plans for renovating the Basic Science quad are now being developed; and a 31-acre Science & Technology Park is under construction now—the first of the biotech park buildings opened in 2008. The Science & Technology Park project includes 1.1 million square feet of lab and office space.[5]

Representatives of the institutions continued to evade the issue of direct ownership of land even as ground was broken for its new graduate student housing complex, renovation of a historic fire station for its bioethics institute, and occupation of the first biotech building occurred in the first 31 acres adjacent to the campus. However, even while it publicly asserts no ownership of land in the 88 acres, its decision making of what occurs in these 88 acres was made clear during the presentation of the third master plan. According to a newspaper article, after the master developer attempted to present the third revised master plan in a public meeting "[the spokesperson for the developer] tried to soothe the fears and protests [of residents] by pledging to work with the residents. He said . . . , Hopkins' president, was committed to working with the remaining residents. 'Johns Hopkins can help this community achieve what it wants . . . or we can fight [the president of Hopkins] for the next 10 years that he's president of Hopkins and I swear we'll all be sitting in this same room 10 years from now."[6]

The major decision makers were JHMI, the mayor and governor's administration (the mayor who initiated the plan in 2001 became the governor in 2007), the city-appointed chair of the EBDI board, the city council members who granted eminent domain for the area, and the major private investor Annie E. Casey Foundation (investing in excess of $50 million—direct financial and otherwise—personnel, training, administration, leveraging power in bringing additional investors to the table) during the first 10 years (chapter 6).

WHERE IS THE "RESPONSIBLE RELOCATION BENEFIT PACKAGE" FOR RETURNING RESIDENTS?

Of more than 800 households forced to relocate out of Middle East Baltimore, only 28 currently have moved into housing in the 220 new units available in the first Phase (31 acres). The only housing targeted for low-income earners in these 31 acres adjacent to the medical complex is rental units for seniors.

The first household moved into a rehabbed house in 2010, 2 years after the first ownership opportunities were promised in writing, in February 2008. By 2011, 37 households still were waiting for these promised houses—none were residents from Phase 1. At this writing less than 5 percent of displaced residents have returned or remained in their historic community. A "plan of return" was neither implicit nor explicit in the relocation of residents out of Middle East Baltimore.

The Save Middle East Action Committee, Inc. (SMEAC) helped residents fight for a right of return by ensuring that one-third low-income housing was part of the housing construction plan, equally distributed between rental and ownership units; this was legislated in 2005. The most recent master plan recommended "a housing plan that responds to our research findings."[7] Their research findings showed demographics for prospected tenants for the rebuilt area with a median income between $30K and $105K. The median income for East Baltimore is less than $18,000.[8]

However, there was no planning done, no policy developed, and no funding earmarked to afford residents to return to their community, to sell the homes outside of Middle East Baltimore they had relocated into, relocate back into Middle East Baltimore, purchase affordable low-income housing in the rebuilt community, and pay the increased taxes. The words "right of return" were on the policy defining relocation out, but there was no systematic effort or planning to ask residents what types of houses or retail shops and amenities they would want to return to. The effort and planning went into the relocation out of the area. It was a one-way ticket out; no ticket to ride a train back into the area was issued and no "responsible relocation packet" back into the community was developed, with or without resident input.

Currently, EBDI and staff provide assistance for relocation back into the community on an individual basis. Instead of following an equitable and consistent process, they have discretion in each interaction. With neither a systematized process guided by policy nor allocated funds, there is no accountability and no expectation of a process of fair relocation back into the community. There were no goals set as to how many residents would be relocated back into the community and therefore no funding to assure such a goal was achieved. Instead there were concrete activities which contradicted the likelihood of successful return of displaced residents.

For example, the discussion regarding renovated homeownership opportunities in Phase 2 was put on the table in late 2006, after the majority of residents from the first phase had been relocated out of East Baltimore. The House for a House and Home Repair programs were the final results of these discussions. It was only in 2008, when EBDI and partners were choosing the developer for construction of these ownership housing, that residents were offered an opportunity to suggest the types of amenities they would prefer in houses. By this time, some residents from the first phase had been relocated for almost 4 years already. Many reported they were still recovering from the stress and frustration of the relocation process and could not imagine moving again. Those who considered returning commented about the

Figure 7.1. Homeownership opportunities in Phase 1 of the Middle East rebuilding area

absence of the type of affordable housing they had requested in the 2001 and 2006 planning sessions.

Others still did not believe that EBDI, Johns Hopkins, the foundations or the other powerful partners truly wanted them to return: "Now you know they don't really want us back there . . . they finally got what they wanted . . ."

The first rehabbed houses did not become available until late 2010, These were the first opportunity for owners to relocate only once and use their relocation benefits to remain in the community.

In contrast, the planning for construction and rehabbing of housing units for new residents involved focus groups and surveys of students and staff of the medical campus and communities outside of East Baltimore in 2010 and 2011. These attempts to learn what types of amenities they wanted to see and build to attract this community were adequately planned and funded. Likewise, the plan to rename the community in an effort to market it to its prospective new residents occurred with no input from relocated and remaining residents—instead, the tentative name was presented to the community after the fact.

Plans to attract staff and faculty from the JHMI to live in the rebuilt area included a partnership between the Johns Hopkins University and EBDI to offer its East Baltimore employees incentives to "live near your work." This took the form of $50,000 grants from EBDI toward homeownership for employees who purchased homes in the first 31 acres.

The first 10 years of rebuilding Middle East Baltimore may be best described as "removing Middle East Baltimore" as it achieved exactly that. With a relocation program assuring residents were displaced according to schedule, partially financed by the public funds guaranteed through the use of eminent domain powers and private investment, the land was cleared and prepared for construction of the new community: Beacon Park (the proposed name). The next phase of planning proposed rebuilding on this cleared land, a community which would benefit the image of the more powerful neighbor. As one resident said: "Hopkins is getting rich off of us, the backs of poor Black people . . . now they don't say 'Hopkins,' they call it 'EBDI' . . . same thing."

Do residents want to return to their community? During 2001–2003, before residents were relocated, 66 percent of residents surveyed in Middle East Baltimore expressed a desire to return to the rebuilt community. In 2006, after relocation of residents from the first 31 acres, 26 percent of these residents did not want to return and another 10 percent responded negatively, stating they may change their mind in the future.[9] Many of these residents who were not interested in returning at the time of the survey in 2006 felt there was insufficient information (cost, housing type) to make a decision about returning. In 2009, EBDI and partners conducted a follow-up survey to assess housing and economic outcomes of residents who had been relocated. In 2011, there still has not been public disclosure of these results. More than 1 year of attempting to learn the results yielded the final response, "The response rate was too low" for public disclosure. It remains curious why the results cannot be reported with a note stating exactly that.

In 2011, EBDI and partners reported a plan to survey residents who had been relocated to learn how they are doing and what types of housing they wanted to see in the rebuilt community they had left. This information they are now seeking was offered 10 years ago, to deaf ears. While this is very late in the process of planning to ensure that residents return to the community, this new effort, if followed through with action and funding, would start a different pattern in the rebuilding of Middle East Baltimore. It would begin to change the message that has been overtly and covertly communicated throughout the previous 10 years.

According to residents, rebuilding Middle East Baltimore has been about "getting rid of us, so Hopkins can feel safe." Reaching out to relocated residents to learn what they would need in order to return begins to equip residents with a ticket on the train running back into the community. A ticket of equity on this train would be fully invested with all the benefits that ushered residents and businesses out of the neighborhood. And the ticket of equity would ensure that residents can return not only to houses in the peripheral communities but throughout the entire 88 acres of Middle East Baltimore. Such intentional and practical steps to ensure movement toward equity for historic displaced residents could begin to assure that the rebuilt community reflects and benefits the historic resident who suffered through the years of disinvestment and abandonment. It begins to recognize the history of racist and classist policies which supported such decay and made it susceptible to speculation and land banking by powerful interests. It would begin to change not only the history of rebuilding in East Baltimore, but similar histories in America.

WHAT ABOUT THE COMMUNITIES PERIPHERAL TO MIDDLE EAST BALTIMORE?

Bridging the gap between the powerful JHMI and its less powerful neighbors is one of the factors that will result in more residents returning to the rebuilt and peripheral communities of East Baltimore. Residents of the entire area of East Baltimore fear that this powerful neighbor will eventually expand to take their homes, up to North Avenue. Elders have seen the evidence of this with their own eyes, as their homes were bought for cheap by those "white people from Hopkins" or their leases were not renewed. The continued accumulation of land by the institution, and its expansion from one block to more than 21 blocks, confirms these fears. Why would a resident return to live with the fear of another displacement in 20 to 40 years?

These peripheral areas, including Broadway East, Madison East End, and Milton-Montford, adjacent to the rebuilt area, are typically affected by the same disinvestment as the ones being renewed (see figure 1.1). It was the same more than 50 years ago as it is today. They are primarily low-income communities, with similar employment, educational, housing, recreational, and health characteristics to those of Middle East Baltimore. Perhaps they are not as abandoned and deteriorated as Middle East Baltimore, but they are on the path. For example, between 1990 and 2000, while the population in Middle East Baltimore decreased by 44 percent, the peripheral neighborhoods saw decreases between 21 percent and 36 percent.[10] In East Baltimore, crime was and continues to be higher than in the city as a whole and in most communities in Baltimore.

In the 1950s Broadway Redevelopment Project, while the majority of residents were displaced to the periphery of the project area, there were no additional governmental services or private dollars for safety and sanitation nor increased businesses to create employment in these areas. In the next big redevelopment in East Baltimore, the 1960s Gay Street I Urban Renewal Project, the majority of residents remained in the rebuilt area. The remainder relocated into the peripheral communities in need of renewal. Some new businesses were established in the rebuilt area, none in the peripheral communities. Today, the majority of renters were relocated into East Baltimore communities. Again, funding for improved services or public infrastructure did not follow them. Neither did opportunities for entrepreneurship or ways of increasing income and move out of poverty.

Relocating residents into peripheral communities to remove the "eyesore" of poverty from the immediate boundary of the campus is no solution to the causes and consequences of poverty.[11] In the past and again in the present, the character of the physical community was changed because different people and businesses were brought to inhabit the "rebuilt" area.

These were place-based rebuilding initiatives, a negative result of urban renewal strategies. The people and businesses who were relocated out continued to live in the same way as before. Their incomes had not changed, their children continued to attend poorly financed schools, and the houses they moved into were maybe a few years away from being as deteriorated as the ones they left behind.

The tax base of the peripheral areas they moved into did not change, so neither did the services offered by the government: sanitation, safety, upkeep of infrastructure, housing inspection, recreation, health, education. The causes of living in an environment of poverty were not addressed—segregating low-income and communities of color into already disinvested and deteriorating communities and abandoning public services for upkeep of schools, health centers, recreational centers, infrastructures. People were simply moved from a "very poor area" to a "poor area." This has been the history of rebuilding in East Baltimore and many similar low-income and African American communities in the United States.

As seen in figure 7.2, the rebuilding processes in the 1950s Broadway Redevelopment project and the current project ignored these peripheral areas with no comprehensive plan to address the continued growth and separation between the rich and powerful neighbor and the poor and disenfranchised neighbor.

To ensure that this does not continue to occur, these communities peripheral to Middle East Baltimore must begin rebuilding now. Residents of these communities

Figure 7.2   Gap between rich and poor

7.2a.   East Baltimore: buildings of Johns Hopkins in the backdrop of de-caying neighborhoods, 1960s

7.2b.   Decaying building four blocks northeast of Johns Hopkins' new graduate student housing, 2010

must participate in a comprehensive rebuilding process linked to the rebuilding and economic and social benefit of East Baltimore. A powerful community of the whole can emerge within these neighborhoods, powerful enough to challenge the medical campus's continued outward expansion—piece by piece or in large measure, as today.

EMINENT DOMAIN AS A POTENTIAL TOOL OF INJUSTICE: WAS IT LEGAL TO USE EMINENT DOMAIN IN THIS WAY?

The use of the power of eminent domain is relevant to understanding how equity in benefit is determined from rebuilding abandoned communities like Middle East Baltimore. The Fifth Amendment of the U.S. Constitution requires that just compensation be paid when the power of eminent domain is used to appropriate private property for public use without the owner's consent.[12] In Middle East Baltimore, more adequate compensation for existing land and relocation processes occurred only after residents organized and challenged the initial acquisition plans and relocation policy. The compensation determined in the first relocation policy was unjust and inadequate and did not reflect the minimal benefit accorded by the Uniform Relocation Assistance (URA) Act, corrected for the current year.[13] The second draft afforded compensation based on where one moved—it was a policy of continued segregation.[14] Therefore, according to the initial planning for rebuilding using the power of eminent domain, there was insufficient compensation and unequal benefit—relative to the benefit gained by the developer of the land taken—to affected residents.[15] The intention was not to assure equity in benefit.

The use of eminent domain powers also requires that "public use" of the acquired property be demonstrated. Today, "public use" includes economic development for the purpose of generating more tax revenue for the local government. In 2005, after a challenge to the existing definition of "public use," the U.S. Supreme Court ruled that private property may be condemned by eminent domain and used for private development projects that are predicted to have a "public benefit".[16] The taking of private property to give to another private entity was the basis of the challenge of the law in the 2005 trial. The outcome of this trial described public benefit as creation of jobs or the generation of increased tax revenue.

This ruling followed a challenge to an attempt by the city of New London, Connecticut, to seize private property to lease to a private development for a biotech park, research and office space, a hotel, a public park, a museum, residences, and a marina.[17] One dissenting judge wrote:

> Any property may now be taken for the benefit of another private party, but the fallout from this decision will not be random. The beneficiaries are likely to be those citizens with disproportionate influence and power in the political process, including large corporations and development firms. As for the victims, the government now has license

to transfer property from those with fewer resources to those with more. The Founders cannot have intended this perverse result.

Studies confirm that eminent domain is disproportionately targeted for use in communities of less educated, poor, and minority populations.[18]

Another justice wrote that the government could not take the property of one person for the sole purpose of transferring it to another, nor take private property under the pretext of public purpose when the purpose is to provide private benefit.[19] It was acknowledged that a taking of private land should be struck down if it is clearly intended to favor a particular private party over another, or if only an incidental public benefit exists.

It is fairly clear that the taking of private property in Middle East Baltimore provides disproportionate benefit to the JHMI—with the construction of the Johns Hopkins biotech building, the Johns Hopkins bioethics institute, and the 365-unit graduate student tower and parking garage. Who will own or occupy the additional 3 to 4 biotech buildings remains unknown—as does when and if they will be built and benefit 7,000 to 8,000 people of Baltimore with jobs. But this inequity in benefit does not stop here.

The Supreme Court's ruling in the case in Connecticut supported the private developer because the majority of justices considered the economic development part of a "carefully considered development plan." The majority in this trial decided that the public interest was being served, viewing the private developer's plan as a "comprehensive redevelopment plan" that considered "the legal rights of all interested parties." Still, three dissenting justices found a lack of "clear and convincing evidence" that the economic development in New London would achieve the described outcomes.

There was no "clear and comprehensive plan" detailing benefit in the initial or subsequent planning for the rebuilding of Middle East Baltimore. The 2011 revised plan described no employment benefit, timeline for employment, or adequacy of a workforce in East Baltimore to match new jobs. It described no target for local hiring in East Baltimore, an area with the some of the highest unemployment rates of the city. It described no apprenticeship programs, living-wage benefits, long-term employment, and short-term employment goals. None of the master plans have had a business or economic plan detailing clear and comprehensive steps by which the community would achieve tangible benefits and outcomes in education, employment, social skills, and income. There have been no goals or evaluation processes set for such outcomes. There has been no plan for long-term follow-up of displaced residents to assess their benefit from the use of public powers to remove them from their land. Further, housing and amenities targeted to a moderate and market-rate income class challenges the definition of "public" in public benefit; are low-income and working-poor people not part of the "public" in East Baltimore and Baltimore?

Although the Supreme Court did not define "comprehensive," previous decisions about rebuilding areas of abandonment have addressed the health of the area and the residents. A comprehensive plan for rebuilding Middle East Baltimore should similarly address the health of residents of both Middle East Baltimore and the larger East Baltimore community and their economic security through jobs, education, social services, recreational services, and elderly services. The health of the neighborhoods to which residents were displaced should be assessed as well as the health of the neighborhoods affected by the rebuilding—all of East Baltimore.

There was no plan projecting how the residents of East Baltimore would have the opportunity to gain economic security from the development of a biotech park. Surveys of the social, educational, and employment characteristics of residents occurred only after the relocation of residents. A comprehensive plan would have required an assessment of the needs of the area and a clear, detailed plan for how these needs would be met through the rebuilding effort. This would show clear evidence of intent to benefit, something a plan with vague, intangible, and incidental "public benefit" did not do.

Because the plan to rebuild Middle East Baltimore has changed twice, and an increase in land acquisition since the initial plan has occurred, the intent of the powerful stakeholders remains unclear. While the city government continues to talk about a biotech park, the JHMI and developers continue to change their plans and to look to the city and state to fund the changed plans. Meanwhile, the city continues to grant requests for the additional land to be taken by eminent domain and for government-supported funding to be readily accessible to EBDI and partners.[20] These changes and contradictions in planning cast doubt on the appropriateness of the use of the powers of eminent domain in this process—a process the benefits of which favor disproportionately the private interests of the JHMI.

The law does not set a number of jobs that must be created for the results to be considered "public benefit." The jobs created by the rebuilding process in Middle East Baltimore have been temporary, most without benefits or opportunities for further training. Many of the biotech park's occupants bring their employees with them. Currently, additional government grants are being offered to ensure that occupants of the biotech park hire local residents. As these practices demonstrate, there is no guarantee that the biotech park will provide increased jobs without additional subsidy from the government.

In contrast to the promises the initial proposal of a biotech park made about bringing jobs to the area, an economic development consultant—coauthor of a report on the biotechnology industry for the prominent Washington think tank the Brookings Institute—described the opportunity for increased employment as a "gamble":

> This is a lottery ticket kind of endeavor. . . . This is kind of an arduous long shot . . . Most biotech companies lose money. Most biotechs fail. A few will be wildly successful. But that doesn't necessarily mean the biotech park is a bad idea. . . . It kind of depends on what your objective is. . . . If the university wants to attract more medical researchers and grant funding, the park will help. But, if the university is hoping for a new industry that generates lots of jobs and tax income, then. . . . It's a pipe dream.[21]

The law does not set an amount by which the tax revenue in the rebuilt area must increase for the results to be considered public benefit. In communities like Middle East Baltimore, where tax revenues are low, developers can claim that a minimal increase in tax revenue satisfies the legal requirement of "public benefit." One way to ensure some equity and balance between private benefit and public good would be to require a minimum quantity of increase projected over time, based on the increasing assets of the developer, also projected over time. Such accounting to the public would begin to offer transparency, demonstrating how much the use of public funds and private and governmental partnerships benefit private interests and how much they benefit the public good.

When private interests stands to benefit substantially from eminent domain–driven redevelopment, how their benefit is redistributed into the affected community should be carefully assessed. The JHMI's medical complex of hospital and university, like others in the United States, maintains a nonprofit status that allows it to expand continuously without paying any property taxes to Baltimore City. Any payment in lieu of taxes (PILOT) and other energy and telecommunication taxes it has contributed to the city in recent years are similar to those paid by other hospitals and universities in Maryland.[22] Meanwhile, it has benefited substantially from its close ties with the city and state during its century of physical expansion. It may be time to assess the benefit of such public-private partnerships which may disproportionately enhance the wealth of institutions like JHMI while diminishing the wealth of its public citizens—specifically those whose land is repeatedly acquired through city and state processes and sold or leased to such private institutions for wealth accumulation.

How will its expansion in this eminent domain–driven rebuilding of Middle East Baltimore benefit the public good by increasing the tax revenue from property taxes? These are the taxes that pay for Baltimore City police to protect the medical institution and its employees and students and pay for the upkeep of streets and infrastructure in the more than 21-block space it occupies. The money the medical institution could pay the city in taxes would contribute to increased services in all of East Baltimore. Levying taxes at a low rate on each of the JHMI's many physical structures alone would contribute substantially to the tax fund, providing benefit to the community of East Baltimore—the public good.

The JHMI recently expanded its interests in selling its medical experience to Walgreens clinics and onsite employee health centers around the United States. This is one example of how continued growth of medical knowledge and expertise fostered by a local expansion of the institution in East Baltimore is marketed for business and financial gain and further asset accumulation. The JHMI business development team plans to develop partnerships with private industry to expand the reach of the JHMI's expertise while also creating new sources of revenue for the institution, moving into a for-profit status. That the medical knowledge the School of Medicine and other research entities develop is now being sold for profit challenges the line between nonprofit and for-profit institutions and the appropriateness of these institutions' designation as nontaxable enterprises.[23] How is the continued growth in wealth through these enterprises directly and indirectly benefitted from such expansions in Middle East Baltimore? How is the opportunity for the co-location of biotechnology enterprises effectively increasing the commercialization of JHMI scientific discoveries (per the third master plan) enhancing the wealth of this already wealthy institution?

How does having a rebuilt community catering to a moderate and market rate population serve to boost the attraction of highly skilled students and scientists to JHMI which in turn contribute to its continued ranking as a premier research, teaching, and health care institution with the highest federal and military research funding in the Americas?

How are the powerful planners and implementers of this plan to rebuild Middle East Baltimore assessing the relative and absolute benefit to the major private developer of JHMI and its low-income and African American community? Will they calculate increase in income, assets, wealth, land ownership by JHMI and individual residents forced to leave their land for their expansion over time? Will they assess the health of the surrounding community 5, 10, 15, 20, 30, 50 years from now and compare it relative to the health of JHMI over these times? Or will they, as in the 1950's public-supported expansion of JHMI in East Baltimore, displace another 800 households and quickly forget the disparity in benefit that was afforded them—then and now? Or if they decide to measure how equitably benefit was distributed, will they acknowledge and remedy the glaring disparity that exists in the current plan?

Such plans to discover the benefit to residents affected by displacement is not new. Previous studies of residents displaced from public housing projects show little or no increase in income over time. If residents were displaced to communities of higher socioeconomic indicators, they face challenges in affording groceries and services which are more expensive than in their previous communities. The barter systems which exist in many low-income communities are absent secondary to the displacement and demolition of their previous communities resulting in displaced residents having to pay for services and products they previously accessed through exchange.

Similar factors must be assessed for residents displaced from Middle East Baltimore. The same must be assessed for those who return. Such follow-up studies will begin to help us understand how rebuilding of abandoned communities benefit the most vulnerable currently and over time.

In its current implementation, the "perverse result" of eminent domain in benefiting private interests is clear. The benefit to displaced residents and those remaining in the rebuilt and peripheral communities of East Baltimore remains illusory; this must be brought to light and a comparison of benefit to the major developer of JHMI and affected community performed and made transparent to begin to move toward the letter and practice of the power of eminent domain to serve the public good.

ABANDONED COMMUNITIES
ARE PREY TO BEING LEFT OUT IN
EMINENT DOMAIN–DRIVEN REDEVELOPMENT

Communities that have been abandoned, such as Middle East Baltimore, are prey to the use of eminent domain powers for redevelopment. In situations in which the private developers have strong bridging relationships with the government, communities without power are at the mercy of the developers' and governments' interests.[24] In the current rebuilding process, every change toward equity for residents resulted from persistent struggle by residents and SMEAC.

In the mid 1960s and 1970s, residents of East Baltimore organized, demanded control of rebuilding their community, and succeeded in rebuilding parts of their community. Residents challenged the JHMI, the major employer and landlord in East Baltimore at that time, to limit its expansion into their community. Their struggles were energized by a political movement of African Americans slowly moving into the system.[25] The movement of public housing activists was also taking place in Baltimore during these times, challenging the traditional neglect by housing authorities.[26] The Civil Rights Act of 1968 was fresh in people's minds, and African Americans in East Baltimore were still optimistic, organizing and doing their part to ensure their right to participate in rebuilding their community.

Half a century later, continued disinvestment and abandonment in East Baltimore, continued expansion on an individual and a large scale, broken promises past and present by the powerful stakeholders to their less powerful neighbors, and diminished political will from elected officials have taken their toll on community activism and organizing.

In these challenging social, economic, and political conditions, placing on the existing community the burden for continuously and consistently holding powerful stakeholders with private interests accountable is unfair.

It seems necessary, then, that in planning to use eminent domain powers in abandoned and powerless communities, a community pact or benefit agreement between the developer and the community be set forth at the beginning.[27] Such intentional organization and administration of a community benefit agreement (CBA) can ensure that the community's needs are as central as the private developer's needs. While making more explicit the current law in regard to "public benefit" is helpful, it still does not address the involvement of residents in defining the needs of their community.[28] Expecting that community residents will organize and challenge the eminent domain rebuilding process and ensure equity is also not enough. Planning based on that expectation builds inequity into the process and places the burden of assuring equity on the residents who will suffer if they cannot hold the powerful stakeholders accountable (box 7.1, box 7.2, box 7.3, box 7.4). In communities with little power, the type of organizing that occurred with SMEAC is challenging.

Therefore, establishing a legally binding document between the private developer and the community—detailing a comprehensive plan for how each will benefit over

Box 7.1. SMEAC requests participation, affordable housing, transparency in rebuilding Middle East Baltimore

Save Middle East Action Committee, Inc.
(SMEAC)
2111 Ashland Ave. (mailing address)**
Baltimore, MD 21205
410-522-3360
smeacbaltimore@verizon.net

Executive Director   Board Chair

To: ...., Chair Housing and Relocation Committee
From: Save Middle East Action Committee, Inc. (SMEAC)

Date: July 10, 2006

RE: Current and Future Policies pertaining to the East Baltimore Redevelopment Project

Listed below are items of concern to the residents affected by the Redevelopment Project of Middle East Baltimore. Some items have been previously addressed in current Relocation Policy of EBDI and require additional attention; others pertain to yet unanswered questions not currently addressed sufficiently or in policy. It is our hope that we receive a response – within the following two weeks- as to a plan for addressing these issues, along with a time frame.

1. In good faith and as an indication of inviting community participation, SMEAC is requesting a copy of the certifications that EBDI provides to HUD accounting for its fulfillment of Section 104(d) of the Housing and Community Development Act (one-for-one replacement of low-income housing).
2. In good faith and as an indication of inviting community participation, SMEAC continues to request community participation in all phases of planning for the number of low, moderate, and market rate units in the East Baltimore Redevelopment Project.
3. SMEAC is requesting a written description of a tracking process for residents who have been relocated from the Middle East community.
4. SMEAC is requesting a written plan as to monitoring and providing a process for relocated renters to be afforded a right of return into the Redevelopment Project area after supplemental benefits have been terminated.
5. SMEAC is requesting that a detailed plan describing the mechanism that will afford all residents who have been relocated due to this Redevelopment project be drafted into policy.
6. SMEAC is requesting a written description of the plan to preserve the 'low-income' housing on a long term basis
7. SMEAC is requesting that 1) the 'first year' begins on the next full tax year; 2)EBDI covers 100% difference from the previous tax year, to complete the 'tax year' that relocation occurs; 3) an extension into a 3rd and 4th year at 50% benefit (as currently described for the 2nd year)

8. SMEAC is requesting a process and negotiation on determining how to afford grants for rehabilitation of houses that will not be acquired and demolished in the 'subsequent' phases.
9. The current 'low-income' definition does not afford real low-income residents of the affected area or of other parts of Baltimore city the ability to own
10. SMEAC is requesting the EBDI and its stakeholders make better efforts to assure that residents who must reside in the Redevelopment Project area during demolition and construction of all phases be afforded a reasonable quality of life.
11. SMEAC is requesting that EBDI and stakeholders become educated and familiar with the cost saving and energy efficiency of 'green housing' and incorporate this in budgeting for the design and construction of subsequent phases and future demolition.

a 20 to 50-year period—would serve to both redefine or make more explicit "public benefit" in tangible ways and ensure community participation and decision making.

This would require that the planning for all redevelopment involve community, from the first intention to use the powers of eminent domain. A clearly stated process of what is required for community participation, involving an organizing strategy to listen to and learn the needs of residents as well as the needs of the developer, must inform all plans equally.

Without something legally binding, promises made in regard to development are just that—promises. The CBA would be the legally binding agreement between the existing community and the developer. The public funding that is included in the use of eminent domain–driven development can be used to benefit the community directly by financially supporting the necessary organizational capacity to develop and carry out the community benefit agreement.

Besides a master plan for physical development and a business plan detailing economic development, a CBA should become a necessary document in all requests for rebuilding using eminent domain powers. Under such an agreement, just as there is an EBDI board, there would be a community board overseeing a comprehensive and sustainable community agreement and plan addressing housing, education, recreation, health, transportation, and all other aspects of a community rebuilding process.

That an entity such as the EBDI board, with all its affiliations and partnerships with the powers of the JHMI, government, and foundations, would hold the interests of the community foremost is difficult to conceive. In the first 10 years of rebuilding Middle East Baltimore, it has not occurred.

This book has also shown in detail the challenges those with less power experience in holding the powerful accountable. The burden of ensuring public benefit is placed on those with less power. The power imbalance between community and developer—in partnership with the government—results in greater benefit to the

Box 7.2.   SMEAC addresses Segregationist tactics by EBDI

SAVE MIDDLE EAST ACTION COMMITTEE INC.
(SMEAC)
2100 EAST MADISON STREET
2111 ASHLAND AVENUE (mailing address)
BALTIMORE MARYLAND 21205-1699

August 9, 2004

President and CEO
East Baltimore Development Corporation
1731 East Chase Street
Baltimore Maryland 21205

Dear Mr. [President and CEO]:

This letter is a follow up on an outstanding concern that has not been resolved to the satisfaction of the residents of Middle East Baltimore: having the relocation restriction (keeping residents in Baltimore in order for them to be eligible to receive relocation benefits) lifted.

You indicated to me that a letter should be sent to your attention so you could go back to the EBDI board with the concerns of the residents. At the July 12, 2004 SMEAC community monthly meeting we had a unanimous vote that confirmed that residents wanted the relocation restriction lifted. The stakeholders of this community want the right to relocate anywhere in the country with full relocation benefits due to being forcibly displaced out of the community that they have a long-term – and in many cases, generational -- investment in.

The stakeholders of this community want their concerns to be acknowledged in a respectful manner that has their best interests at heart. As far as we are aware, there is no federal or state mandate that states stakeholders must relocate back to the city in order to receive full benefits. If there is, we should be informed of that so that we can pursue a change in policy. If there is not, the relocation restriction should be released for our community. We seriously doubt that residents in another community, such as Roland Park, would be held to the same restrictions.

We would like the decision makers to consider this: that the stakeholders of this community want the freedom of choice regarding where they move just like any affluent Baltimore community resident would be afforded. The relocation benefits for residents being shoved out of their community in order to make way for gentrification should not be held hostage to any particular area of relocation. (And as you know, [Mr. President and CEO], most residents would prefer to come back to Middle East Baltimore. But that is another letter...)

Sincerely,

Board Chair

Box 7.3. Residents request safe demolition processes

Save Middle East Action Committee, Inc.
(SMEAC)
2111 Ashland Ave. (mailing address)
Baltimore, MD 21205
410-522-3360
smeacbaltimore@verizon.net

Executive Director   Board Chair

March 15, 2005

Vice President, Operations and Community Services
East Baltimore Development Inc
1731 E. Chase Street
Baltimore, MD 21213

Dear   ,

During the March monthly membership meeting of SMEAC, residents expressed their concern regarding the current plan for demolition practices in the Phase I area. They were unanimous about the need for relocation of residents in this area, before demolition occurs. Please find attached a list of signatures by residents in attendance. Some residents resisted signing for fear of repercussion by EBDI and the city in their personal relocation process.

   SMEAC continues to advocate on behalf of residents to assure the optimum outcome in housing, health, and safety throughout this redevelopment project.

Sincerely,

Board Chair, Save Middle East Action Committee

Executive Director, Save Middle East Action Committee

Box 7.4. SMEAC requests responsible action from EBDI

January 5, 2009

President and CEO
East Baltimore Development Inc.
1731 E. Chase Street
Baltimore, MD 21205

Dear Mr. [President and CEO],

This letter is in response to your letter of December 30, 2008 concerning the upcoming SMEAC GENERAL MEMBERSHIP MEETING on Monday, January 12th. Mr. [President and CEO], you indicated that [EBDI's board chair] has proposed a meeting of 90 minutes structured into three sections. The first section would involve input from community members; the second section would provide an opportunity for EBDI Board members to give their views on SMEAC and community concerns; and the third section would start a discussion about a productive relationship between EBDI and SMEAC going into the future.

SMEAC certainly is interested in members of the community being about to speak their minds to the EBDI Board about pressing issues concerning the EBDI project. But we would like the EBDI Board and yourself, Mr. [President and CEO], to realize that the EBDI Board members have already gotten specific and thoughtful concerns, proposals, and input from the SMEAC and community leadership at the December 11th meeting. In fact, following up from that meeting, SMEAC once again put our concerns and proposals in writing. This was the letter that we forwarded to you, for Mr. [EBDI board chair], on December 12th. EBDI, and its leadership, have been fully informed of the community's concerns and desires.

We are now awaiting the response from EBDI and its leadership, the EBDI Board.

The EBDI Board members will need to present EBDI's response to the concerns stated within SMEAC's December 12th letter during the second portion of the meeting. The members of the EBDI Board, as well as the EBDI staff attending on January 12th, need to come to this meeting prepared to state what EBDI intends to do.

SMEAC is interested in specifics.

SMEAC knows that that "stronger and more productive relationship" can only happen within the context of the resolution of SMEAC's concerns as stated in our December 12th letter. EBDI's response will determine everything.

Please do not hesitate to write or call if you have any matters needing clarification.

With regards,

, President
Save Middle East Action Committee, Inc.

, Executive Director
Save Middle East Action Committee, Inc.

developer and should be addressed from the beginning. Therefore it is more efficient and effective to treat the interests of the developers and of the residents as separate and to organize, administrate, and evaluate the functions that serve them separately to ensure more equitable benefit to both.

MOVING AND CONCENTRATING POVERTY OF PLACE AND PEOPLE

In 2001, the first master plan recommended a place-based strategy similar to those of earlier efforts in the area, one that would simply move the "eyesore" of the low-income and working poor people away from the view of Johns Hopkins and remedying the infrastructure of buildings, streets, services, schools, businesses, recreational and wellness centers to places of nonpoverty. Moving residents to adjacent neighborhoods not as "poor" did not address the root causes of poverty and there was no strategy to prevent the same outcome that had been seen over the past 60 years.

Surveys conducted by EBDI and partners showed that approximately 40 percent of residents from the first phase were relocated to neighborhoods within East Baltimore; the majority were renters.[29] In addition, 21 percent of these relocated residents with children were sending their children to the same schools as they attended before they were relocated. The neighborhoods they were relocated to were neighborhoods the first master plan of 2001 initially identified to help stabilize East Baltimore. These areas, with similar standards of education in economically disadvantaged school systems, were not areas of improvement. Yet the law requires that residents forced to relocate due to eminent domain be moved to areas that show an "improvement" in living conditions (education, income, employment, safety, housing, etc).

Another 10 percent of residents from the first phase were relocated outside of East Baltimore but into similarly economically disadvantaged neighborhoods. Follow-up with these residents, this portion of the "public," is crucial to assess whether they are benefiting through the use of eminent domain as the law says they must.

When residents were displaced from Middle East Baltimore, the drug dealers living off the abandoned place simply moved to the next available community, similarly abandoned. As the communities of East Baltimore as a whole continue to experience higher crime rates than the city of Baltimore, the 88-acre area of the rebuilding effort has been made reasonably safe through extra security: an extension of the security efforts present at the JHMI, paid for by EBDI, has extended the gated community of the JHMI into the rebuilt community of Middle East Baltimore. Addressing the peripheral communities in a comprehensive way will begin to address the crime affecting both rebuilt and peripheral communities. If the peripheral communities continue to be areas of increasing concentration of poverty, with more low-income households relocated for the benefit of rebuilding Middle East Baltimore and the JHMI's expansion, these communities must benefit.

Approximately half of the more than 800 relocated households have been relocated into communities with higher socioeconomic status. It will be important as well to follow up in these neighborhoods, such as the northeastern and western areas of Baltimore, where a majority of this half of relocated residents were moved. The creation of increasing pockets of low-income dwellers outside of the now revitalized downtowns of U.S. cities has resulted in a growing concentration of poverty in the suburbs.[30] The likelihood of similar outcomes must be assessed in this rebuilding effort.

There are several reasons for these effects. Homeowning residents who moved into communities with higher property value have been challenged with property taxes that are 3 to 5 times the amount they paid in Middle East Baltimore. From houses valued at an average of $21,000, some residents moved into houses valued between $100,000 and $150,000. They must now pay the taxes assessed on this increased property value, when there has been no parallel increase in income. This is a severe hardship; affected residents are paying more than one third of their income for mortgages and taxes. How will these residents benefit from the rebuilding of Middle East Baltimore in the next 10 to 20 years?

Let alone the future, more than 30 residents are facing the risk of foreclosure today; 3 have already lost their homes to foreclosure.[31] After their benefits terminated, almost 40 rental households have been evicted, and more than 100 more face the risk of eviction. They must be followed up for longer periods as well.[32] What of those who were lost to follow-up? EBDI has not committed to long-term follow-up and complete assessments of health, economic, education, and social welfare which would help to assess how displaced residents benefit.

Another negative effect of concentrating low-income residents is the effect on payment into the property tax funds. Because different tax credit programs offer some decrease in tax payment, based on income, some residents pay less into the tax fund. When an increasing number of people contribute less to the tax fund, the fund decreases.

Because many public services are funded by the value of assessed property and level of income of the residents, the effects on services of a significant shift in the income level of these neighborhoods must be tracked. Such changes in the services in a neighborhood, such as reduced security or sanitation services, pose a risk for slow depreciation of housing value and increase the risk of crime, drug use, and eventual abandonment by those who are able to leave. This is the cycle of disinvestment that can be initiated without attention and care to the increasing concentration of low-income households in moderate- and market-rate neighborhoods. Such follow-up is necessary to assess how displaced residents are benefiting in the short and long term from eminent domain–driven rebuilding processes in abandoned communities of America.

This type of follow-up will help future rebuilding efforts in defining and assessing equity for developer and impacted residents. Only if future planning sets benchmarks and goals as to what it wants to accomplish, and accounts for the history of disinvestment in segregated communities of race and class, can it move intelligently toward addressing the root causes and consequences of poverty. Without acknowledging the consequences of this history, rebuilding efforts like the current one in Middle East Baltimore risk continued race and social segregation resulting in disinvestment and abandonment, in the new communities. The question of which came first, "poor people or poor communities," adequately sets the framework to understand that disinvested and abandoned communities existed before low-income and African Americans moved into them. The disinvestment continued because low-income residents did not have the income and power to reverse the declining tax base which assured public services would be updated. For African American communities, the racist laws, policies, and institutionalized behaviors contributed even more greatly to the disinvestment. This cycle can be stopped only when the history of segregation and its current-day consequences are included in strategies and funding for addressing not only the place, but the people of abandoned communities of America. Hoping that moving low-income and working poor people to communities with improved socioeconomic indicators will increase their socioeconomic status has not been proven in previous rebuilding processes where this occurred. Studies of economic mobility of low-income residents from public housing displacement suggest there is little or no upward mobility.[33,34]

Therefore a rebuilding plan which displaces residents to address the poverty of the area and the people must assure that residents can afford their homes, services, food, health care, employment, and education in the new community over the long term. If not they have simply been moved from a poor community to a not-poor community. Now they are low-income and working poor people living in non-poor communities. While this may increase their likelihood of improved health outcomes the disadvantages from being marginalized for being low-income, disconnected from your home community, unable to afford living in the new community, and not being part of the new community may diminish such likelihood (discussed in chapter 9).[35] Studies to date reflect many residents with no health benefit after similarly large-scale displacement from disinvested communities. [36,37,38,39]

A comprehensive plan to rebuild Middle East Baltimore to equally benefit all the residents of the area must address the conditions that contributed to the abandonment of the area. In the case of residents moving to peripheral areas, the buffer zone created around the rebuilt area continues on its path of abandonment. Ensuring that sufficient resources (financial and otherwise) follow the residents wherever they are relocated must be part of the relocation and benefit plan for individuals and communities affected by rebuilding.

Just as developers are offered a "tax-free" period, tax credits, state-guaranteed loans, government bonds, federal block grants, and other incentives to build in areas of poverty, so must "tax-free" periods and other incentives be offered to those who lived through the causes and consequences of poverty and then were forced to give up their homes for the public benefit. This would begin to address the issue of making the benefit equitable between the private developers and the community.

Additionally, the tax credits, federal community block grants, state loans, city and state bonds, tax-incentive financing, and other generous public means that have financed almost half of the rebuilding of Middle East Baltimore must be analyzed for equity of benefit. Based on a projected assessment of benefit to the developers similar benefit to displaced residents, following them directly and into the communities they relocate into can begin to assure that the long-term effects of past segregationist laws and policies do not follow residents. A thorough accounting must be provided, showing the asset increase for the developers and businesses who are benefiting from the rebuilding process and its outcome compared with the asset increase determined broadly to incorporate the place and the people. There must be some normalizing of equity to produce benefit for all and stop the cycle of poverty of place and people.

Other remedies can include imposing taxes on existing nonprofits in the East Baltimore area or creating tax funds that can be used to assist residents who cannot afford the new taxes or who face eviction. These resources can also be used to provide social and health programs, vocational education, entrepreneurial skills and business development, and other opportunities that help residents gain greater income potential in whichever community they are relocated.

Lastly, the assurance that low-income housing is replaced on a one-for-one basis must be transparent to substantiate its occurrence. There are two ways to assure that not replacing every low-income house that was demolished will not negatively affect low-income people. The first is that every low-income person who was displaced is assured comparable low-income housing or the means to afford moderate or market-rate housing (through subsidized housing, public voucher, tax credit or subsidies, increased income, gain in asset, etc). Unless this occurs, the long-term effect of expiration of 5-year rental subsidies—which afforded this same period of moderate-rate dwelling—will result in less housing available for this resident when required to relocate again. The same is true for owners who cannot afford their taxes or mortgages in the long term and must seek low-income housing in the future. If EBDI and partners cannot guarantee that this will not occur, every low-income home must be replaced or the short and long-term benefit of rebuilding Middle East Baltimore has simply continued the cycle of poverty, under cover of a "responsible relocation packet".

ACKNOWLEDGING THE DIFFERENCE IN POWER AND ITS EFFECT IS BENEFICIAL

Once this difference in power is acknowledged and policies and procedures are enacted to bring some balance, we begin to negotiate with more transparency. The elephant in the room has been acknowledged and something is being done to ensure that he does not sit wherever he pleases.

After all, it is the nature of capitalism to continue to expand and to grow where one can. This growth is perceived as productive and is supported by the larger society. In that light, an aspiring politician may see expansion of a new or existing private development into abandoned areas of a city as a feather in his or her cap, having given insufficient thought to the welfare of the existing community. Acknowledging that many abandoned communities lack the power to secure a decision-making place at the table in rebuilding efforts is a step toward ensuring equitable participation.[40] Their being at the table, having decision-making power, increases the likelihood of equitable benefit to all stakeholders.

Powerful neighbors are expanding into the abandoned communities around them in many parts of the country (discussed in the next chapter). At the same time, the less powerful communities continue to be removed, segregated, hidden, and forgotten. This relationship between these two types of neighbors continues the age-old question of balance: must one community's history be lost to build the legacy of another? As one stakeholder put it, "How do you make progress without screwing over the little guy?"[41]

How do we bring balance into this dynamic of poverty and wealth and the growing inequality of incomes? For decades, those affected by poverty have been pointing out the gap between the rich and the poor, and recently one Federal Reserve Board governor had this to say about the continued growth in income inequality over the past 90 years:

> The inequality is destabilizing and undermines the ability of the economy to grow sustainably and efficiently. Income inequality is anathema to the social progress that is part and parcel of such growth . . . growing levels of income inequality are associated with increases in crime, profound strains on households, lower savings rates, poorer health outcomes, diminished levels of trust in people and institutions . . . those are all forces that have the potential to drag down economic growth. It seems to me that trying to build communities, bring people together from different parts of the spectrum and different parts of the country, probably has, long term, the best likelihood of bringing down inequality.[42]

In East Baltimore in 2000 the jarring inequality of power indicated by disinvestment and abandonment and the lack of an organized base of residents resulted in the community's being at risk and at the mercy of the organized powerful stakeholders of the JHMI; city, state, and federal representatives; and foundations. This coalition of forces was unchecked and had a free ticket of "eminent domain" with which to carry out its intentions of gentrifying the Middle East Baltimore community, pushing the consequences of poverty farther away from its sight. SMEAC forced the powerful stakeholders to define their perception of "just compensation" and "public benefit" and make good on their promises.

It was clear that there would be "private benefit" to the JHMI. Its history of strong relations with the city and state government in regard to expansion was evidence of this. What was not so clear was how the taking of private property from residents by the city, and the project's being almost 50 percent financed through tax credits, general bonds, bonds paid back from the increased tax revenues in the rebuilt area, and government-backed loans and grants, would eventually benefit the displaced community. The JHMI's plan was not clear, comprehensive, nor tangible.

Without strong community organizations challenging the powerful stakeholders and holding them accountable in the application of eminent domain, as they did in Middle East Baltimore, it can become a powerful tool of injustice, continuing the history of racial and class oppression.

To benefit the community of East Baltimore, rebuilding efforts must give priority to dealing with the historic and current causes and conditions of poverty. This includes greater participation of residents in decision making and planning; a fair relocation plan for residents wanting to leave, remain, or return to the rebuilt community; and planning for the peripheral communities.

The next chapter will discuss other types of rebuilding efforts in the USA and abroad.

NOTES

1. Historic East Baltimore Community Action Coalition. May 1994. "Community Revitalization Plan." Baltimore, MD.

2. Crowder PA. (2007) "Ain't no sunshine: Examining informality and state open meeting acts as the anti-public norm in inner-city redevelopment deal making." University of Tulsa Legal Studies Research Paper No. 2008–01; *Tennessee Law Review*, 74:4.

3. ABT associates. (2008) East Baltimore Neighborhood Revitalization. Phase 1 Baseline Summary Report. 2001–2005.

4. *Baltimore Sun.* May 31, 2001. "Planned Hopkins biotech park draws guarded response from community."

5. Johns Hopkins Medicine. www.hopkinsmedicine.org/graduateprograms/campus.cfm. Accessed May 2011.

6. *Daily Record.* August 1, 2011. "New EBDI plan increases size."

7. EBDI (2011) Revised Master Plan.

8. Baltimore Metropolitan Council. (2000) Census tract data: Baltimore neighborhoods. www.baltometro.org/C2K/SF3medincome.pdf. Accessed May 2011.

9. ABT associates. (2008) East Baltimore Neighborhood Revitalization.

10. EBDI. (2009) The workforce supply and demand characteristics of the East Baltimore Development Inc. redevelopment effort.

11. Valparaiso. "Judicial Review of Displacee Relocation in Federal Urban Renewal Projects: A New Approach?" (1969) 3 *Val. U. L. Rev.* 258. Available at: scholar.valpo.edu/vulr/vol3/iss2/7. Accessed July 2011.

12. Kelly Jr, JJ. (2008). "Taming eminent domain." *Shelter Force.* Spring #153.

13. EBDI. (2001) Draft of Historical East Baltimore Community Relocation Policy and Benefits.

14. EBDI (2002) Homeowner Acquisition/Relocation Process Guide.

15. Talley B. (2005) Restraining eminent domain through just compensation: Kelo v. City of New London, 125 S. Ct. 2655.

16. Sheridan PG. (2005) Kelo v. City of New London: New Jersey's Take on Takings 38.113.83.199/Students/academics/journals/law-review/Issues/archives/upload/sheridan.pdf. Accessed May 2011.

17. Lopez, A. (2006) Weighing and reweighing eminent domain's political philosophies post-Kelo, 41 *Wake Forest L. Rev.* 237: 243.

18. Carpenter DM, Ross JK. (2009) "Testing O'Connor and Thomas: Does the use of eminent domain target poor and minority communities?" *Urban Studies.* 46:2447.

19. Sheridan PG. (2005) Kelo v. City of New London.

20. *Daily Record.* September 18, 2011. "Baltimore finds funds for EBDI TIF."

21. *Miami Herald.com.* June 9, 2008. "UM bets on biotech future." www.miamiherald .com. Accessed March 2011.

22. Sicher P. (2010) "Hopkins and other institutions pay Baltimore $20.4 million to avoid tax increases." *The News-Letter.* July 15, 2010. Accessed March 2011.

23. *Hopkins Medicine.* Spring/Summer 2011. "A new prescription for partnerships."

24. Gomez MB, Muntaner C. (2005) "Urban redevelopment and neighborhood health in East Baltimore, Maryland: The role of Institutional and communitarian social capital." *J Critical Public Health.* 15:83.

25. *Baltimore Sun.* October 8, 1973. "We live here."

26. Williams RY. (2011) *The politics of public housing: Black women struggle against urban inequality.* Oxford University Press, UK.

27. Rubin RL. 2008. *Shelter Force.* "Take and give." Spring #153.

28. Kelly Jr. JJ. (2006) "'We shall not be moved': Urban communities, eminent domain and the socioeconomics of just compensation." *St. Johns's L. Rev.* 80:923.

29. ABT Associates. (2007) Final Report. East Baltimore Development Initiative. Post relocation satisfaction survey.

30. Smith N, Caris P, Wyly E. (2001) "The 'Camden Syndrome' and the menace of sub-urban decline: Residential disinvestment and its discontents in Camden County, New Jersey." *Urban Affairs Review.* 36: 497.

31. EBDI. (2011) Housing and relocation report.

32. EBDI. (2011) Housing and relocation report.

33. Keene DE, Geronimus AT. (2011) "'Weathering' HOPE VI: the importance of evaluating the population health impact of public housing demolition and displacement." *J Urban Health.* 88:417.

34. Levy D, Kaye D. 2004. *How are HOPE VI families faring? Income and employment.* Washington, DC: Urban Institute.

35. Keene DE, Geronimus AT. (2011) "Weathering" HOPE VI.

36. Keene DE, Geronimus AT. (2011) "Weathering" HOPE VI.

37. Acevedo-Garcia D, Osypuk T, Werbel R, Meara E, Cutler D, Berkman L. (2004) Does housing mobility improve health? *Housing Policy Debate.* 15:49.

38. Manjarrez C, Popkin S, Guernsey E. (2007) *Poor health: Adding Insult to Injury for HOPE VI Families.* Washington, DC: The Urban Institute Press.

39. Price D, Popkin S. (2010) *The Health Crisis for CHA Families.* Washington, DC: Urban Institute.

40. Keene DE, Geronimus AT. (2011) "Weathering" HOPE VI.

41. Barbush E. (2009) *Middle East Baltimore Stories: Images and words from a displaced community.* SMEAC, Art on Purpose.

42. NPR National Public Radio. July 12, 2011. As income gap balloons, is it holding back growth? www.npr.org/2011/07/10/137744694/as-income-gap-balloons-is-it-holding-back -growth?ft=1&f=1001. Accessed July 2011.

8

Rebuilding Communities Across the United States and Abroad: What Can East Baltimore Do Better?

"People can't heal until they feel they have some control; people need to feel something is for them, something is made right, before they can heal." —displaced East Baltimore resident

"The test of our progress is not whether we add more to the abundance of those who have much; it is whether we provide enough for those who have too little." —Franklin D. Roosevelt

This chapter will review several community rebuilding projects in the United States and abroad. The following examples of community rebuilding processes highlight several types of rebuilding efforts in the United States, Australia, and Europe. While the historic race and class dynamics in the United States differ from those of other countries, examples from Australia and Europe are presented to emphasize specific strategies in their community rebuilding efforts. These examples illustrate the characteristics that determine the degree of resident participation in and directing of the rebuilding process, along with economic and social benefit for existing and new residents during and after these rebuilding processes.

COMMUNITIES PARTICIPATING AND NOT-PARTICIPATING IN REBUILDING THEIR COMMUNITIES

Community participation in community rebuilding or redevelopment is not new to East Baltimore. It was something the city of Baltimore strove to achieve in the 1960s Gay Street I Urban Renewal Project. While community participation was an aspect of that rebuilding effort, increased economic opportunities or educational and social services to address existing social, employment, and educational needs were not. In

195

addition, the lack of public services present before and after rebuilding continued to plague the Gay Street I area and the surrounding communities of East Baltimore.

In this discussion of the rebuilding of Middle East Baltimore, a key characteristic focused on has been community participation, including decision making, by residents in this low-income and African American community. Because of current and historic racism and classism in housing and redevelopment policies and law, this type of community participation seldom occurs in rebuilding low-income African American communities or other communities of color. When it does occur, the ideas and advice can easily be co-opted or forgotten by the more powerful stakeholders, as occurred in Middle East Baltimore during the first 10 years of its rebuilding.

The current practices of community rebuilding and change in most low-income communities are in line with urban renewal of the 1960s and 1970s in the lack of sufficient participation and planning for the consequent of displacing residents from their homes.[1] The underlying assumptions of these types of rebuilding practices have been the outsider's perception of targeted communities: they have no implicit or explicit value of their own, so they can be easily removed; their residents have no ability to inform and to make decisions about what is a healthy community, so their participation is not necessary; they cause their own abandonment, so whatever little is done for them is sufficient. Over the decades, these wrong assumptions have resulted in mass relocation of low-income communities and their replacement with new structures and higher-income residents, a change in place and people.[2,3] Now a gentrified place, it is considered rebuilt or redeveloped—for the gentrified population who come to inhabit it.

Trying to use mixed-income housing development as a means to rebuild low-income areas, theoretically increasing the tax base in a neighborhood, came into favor in the early 1990s. However, the approach of dispersing concentrated poverty through scattered low-income housing development has been in existence since the 1960s.[4] For example, the Section 8 program, supported by federal dollars and administered by city housing departments, provides voucher assistance that enables residents to live in market-rate rental housing.

While many studies have reported that mixed-income housing redevelopment benefits the existing low-income residents only minimally, the rebuilding of Middle East Baltimore is based on this model.[5] These past examples of mixed-income housing redevelopment show that the degree to which these types of rebuilding efforts involve community participation, control, and decision making and provide opportunity for increased asset and educational attainment for low-income residents helps to determine the degree of benefit they provide to the low-income resident.[6]

The effort in Middle East Baltimore has attempted to use a biotech park as an economic engine for the area, with half-hearted and insufficient attempts at preparing the local community to benefit from that engine. It has proposed mixed-income housing to increase the income in the area without ensuring that historic residents are able to return and to remain after doing so. And it has ignored the role of racist and classist policies in creating and maintaining communities disinvested of public services like East Baltimore, thereby ignoring their continued consequences in East Baltimore and adjacent communities.[7,8]

The focus of these examples is community rebuilding to include and benefit the existing and new residents and the social and economic factors that will enable them to thrive equally. While no one of these rebuilding efforts is perfect, each offers evidence of some of the possibilities for what can occur.

The discussion of these examples draws out some of the similarities and differences and their application to Middle East Baltimore. But it is up to us to envision how the most beneficial aspects of each can occur together in rebuilding abandoned communities like Middle East Baltimore.

OLDTOWN, BALTIMORE

Less than 5 miles from the Middle East Baltimore community is the Oldtown community of East Baltimore. Like its Middle East Baltimore neighbor, it experiences the consequences of abandonment and subsequent intergenerational poverty. In an experience different from that of its neighbor to the east, however, several stakeholders have come together to plan and implement a different kind of community rebuilding in Baltimore. This effort, Change4Real, recognizes that past and present rebuilding efforts in Baltimore have led to gentrification: replacement of the historic low-income and African American residents with white and higher-income residents.

Change4Real, a coalition of people and core institutions connected to the existing Oldtown community—including local residents, local congregations, and Sojourner-Douglass College—has put forth a rebuilding plan based on an alternative microeconomic local economy capable of addressing the historical barriers facing existing residents. It insists that past rebuilding efforts' dependence on existing economic engines of downtown Baltimore, the JHMI, and the East Harbor has not adequately secured levels of prosperity for historic residents under mixed-income models of development. In fact, it suggests these present economies have simply maintained existing residents at current income levels, making it difficult for residents to sustain transformation in their communities.

In contrast to the practice of the first 10 years of rebuilding in Middle East Baltimore, Change4Real's plan embodies five core values: a comprehensive planning process, a model that will eliminate poverty, new rules of engagement to prevent exploitation of the community's assets by outsiders, resident engagement from the very beginning and at all levels of the process, and a replacement economy based on self-determination.[9]

A four-phase plan outlines skill development, redevelopment of the Oldtown economic environment, skill enhancement, and economic expansion as the framework within which the physical infrastructure is changed. The plan promotes local control of the process in all aspects of the rebuilding: self-employment and microbusiness enterprises, including a community land trust, a community development corporation, a community development financing institution, and a community economic broker to monitor and oversee the successful interaction of the existing economy with the alternative created in a rebuilt Oldtown.

Change4Real's medium- and long-term visions include a community-owned health care delivery system; hotel and related enterprises in the field of hospitality; an infrastructure of housing maintenance, including skilled trades in plumbing, electrical, construction, and rehabilitation contracting; green/environmental installations; significant ownership of retail stores; a community-based professional business infrastructure, including management consultants, accountants, lawyers, insurers, and financing specialists; and a network of support trades and retailers, including suppliers of office equipment, custodial services, security services, computer services, etc.

Using specific benchmarks to assess progress, Change4Real advocates monitoring income change, self-employment, and business ownership as well as home equity to ensure that self-sufficiency is occurring and growing in a healthy rebuilt community. Who benefits from this planned rebuilding in Oldtown, this people- and place-based initiative, is clear; it is confirmed by asset increase for existing residents.

Change4Real's plan is clear and comprehensive. It details the steps to economic self-sufficiency and sustainable development. And it recognizes that rebuilding communities must offer tangible changes in the economic prospects of residents and businesses. The reality of the history of urban poverty and its current consequences is foremost in the planning of rebuilding Oldtown.

These community planners assert, "The only true antidote to hopeless poverty is emerging wealth." A guiding principle in their planning is "creating an economic framework to meet this challenge."

Furthermore, they openly acknowledge the disconnect between "corporate and community partners" in rebuilding abandoned communities like Oldtown and Middle East Baltimore. They have began a series of workshops aimed at addressing this divide: "We have designed the Institute to join participants from two cultures that have not worked well together in the area of urban redevelopment to rethink existing strategies of partnerships as an alternative to the existing climate of uneasy-to-outright-hostile interaction."[10]

This type of planning did not occur in the rebuilding of Middle East Baltimore. EBDI and partners are aware of the plans for the rebuilding of Oldtown; they could benefit from using similar processes to bridge ties between the existing stakeholders in Middle East Baltimore and begin a comprehensive planning strategy for real economic sufficiency for historic residents.

SANDTOWN-WINCHESTER, BALTIMORE

In the western part of Baltimore city, the community of Sandtown-Winchester has social and economic characteristics similar to those of many neighborhoods of East

Baltimore. It has primarily African American and low-income residents, and it also experienced abandonment by government and flight of those able to leave. In the early 1990s, this 72-block area initiated a community rebuilding strategy—Community Building in Partnership—that involved city offices, neighborhood organizations, a national community leadership organization, a community development enterprise, and Habitat for Humanity.

Unlike the rebuilding of Middle East Baltimore, which has focused on large-scale economic development at the expense of the residents it displaced, this strategy took a community-first approach. Its intention was to unite new and existing faith-based and neighborhood organizations to act as community organizing entities through programs for education, employment, health, public safety, economic development, and community development.

The rebuilding of Sandtown-Winchester was a neighborhood transformation initiative, with a comprehensive vision for ending poverty. This strategy attempted to address the social, economic, and physical conditions of the people and the place. To do so, it focused initially and consistently on building community capacity to lead the rebuilding process and to sustain the efforts after the project ended.[11]

One of the faith-based community development organizations in the initiative has contributed to rehabbing more than 280 houses in a 15-block portion of Sandtown-Winchester. Its efforts focused on rebuilding the existing community with increased homeownership by existing and new residents. Some of the community-building outcomes in this 15-block area are a new $5 million public school for K–8, a job center, a health center, and a transitional home for women. Very few residents have had to relocate, and some residents have seen the result of their sweat equity in rehabbing their first homes. The high involvement of parents—more than 75 percent usually attend meetings and events—in the parent-teacher organization indicates how the rebuilding of community, using a community-first and participatory approach, affects social engagement and control of community networks by residents.

In the 72-block area, more than 50 churches worked together to engage residents in social and political community development efforts: youth programs, voter registration, neighborhood upkeep, community leadership, and more.[12] The positive indicators include increased homeownership, median income, school performance, community organizations, and community participation in community change efforts and decreased crime and unemployment.[13]

This community rebuilding process has taken the slow, nongentrification approach: a time-consuming, community-engaged approach whose priority was to improve the opportunities for existing residents without displacing them. It worked at increasing bonding within the community while improving the physical conditions one project at a time. Nearly 20 years since the process began, many of the original problems common to areas with a history of low income and disinvestment still exist—but to a lesser degree. The biggest challenge is continued economic investment in local businesses and increased local leadership capacity.

After the first 10 years of the rebuilding of Sandtown-Winchester, more than 1,000 houses had been built or rehabbed. In comparison, 10 years into the Middle East Baltimore rebuilding process, 220 units have been constructed or rehabbed.

Nearly 20 years into the process, Sandtown-Winchester remains the "community of people and place" it set out to rebuild, in people and collective memory. The community stakeholders are more hopeful about their future and the neighborhood because of the process of change even while they continue to be challenged by some of the same conditions that existed previous before the project began. In contrast, Middle East Baltimore is no longer a historic "community of people and place." Instead, it is a gentrified community as a result of the removal of the low-income community and complete demolition of the physical structures—the intentional clearing away of low-income, African American people hidden behind the language of "mixed income."

As different as they are, these two community-building initiatives face two of the same obstacles to success—each for different reasons. Neither community has an umbrella community organization or leadership representing a shared vision of rebuilding by the residents. In Middle East Baltimore, one reason for this is that the affected residents have been displaced, or cleansed, from the community.[14] Another is that residents who have been relocated are reluctant to commit to returning, citing the lack of their social network in the rebuilt area and of new or rehabbed houses for them to live in.

And, as in Sandtown-Winchester, in the 88 acres of Middle East Baltimore there are almost no local businesses established or planned. Yet, unlike in Sandtown-Winchester, in Middle East Baltimore there has been ample funding for such initiatives. Lack of political will by the powerful stakeholders and lack of a grassroots community base to challenge the process remain giant obstacles to achieving a people- and place-based rebuilding outcome.

The initiative in Middle East Baltimore, effectively propelled by the JHMI, seeks to "strengthen" the neighborhoods surrounding the institutions. Removing the signs and symptoms of poverty from the physical space may surround the JHMI with economic strength, but it does not address the causes or consequences of poverty of the place and people. The JHMI's refusal to acknowledge its current motives, as well as past disinvestment, and its long-running practice of buying and boarding up houses or leasing them until it is ready to occupy the property continue to contribute to the lack of belief among the historic residents that this is a rebuilding effort to benefit them. Nothing in the past or the present has given them a basis for such trust. Without a shift in behavior by the JHMI, this adversarial relationship will continue to affect the next 10 years of rebuilding Middle East Baltimore.

Of interest is that the major philanthropic partner in the Middle East Baltimore initiative—the Annie E. Casey Foundation—financially supported the evaluation report for Sandtown-Winchester's first 10 years.[15] This report highlighted the challenges of acknowledging and altering the balance of power, acknowledging and removing inherent racism and classism between communities of color and mainstream institutions, and respecting and honoring competence in resident leadership and spiritual strength. To date, the powerful stakeholders in the Middle East rebuilding initiative have overwhelmingly acted contrary to these suggested "lessons learned." Many questions about the practical expertise, lack of awareness, and intention being brought to the process arise when the racist and classist interactions critiqued in the report of Sandtown-Winchester's rebuilding initiative continue in the open- and closed-door meetings of the Middle East Baltimore rebuilding initiative. They highlight the inconsistencies between the actions and the words of the stakeholders involved in rebuilding Middle East Baltimore.[16]

BOSTON, MASSACHUSETTS

In the mid-1980s, the Dudley Street Neighborhood Initiative (DSNI) was formed as a coalition of residents and local service providers in a 1-square-mile area of one of Boston's most deteriorated neighborhoods, Roxbury.[17] The area was a multiethnic and primarily low-income community, with a history of abandonment, arson, and illegal dumping in almost half of the vacant land. After learning that the city planned to use eminent domain to redevelop the area, residents organized across racial and ethnic lines to challenge this process and create a community land trust (CLT). This was the first community-owned and -driven rebuilding initiative in the United States to use eminent domain as a vehicle for community rebuilding.[18]

Twenty-five years later, the DSNI continues to thrive in this still multiethnic neighborhood, made up about equally of African Americans, Latinos, Cape Verdeans, and white Irish and Italian Americans. In an effort coordinated by the DSNI, the area has been transformed with hundreds of affordable rebuilt homes, park and green spaces, murals of its history, and local- and minority-owned small businesses—a thriving example of a community-driven people- and place-based initiative. The DSNI has managed to prevent gentrification, and small- and large-scale speculation, through the CLT and by protecting areas that have not yet been fully developed.

In addition to the physical rebuilding, community residents have maintained a high degree of participation in activities of the DSNI, as well as in other locally sponsored events (youth-based, team sports, volunteering). Community control has been the basis of the DSNI's existence: resident voice and decision making in all aspects of change continue to be the way it maintains strong and vibrant community involvement in all aspects of the neighborhood's change.

Involvement of youth at an early stage in the organization is evident from the presence of teenagers on the board, right alongside the elders. The board's membership is defined to maintain representation from all racial and ethnic groups in the neighborhood. And residency in the neighborhood, as a homeowner, tenant, business owner, nonprofit organization, or other entity, is required for participation on the board. This clear direction of who can decide how the community changes has ensured that residents maintain control of the rebuilding of their community through equal access to decision making. This has continued to strengthen existing bonds while building new ones in the neighborhood. And it has multiplied the community's bridging relationships with a significant number of outside organizations over the years.

Such strong bonding and bridging relationships have given the community continued access to external resources while maintaining an internal base with clear objectives for how the collective defines and sustains itself. This self-determination and -definition allow the individuals and the collective to support each other, growing stronger together.

Unlike in the Middle East rebuilding process, in Roxbury there was no powerful stakeholder with a vision of how community rebuilding could support its priorities. Once the DSNI was formed, without the challenge of an existing plan of gentrification engineered by strong ties between government and private interests, it had the opportunity to organize and build community leadership and capacity.

The DSNI continues to be a model of community-owned and -run rebuilding in a previously abandoned neighborhood. It provides a lesson on how leadership development and community engagement can address the community's needs, and it offers an example to the remaining communities of East Baltimore. With organizational development and leadership capacity, this model of land acquisition and governmental support for rebuilding, provided directly to the community, could empower the rebuilding of all of East Baltimore.

MIAMI, FLORIDA

In 2008, the University of Miami, in Dade County, Florida, presented a plan to the area's planning commission to build a biotech park in the neighboring community of Overtown—a historically African American community with high rates of unemployment, drug use, and abandoned buildings. It was a place-based initiative. And, like the JHMI, the University of Miami did not engage the community in the plan to develop a biotech park or to discuss its effects on the community, positive and negative. The university and developer planned to use the benefit of tax increment financing (bonds sold to private interests and paid back over 20 to 30 years from the increased tax revenues in the rebuilt area), tax credits, and other publicly supported bonds to construct the first of four planned biotech buildings.

In 2009, the Overtown Alliance, a coalition of community organizations—resident stakeholders—working with several ally organizations from the neighborhood and university, requested that the University of Miami and the developer engage in regular meetings with the community to develop a sustainable community benefits agreement (sCBA). The developer and the University of Miami refused to engage with residents in regular meetings to negotiate a formal sCBA. Following a series of community organized events with student allies at the university and local churches, much media coverage, rallies, and demonstrations, the powerful stakeholders met with the community groups.

After several meetings, the Overtown Alliance presented the powerful stakeholders with a sCBA. The sCBA requires that the University of Miami fulfill the promises it made to the community when it received $100 million in public funds to construct the first of four biotech buildings.[19] The demands include benefits of land use, housing, employment, and education to the neighbors of the University of Miami. The introduction of the document states:

> Two years ago, before construction of the 8.6 acre UM Life Science and Technology Park started, students and community members approached the University of Miami administration and Wexford officials about developing a Sustainable Community Benefits Agreement with the local area. . . . They were told that the University of Miami doesn't sign agreements with communities. However, less than a year later the University of Miami signed a development agreement with Coral Gables [a majority white community] guaranteeing their residents over $22 million in benefits. Overtown residents perceive the university's lack of commitment to Overtown as a demonstration of institutional racism."[20]

In 2011, the University of Miami responded with an edited version of the original sCBA. As of 2011, the sCBA has not been signed and the community continues to organize to keep pressure on the powerful stakeholders to reach a shared agreement that would benefit residents. Currently, the community is suggesting a task force consisting of representatives of all stakeholders, which would serve as the overseer of the sCBA.

While the initial response from the University of Miami was negligent, consistent organizing changed this. The media, along with support from student organizations at the university, challenged the university to respond to the demands of residents to be made whole. The organizing efforts in Overtown, like those in Middle East Baltimore, kept the pressure on the powerful stakeholders to respond to the demands of residents and remain consistent in actions and words.

The public funding benefiting both of these biotech park initiatives is available to the developers only because they are building in areas of slum and blight. And neither city government requested a detailed plan describing benefit to the community. With an organized effort of residents in the East Baltimore community, a sCBA can be the tool used, as it was in Overtown, to hold the powerful stakeholders accountable to the community for the recent—and any future—master plan, with tangible goals of housing, employment, educational, social, and economic sufficiency.

NEW YORK, NEW YORK

In 2003, a community organization representing residents in New York City's West Harlem (Northern Manhattan) presented a plan for rebuilding a section of their community to the Planning Commission of Harlem. The residents were unaware that Columbia University had also presented a plan for expansion into the same section of their community. While the university's plan described increased employment, it neither quantified nor detailed specific benefit in economic and educational needs in the community.

A community development corporation, West Harlem Local Development Corporation (LDC), representing and accountable to the residents of West Harlem, was formed to negotiate for a CBA with the university. The organization had powerful allies on board and represented an area that was still thriving, with locally owned businesses and working-poor, low-income, and middle-income residences. Residents organized through door-knocking and listening projects, bringing their previously unsolicited voices to the negotiation table. Their suggestions for their community informed the CBA negotiations.

In late 2007, despite sustained public opposition to Columbia's proposed change in land use and testimony to this effect by residents at the Planning Commission's hearing, Columbia's plan for expansion was approved. During this period, the city committed to providing $150 million for affordable housing in Northern Manhattan to counteract the effects of gentrification that Columbia's expansion would bring.

In 2009, Columbia signed a memorandum of understanding with the LDC.[21] It provided $150 million in community benefits to West Harlem, including $24 million for an affordable housing trust fund, $30 million for a community public school in Manhattan Community District 9, community access to Columbia facilities and services valued at $20 million, and $76 million in installments to go toward programs designated by local community organizations.

While residents did not support Columbia's expansion into their community, the negotiation and achievement of this CBA offer an example, to both EBDI and partners and the community, of what types of specific outcomes can be agreed upon. Now that the JHMI has publicly declared its control of the current master plan, this offers the community an entity with which to negotiate.

Still unknown are what processes the LDC will use to ensure that the agreed-upon benefits materialize and what independent monitoring agency will hold Columbia accountable. As reported by one scholar who studies the successful implementation of CBAs: "Developers are notorious for breaking promises . . . [Referring to Columbia] I don't expect it to act any differently from another employer-developer just because it's a university."[22]

EBDI, a public-private partnership, is accountable to the public, but its private designation allows it to maintain privacy in its financing, planning, and negotiations with special and private interests that may not benefit the public interest. Like the LDC in West Harlem, EBDI is supported by the mayor's and governor's administration and city and state politicians representing East Baltimore.

The private and public bridging between Columbia and the New York City government is similar to that between the JHMI and the governments of Baltimore and Maryland. Like Columbia, the JHMI recently published a listing of its financial contributions to the city in which it is located, in its attempt to show its benefit to the public. It would be transparent and beneficial to the public for each to publish a listing of all the publicly financed contributions (tax credits, government bonds for expansion, government loans, etc.) it has received, with an accounting of how each benefit has enhanced its assets, physically and economically over time.

PORTLAND, OREGON

In 2001, Columbia Villa in North Portland, Oregon, an 82-acre site of 1,300 low-income and multiethnic residents, was targeted for redevelopment into a mixed-income community through the Housing Authority of Portland.[23] After receipt of funding from the federal HOPE VI program, and additional funding from multiple sources, a $151 million project began to relocate almost 400 households over an 8-month period.

The planning and design of "New Columbia" were based on the principle that past rebuilding efforts of this size mostly resulted in displacement of residents, little or no real resident involvement in the design and implementation of the rebuilding process, and no opportunity for residents to benefit from the rebuilt community— through housing, employment, education, or other social services. With this in mind, resident engagement became a large part of the planning and rebuilding of New Columbia's 854 new homes. The relocation team was informed by a relocation plan and advised by a 15-member group consisting of residents, housing advocates, and social service and public school representatives.

Services provided before, during, and after the 8-month relocation process were aimed at increased self-sufficiency of residents who chose to return. These included case management, employment assessments, education, workforce training, rent and utility assistance, family counseling, and resident workshops. These services would continue for 5 years after relocation.

During the design and planning phase, residents were offered a choice of return-ing within 2 years of the time of relocation. More than 100 of the original 400 fami-lies chose to do so. Some became homeowners in the process, through participating in constructing their new homes (sweat equity).

The process included economic development, in the form of construction oppor-tunities and small business development, along with a section of mixed-use develop-ment that includes retail space and a community college lifelong learning center. A new elementary school, funded by an additional $2.7 million of state funds, is part of the rebuilding project, as is a Boys & Girls Club offering recreational facilities adjoined to a city-owned community center with a gymnasium.[24] And half the trees from Columbia Villa were preserved in New Columbia, throughout the various parks and open spaces, providing tangible memories for those choosing to return.

The planning of this mixed-income community of New Columbia focused on a people- and place-based initiative. It used a broad approach in involving a diverse group of stakeholders advising the design, planning, and implementation of all as-pects of the rebuilding process. They included housing, social services, transportation, environmental, private, and nonprofit partners; community liaisons; community advisors; and—most importantly—residents. While some residents wondered what would happen to them after relocation from their close-knit community of support, many felt inspired to return and become part of the new community.

Where Columbia Villa had 462 units of public housing, New Columbia has 853 units of rental and for-sale homes.[25] Fewer than one third of its housing units are homeownership units for non-low-income families, one third are affordable rental units, and one third are public housing units. As planned, the physical layout shows no external signs of these differences in house value to the observer. The design includes public space flowing through the community to encourage easy mixing of residents of the area, an intentional design in mixed-income developments.

By 2007, less than 2 years after old and new residents moved into New Columbia, tensions between the old and new neighbors became palpable and resulted in open hostilities. Over this short time, the new community had divided primarily by class and race differences or between owners and renters. Fear of gangs was on the minds of many in New Columbia after several large meetings of youth in the park, one resulting in violence.[26]

Like many reported attempts at mixed-income developments in the United States (Illinois, North Carolina, Tennessee) and abroad (England, Netherlands), the planned social mixing of residents from different races and classes brought together as neighbors was not readily successful.[27] In these developments, targeting disinvested neighborhoods that are low-income, communities of color, or both, the new socially mixed communities often remain segregated generally by race and class or between old and new residents.

In New Columbia, this separation continued despite attempts at community gatherings organized by the city's property management team, resident associations, outside nonprofits, and others. As described in several reports on similar mixed-income developments, renters attended these functions, while owners mixed mostly with other owners. In addition, renters had their own meeting spaces and times separate from those of the owners, which contributed to a generally accepted attitude of "us" and "them" in both gatherings. No overarching and viable community association developed over the next 3 years, and perceptions of the "other" continued to reflect the stereotypes both groups previously held. And, at times, each group's actions confirmed the other's perceptions and stereotypes of it.

The question of "appropriate behavior" divided the two groups along lines of class. Some of the disputed behaviors were hanging clothes in the backyard, having furniture on the balcony, gathering on the street corners and porches, and smoking in the buildings.

Between 2007 and 2010, youth violence escalated. This led to two shootings in 2010, one resulting in the death of a teenager.[28] This spiraling violence, triggered by gang presence, confirmed the fears that many of the new residents and owners openly or subtly held about their lower-class neighbors. Now they had reason to support their stereotypes and discrimination and their desire to maintain greater distance to ensure safety. While old tenants also feared violence in their community and lack of safety for themselves and their children, they were perceived as the direct or indirect cause of the violence.

Still, in New Columbia today, residents old and new continue to live side by side. As they do in many other attempts at engineering mixed-income communities, some hope that in time the school and the children will be the keys to bringing families together. In the meantime, increased safety measures in the form of greater police presence and mentoring programs are being used to try to ensure that seeds of community building will root and grow.

This large-scale mixed-income rebuilding initiative is similar in size to Middle East Baltimore. It was a people-first approach with an economic initiative to foster movement to self-sufficiency, through social services aimed at addressing existing obstacles to employment, education, and health. While it did not promise the number of jobs the Middle East Baltimore initiative did, its focus from the beginning of the rebuilding process was to enhance the likelihood of self-sufficiency, as was evident in the planning process. Residents trusted this intention and were more responsive to these efforts than their Middle East Baltimore counterparts were, as indicated by high enrollment in the different programs. Programs offered by and through EBDI have not had similar response rates, with Middle East residents seeking assistance through sources they perceive as more trustworthy.

Like the Middle East rebuilding initiative, New Columbia did not focus on how the transition of residents of different races and classes in a mixed-income community would occur. The perception that "bringing these different groups together will result in benefit through some natural bridging force" remains unproven.[29] The supposed benefit of shared relationships and role modeling by upper-income residents for economic benefit to the low-income person is shortsighted and not supported by previous attempts over the past 15 years in similar rebuilding projects.[30,31,32]

Implicit in the assumption that these benefits exist is that the low-income and person of color resident will benefit from living near non-low-income and white residents.[33] Past attempts at engineering mixed-income communities have not confirmed this. Instead, they report that segregation of the old and new residents eventually evolves and becomes the new norm of the rebuilt community. For those who do not return, dispersion of residents in similar HOPE VI projects has not shown consistent improvement in economic stability and or benefit.[34,35,36]

Attempts to address the underlying belief systems and resulting discrimination that contribute to these patterns of "natural segregation according to perceived similarities" would benefit the rebuilding processes in both cities. Direct attempts to acknowledge and emphasize the similarities and dissimilarities in unspoken beliefs and values across race and class differences through antiracism oppression trainings would begin to forge new relationships of understanding and trust.

The Annie E. Casey Foundation has visited and offered resources directly and indirectly to support New Columbia's effort. This powerful stakeholder of the Middle East Baltimore rebuilding process is aware that the claims of ease of social integration and a new thriving and cohesive community are not supported by the practice and evidence to date, at New Columbia or in previous mixed-income developments. Still, the foundation and its partners—EBDI, the JHMI, and others—continue to assert these claims.

Unlike Middle East Baltimore, New Columbia has consistently offered full transparency of its process and outcomes, when it was successful and when it was challenged. Accounting of the finances that have funded the building of New Columbia and the relocation and return of residents, along with the cost for relocation assistance, has been detailed in full. The sources and breakdown, timelines in achieving or not achieving set goals, and provision of individual-level information on request from many different observers have been timely and forthcoming.

Because the New Columbia effort engaged independent researchers from the nearby university to collect baseline and follow-up information regarding social, economic, and health consequences, assessment of the outcome of this massive displacement of residents will be available.[37]

Other follow-up surveys openly reported residents' feelings, both positive and negative, about being relocated, highlighting the risks and fears for those leaving public housing living assistance.[38] It starkly portrays that almost half of relocated residents faced risk of losing the housing they were relocated into. They faced increased economic hardship in the form of meeting utility and rental bills and having no increase in income despite an increase in rent. And landlords sometimes imposed rules that were difficult to live with. This information was as available and transparent as the success stories of the number of residents graduating from their "family self-sufficiency programs," becoming new homeowners, achieving increased income, or graduating from the "trades pre-apprenticeship program."

This kind of transparent information and follow-up with residents have been important in helping the stakeholders of New Columbia determine how best to increase successful initiatives while tweaking insufficient ones. The stakeholders involved in New Columbia maintain a resident focus in the rebuilding initiative and appear to welcome the challenges as lessons that will increase the likelihood of low-income and poor residents becoming integrated in all aspects of society. Similar transparency and willingness to acknowledge the necessary risks and challenges would be welcomed in the Middle East Baltimore rebuilding initiative.

Recently, the Baltimore City Council requested that EBDI and its partners account for the more than $500 million of public and private funding they have received to date. During the hearing the council continuously requested more detail about the number of residents benefiting from the rebuilding process through permanent jobs, more truthful disclosure, greater transparency and communication, and construction of affordable homes. Feeling that questions about progress made to date were still unanswered, the council planned another public hearing to continue this oversight of the rebuilding process in Middle East Baltimore. The council expressed hope that in the future there would be more information that shows benefit to residents alongside the already apparent physical and capital development benefit to the JHMI and its partners. Unlike the New Columbia project, EBDI is protected by its semi-public-private status and does not have to reveal its records to the public. This hinders the transparency being encouraged by the community and public officials which roots and builds trust between community and other stakeholders.

SAN DIEGO, CALIFORNIA

In one of San Diego, California's most disinvested multiethnic communities—Diamond Neighborhoods—a community-based empowerment model of community rebuilding began in the late 1990s. Led by the Jacobs Family Foundation, through community engagement activated by resident-led teams, residents envisioned, planned, and learned the skills necessary to implement plans for rebuilding their community. Building community capacity has been a basic principle of the effort's implementation arm, to ensure that residents "envision, drive, and own change" in their community.[39]

The initiative began when an arm of the foundation, the Jacobs Center for Neighborhood Innovation, established offices in the neighborhood and organized the community through a door-knocking and listening project. After identifying existing and potential leaders in the community, it convened meetings to envision and plan the rebuilding of their communities. Using community-based entrepreneurial relationships, hands-on training, and the creative investment of resources, it provided opportunities for residents to learn about financial management and growth through investment in community improvements and change. In 2001, a 10-acre shopping plaza was built at a former dump site. More than 400 residents learned about and participated directly in investing in the new plaza, owning 20 percent of the shares. They have consistently realized a return on their investment, creating a joint fund for ownership of future community development.

Residents felt engaged in the rebuilding effort, even though it was initiated by outsiders to the community. They report that the initial community organizing process encouraged residents to envision the change they wanted to see in their community and commit to making it happen. This process of engagement created trust between residents and the foundation's representatives. Working with other residents increased the bonding relationships in the community.

The new community organizing and engagement offered a different model for their children, of parents' and families' involvement in neighborhood change. When residents were able to decide which retailers would occupy the new shopping plaza, they felt a direct ownership in how their community would grow: "We wanted a pizza place that wasn't afraid to deliver in our neighborhood; so we told them if they didn't do this, they couldn't come."

This sense of community ownership has fostered greater pride and willingness to engage in other rebuilding efforts, such as programs to engage youth; planning for new affordable housing; and participation in workshops on energy conservation, financial management, and employment training. A comprehensive development plan to transform approximately 45 acres of underused land around the existing shopping plaza is planned. The plaza will include a conference and community center, retail businesses, service providers, educational hubs, affordable housing, and a variety of marketplaces.

It is hoped that the past successes of community engagement continue to fuel the ownership in planning and driving the next round of physical community development. As the financial investment and benefit from the first shopping plaza continue, it is anticipated that more residents will invest and therefore continue to drive greater economic self-sufficiency.

The community organizing aspect of these rebuilding initiatives has been maintained through regular door knocking, constant communication, and regular meetings. Resident and nonresident community organizers are seen as a valuable part of the rebuilding process, not just at the beginning, but continuously. The meetings have offered a place for residents to share the personal changes experienced in their families: self-transformation through ownership and control of community transformation.

This personal transformation can become the root of ongoing social transformation in the larger community as it reinforces the internal and external interactions necessary for sustaining healthy community change. A cycle of individual and collective transformation therefore ensures that each reinforces the other.

This model of community rebuilding in the Diamond Neighborhoods of San Diego offers evidence of successful rebuilding through community planning and ownership sustained by training in local economic investment as a means for moving away from poverty. This people- and place-based initiative addressed economic growth within the current neighborhood while building bonding and bridging relationships within the community as the physical building supported the economic initiative.

Currently, neither former and remaining East Baltimore residents nor EBDI and partners have any plans for resident-driven local businesses, small loans to initiate new local businesses, or economic investment in new and existing businesses. This is especially surprising given the Annie E. Casey Foundation's financial support for the rebuilding efforts in Diamond Neighborhoods and its documented support of economic entrepreneurship as an important means of rebuilding low-income communities—for children and families.

MILLER, LIVERPOOL, AUSTRALIA

In a suburb of New South Wales, Australia, Community 2168 is a project targeting the 2168 postcode area that includes 8 suburbs in Liverpool Local Government Area. This multiethnic "locationally disadvantaged area" and previously open drug market community shared some social and economic characteristics with disinvested and low-income inner city communities of color in the United States.[40] Of area residents surveyed in 1999, a majority lived in rental households (with more than half in the public sector), less than half had completed high school, a high proportion lived in single-parent-headed households, approximately one quarter were working, and almost one half were receiving a pension or benefit.

That same year—after closing of several key establishments, increased safety concerns, and requests by residents and frontline service providers—several key stakeholders came together to develop a "community renewal and capacity building project" in Miller. The local city council, the state housing department, and the local health service brought funding to bear on the issues facing the community. Residents were surveyed regarding their perceptions of community connectedness, security, and challenges. Since this initial survey, also in 1999, three more have been conducted. The most recent, in 2007, was used to examine changes in residents' perceptions since the beginning of the community rebuilding initiative.

This community rebuilding initiative started by focusing on bringing residents together with different service providers to identify problems and develop practical approaches to address them.[41] These efforts resulted in a focus by local agencies on community-identified challenges. They initially resulted in increased security through policing, youth programs, and improvement in existing open spaces and parks. Aspects of social sufficiency were addressed through job training workshops, arts and cultural activities, various social services programs, youth activities and programs, migrant resources, and opportunities for small grants to involve residents in community improvement efforts.

A neighborhood center has become the place where residents go to access other types of services and find out what is going on in their community. It is the focus of community volunteerism, cultural and art activities, neighborhood garden projects, after-school programs, health activities, and various workshops and trainings. It also houses regular meetings of the Community 2168 management committee, which acts as the coordinating body, or central overarching group, for planning the implementation of the strategic plans of the project. The committee consists of 6 resident representatives and 9 representatives from different stakeholder groups—including health, social services, local and state government, and migrant services.

The project has enacted a new strategic plan every 3 years and set priorities to increase the community's participation, capacity building, and leadership. Its work is guided by the perception that the issues of social and economic disenfranchisement affect the well-being of the individual and the community.

Several working groups act on the implementation of the priorities set by the strategic plans: youth, employment and education training, participation, and community action group. They have organized health and family fairs, employment fairs, recreational activities, opposition to alcohol billboards and taverns in their neighborhoods, and more.[42] More than 10 years into its existence, Community 2168 is turning to projects of entrepreneurship through resident involvement and development of enterprises that will build economic sustainability for participants and benefit the larger community.

The basic framework of this initiative has been community participation and diverse stakeholder involvement. This reconnects residents to existing services while increasing different stakeholders' awareness of the needs of the community. This strategy reduces the feelings of abandonment and isolation that residents have reported over the years.

The Community 2168 initiative has been successful in increasing residents' perception of their community as a secure place to live. Specifically, compared to 1999, residents perceived a decrease in all forms of crime—even while local statistics reported no significant change—felt safer in their homes and walking their streets in the daytime, and felt that litter and discarded needles had decreased.

They did not feel there was much improvement in the neighborhood infrastructure: lighting, houses empty or in disrepair, walking paths, gardens and open spaces, or recreational or safe places for children.[43]

Residents felt that racism had increased over the years, and in 2007, a majority felt that differences in ethnic background, spiritual beliefs, mental health and drug problems, age, and length of residence divided the neighborhood. Of interest, fewer felt that indicators of class (education, social status, wealth, landholdings) divided the neighborhood. These perceptions of community cohesion offer all stakeholders guidance in future rebuilding efforts.

While the Community 2168 rebuilding initiative continues to face some of the same challenges as it did at its beginning, it has increased resident participation in shared activities, increased services to the area, and increased resident leadership in identifying and producing change in the community. Emphasis on increasing community control through greater capacity building has evolved in tangible ways to help residents learn the skills for this type of individual and social transformation.

The current project officer of Community 2168 described this emphasis on greater community leadership and control through capacity building:

> We are at a stage where we are looking at strategies for sustainable community ownership such as leadership skills training, management and governance and facilitation strategies for and by residents. This project has been successful to train and guide residents to this level of leadership. In many cases the project has a support role and residents have the leading role, such as the Resident Action Group and The People's Shed. I see the project not as designer and developer, but in a support capacity that provides resources and expertise when it is called upon by residents.

Together, the outside stakeholders and community members continue to relearn better ways of communicating, with each other and among themselves.

Community 2168 did not face the massive physical abandonment that Middle East Baltimore did. The 1999 survey showed less than 5 percent of houses abandoned. Yet the social and economic abandonment was similar, and was, as it was in Middle East Baltimore, created by systems that neglected the people and the place.

The Community 2168 rebuilding effort has increasingly focused on finding ways to help address the effects of this abandonment through a resident-informed and

-controlled process aimed at addressing the needs of the people. As residents participate in events together they increase the bonding relationships within the community, and that allows for greater bridging with the diverse stakeholders outside. These new relationships with external stakeholders have connected the local needs with the larger structures that can address them through dialogue and relationships across the diverse systems of health, housing, social services, employment, education, and recreation.

No such comprehensive effort has been attempted in Middle East Baltimore or the East Baltimore community—not before the increasing abandonment of housing, not during the small-scale rebuilding projects in the past, nor during the large-scale one occurring now. Such a broad-scale attempt to address the health, employment, education, and recreational needs of abandoned communities like Community 2168 and East Baltimore is equally as important as addressing the housing needs. These factors are connected in ensuring that a community thrives, having the freedom, skills, and resources to identify its needs and control the way they are met.

Because these factors are interconnected, when one is abandoned, it affects another. In addition to lacking a comprehensive plan such as this, the current rebuilding in Middle East Baltimore did not set capacity building as a priority. With the intention to remove residents from the area, there was no need to build capacity for the existing residents. Still, the neighborhoods of the peripheral communities would benefit from such a comprehensive initiative as Community 2168's.

Such a plan would begin to address the path of sufficiency for each individual as well as the collective—the larger East Baltimore community. A similar plan focused on resident ownership of community change, capacity building, leadership development, and the diverse needs of residents would help to ensure that, along with an increase in housing value, an increase in an individual's capacity to upgrade his or her skills or become an entrepreneur occurs.

This process begins to move the individual and collective out of a path of poverty and onto a new path of self-reliance and economic development. Addressing the capacity of a community to mobilize itself through participatory processes, both socially and economically, increases the sustainability of healthy community change.

FRANCE

Perpignan, a city in southwestern France, faced serious economic and social challenges. The city was isolated from the center of French economic life and had deep ethnic divisions among its citizens.[44]

A comprehensive approach was developed under the leadership of the mayor's office. The mayor's policy on urban renovation emphasized resident participation in all planning activities. Through establishment of an urbanism center, called "L'A," neighborhood residents, politicians, architects, and urbanists gathered to talk about and assess the community's needs and possible solutions to them. The planning process also emphasized the many levels of rebuilding the city, including the position of the city in the nation and in the region, as well as the location of neighborhoods in the organization of the city.

As in many cities in France, Perpignan had concentrations of people from North Africa and the Middle East. In addition to those groups, Perpignan has for hundreds of years been home to sedentarized Romani—formerly known as Gypsies. They have long inhabited the old center city. As in the United States, tensions existed between these different groups of citizens. (French policy prohibits the use of race or ethnicity in referring to citizens—everyone is simply "French.")

To address these problems, a multipronged strategy was developed out of the planning process. In the old center city, the housing occupied by the Romani was very dilapidated. These buildings were renovated, with some modernization. New plazas and improved passageways and stairs were created to connect the old center to other parts of the city and to provide green space and places for people to gather.

Perpignan's public housing outside of the center city had been situated in cul-de-sacs that made it difficult for residents to feel—and to be—connected to the rest of the city. One of the urbanist stakeholders addressed this clear physical marginalization faced by residents in three sets of housing projects. In two projects, buildings were modified to create space for a road to connect to a highway that, though only a few feet away, had been inaccessible in the existing street plan. In another project, the old high-rise buildings were demolished and replaced with townhouses for the existing residents.

To connect the city to the larger region, a train track was constructed for the existing high-speed train system. This connected the city to Barcelona and other nearby cities. This physical connection has reconnected these two ancient capitals of Catalonia, already connected in history and language.

This comprehensive approach to urban rebuilding offers many lessons to East Baltimore. The planning process began with involvement of residents from the different neighborhoods. While no major economic engine was planned, reconnecting the city with the larger region offers greater opportunity for employment and exchange of goods and services. Unlike in Middle East Baltimore, in Perpignan, displacement was avoided by ensuring that residents affected by the rebuilding in each neighborhood were involved in the design and planning of their new community.

These examples of community rebuilding in other disinvested and marginalized low-income communities have highlighted various tools that could be used to improve the results of the rebuilding effort in Middle East Baltimore (table 8.1).

The final chapter will highlight some of the initiatives discussed that may benefit the next 10 years of rebuilding Middle East Baltimore.

The next chapter will focus on the health consequences of disinvestment in communities and the populations living in these abandoned communities.

Table 8.1. Community rebuilding initiatives

City / Community	Initiative	Core Values
East Baltimore Middle East community	Place-based	Resident displacement Economic engine of a Biotech Park Self-sufficiency
East Baltimore Old Town	People and place-based	Resident engagement and ownership Comprehensive strategy Micro-economic employment strategies Alternate economy
West Baltimore Sandtown-Winchester	People and place-based	Resident engagement Small scale and self employment Comprehensive strategy
Boston Roxbury community	People and place-based	Resident engagement and ownership Self-employment Comprehensive strategy
Miami Overtown community	Place-based	Economic engine of a Biotech Park
Portland New Columbia community	People and place-based	Resident engagement Small scale employment Self-sufficiency
San Diego Diamond Neighborhoods	People and place-based	Resident engagement and ownership Small scale employment Resident business entrepreneurship and investment
Australia Miller community	People and place-based	Resident engagement Comprehensive neighborhood strategy/planning
France Perpignan	People and place-based	Resident engagement and ownership

NOTES

1. Popkin S, Katz B, Cunningham M. (2004) *A decade of Hope VI: Research findings and policy challenges.* Urban Institute, Washington, DC.

2. Wilson WJ. (1996) *When Work Disappears: The World of the New Urban Poor.* Random House, NY.

3. Fullilove MT. (2004) *Root shock: How tearing up city neighborhoods hurts America, and what we can do about it.* Random House, NY.

4. Wallace R, Fullilove MT. (2008) *Collective consciousness and its discontents: Institutional distributed cognition, racial policy and public health in the United States.* Springer, NY.

5. National Housing Law Project. (2002) *False Hope: A critical assessment of the Hope VI Public Housing Redevelopment Program.*

6. Fraser JC, Kick EL. (2007) "The role of public, private, non-profit and community sectors in shaping mixed-income housing outcomes in the US." *Urban Studies.* 44:2357.

7. Massey D, Denton NJ. (1993) *American apartheid: Segregation and the making of the underclass.* Harvard University Press, Boston.

8. Bullard, R. (2007) *The Black metropolis in the twenty-first century: Race, power, and politics of place.* Rowman & Littlefield Publishers, Inc., Lanham, MD.

9. Change4Real. (2009) The community's response to the Oldtown Redevelopment Plan. Draft.

10. Sojourner-Douglass College. 2001. Fundraising letter.

11. *Baltimore Sun.* March 5, 1994. "Fast-track in Sandtown-Winchester."

12. Mcdougall, HA. (1993) *Black Baltimore. A new theory of community.* Temple University Press, Philadelphia, PA.

13. Annie E. Casey Foundation (2001). "The Sandtown-Winchester neighborhood transformation initiative: lessons learned about community building and implementation." www.chapinhall.org/sites/default/files/old_reports/104.pdf. Accessed January 2011.

14. Blomley N. (2004) *Unsettling the city: Urban land and the politics of property.* Routledge, NY.

15. Annie E. Casey Foundation (2001). "The Sandtown-Winchester neighborhood transformation initiative."

16. *WBAL News.* March 30, 2011. "EBD-Ire—Residents of Middle East (an E. Balto. neighborhood) attack quasi-public corporation renovating their community, at City Council hearing."

17. Dudley Street Neighborhood Initiative. www.dsni.org. Accessed September 2010.

18. Medoff P, Sklar H. (1994) *Streets of Hope. The fall and rise of an urban neighborhood.* South End Press, Cambridge, MA.

19. *South Florida Business Journal.* June 2, 2010. "Overtown residents demand UM commitment."

20. Overtown Alliance. (2011) Sustainable Community Benefits Agreement. A visionary partnership between Overtown, University of Miami Life Science and Technology Park & Wexford Science and Technology 2011.

21. WEACT for Environmental Justice. Columbia University Expansion Project. www.weact.org/Programs/SustainableDevelopment/ColumbiaUniversityExpansionProject/tabid/216/Default.aspx. Accessed February 2011.

22. *Morningside Post at Columbia University.* "Columbia signs benefits agreement." themorningsidepost.com/2011/03/columbia-promises-benefits-agreement/. Accessed May 2011.

23. Housing Authority of Portland. (2010) Report to the community. Measuring success 2002–2009.

24. Housing Authority of Portland. (2007) New Columbia: Report on development goals.

25. *Portland State University Magazine.* Winter 2006. "A new way home."

26. *The Oregonian.* June 20, 2007. "Old mind-set hobbles New Columbia."

27. Lees L. (2008) "Gentrification and social mixing: Towards an inclusive urban renaissance?" *Urban Studies* 45:2449.

28. *The Oregonian.* June 23, 2010. "Killing spurs increase in security at Portland's New Columbia."

29. Greenbaum S. (2008) "Poverty and the willful destruction of social capital: displacement and dispossession in African American communities." *Rethinking Marxism.* 20:42.

30. Keene D, Padilla M, Geronimus AT. (2010) "Leaving Chicago for Iowa's 'Fields of opportunity': community dispossession, rootlessness and the quest for somewhere to 'Be OK.'" *Hum Organ.* 69:275.

31. Levy D, Kaye D. (2004) *How are HOPE VI families faring? Income and employment.* Urban Institute, Washington, DC.

32. Steinberg S. (2010) *The myth of concentrated poverty.* In: *The integration debate: Competing futures for American cities,* ed. by Chester Hartman C, Squires GD. Routledge, NY.

33. Greenbaum S. (2008) *Poverty and the willful destruction of social capital.*

34. Levy D, Kaye D. (2004) *How are HOPE VI families faring?*

35. Steinberg S. (2010) *The myth of concentrated poverty.*

36. Keene DE, Geronimus AT. (2011) "'Weathering' HOPE VI: the importance of evaluating the population health impact of public housing demolition and displacement." *J Urban Health.* 88:417.

37. Gibson K. (2007) "The relocation of the Columbia Villa community: views from residents." *J Plann Educ Research.* 27:5.

38. Housing Authority of Portland. Report to the community (2010) Measuring success 2002–2009.

39. Diamond Neighborhoods. www.jacobscenter.org. Accessed October 2010.

40. *Inside Story.* March 28, 2011. Understanding Miller. http://inside.org.au/understanding-miller/. Accessed March 2011.

41. *Inside Story.* March 28, 2011.

42. Community 2168 Working Parties. www.liverpool.nsw.gov.au/LCC/INTERNET/me.get site.sectionshow&PAGE1815. Accessed April 2011.

43. Harris E. (2008) Community 2168 Stakeholder Interviews. Centre for Health Equity Training Research and Evaluation and Community 2168, Liverpool NSW.

44. Fullilove MT. *Elements of urban restoration: Rebuilding America's cities after blight, flight and disinvestment.* In press. 2011.

9

Poverty of Health

"When they move these old people they die." —East Baltimore resident

"Don't forget the seniors, us old people, feels like they just put us out here and left us . . . no work to do, can't walk around anymore, no body knows us." —displaced Middle East Baltimore resident

"This great, rich, restless country can offer opportunity and education and hope to all—all black and white, all North and South, sharecropper and city dweller. These are the enemies—poverty, ignorance, disease—they are our enemies. . . . And these enemies too—poverty, disease, and ignorance—We Shall Overcome." —Lyndon Johnson

This chapter will describe in greater detail the role of race and class segregation in building unhealthy communities of disinvestment and abandonment and the potential health consequences of living in these communities. The health of individuals living in these communities and the individual health risks posed by unjust and nonparticipatory rebuilding processes are discussed.

STRUCTURAL INEQUALITY AND HEALTH

Building communities of poverty, concentrating poverty, is the result of institutions and laws which created separate and unequal places for people to live, work, worship, travel, eat, learn, and play. The pervasive effects of such segregationist policies and procedures in all the systems that affect the individual and population—education, housing, real estate, spiritual, recreational, transportation—resulted in a system of separate and unequal places for African Americans to congregate when engaging

219

in the functions of these systems. The consequence of continuous unequal benefit, disinvestment in the place and therefore the people living in the place, is dilapidated schools, streets, houses, businesses, recreational and health centers—places of poverty. This poverty of place becomes unhealthy environments for people to live, work, learn, and play in. The *structural violence* of having institutions and policies that cause and maintain these unhealthy conditions has been accepted as normal in the United States.[1] In Baltimore and East Baltimore the growth of places of poverty have been consistent and evident by the number of boarded and unboarded abandoned buildings, dilapidated schools and infrastructure, disinvestment in infrastructure of streets, lighting, pavements, housing inspection for lead and other health and safety requirements, fire stations, police stations, recreational facilities, mental health and substance abuse prevention and treatment centers, and grocery stores (chapter 1). These conditions starkly violate the health of a place.

A particular dynamic which contributed to greater poverty and unhealthy living conditions in East Baltimore is the presence of a powerful teaching, research, and health care institution—JHMI—who bought houses and boarded them over time and expanded into the neighborhood with resultant displacement of residents into peripheral places of poverty (chapter 2).

The attempts of rebuilding parts of East Baltimore have been guided by policies which displaced residents while offering the JHMI freedom to expand at its whim. These institutional practices of public-private partnerships have contributed to the poverty of unhealthy communities in East Baltimore.[2]

This pattern of mass displacement and demolition of places or communities of poverty is not unique to Baltimore.[3,4,5,6] The effects of these disinvestment may result in creating communities which increase crime, drug dealing, prostitution, gang activity and overall unsafety for residents living in these places. These activities increase the unhealthy and challenging conditions in which its residents must live, work, and play.

How these unhealthy places increase the likelihood of poor health outcomes of those who live there is important to understand.

HEALTHY PLACES AND HEALTHY PEOPLE

An individual's health is determined by many factors: socioeconomic factors, biology, behavior, and environment. Health can be broadly understood as the freedom to do the things that lead to wellness. Poverty, or scarcity of money or resources, results in the loss of freedom to access the conditions or factors leading to health in oneself or in one's community. When the environment one lives in is disinvested, it provides inappropriate resources for shelter, food, education, health care, and regular public services necessary for healthy daily activities.

Biology includes inherited genes, which predispose individuals to certain illnesses or their absence. For example, some forms of breast cancer are linked to genes that can be inherited from the mother. Females inheriting this gene have an increased chance of having breast cancer at some point in their lives. Their behavior and their environments together help to determine whether this gene will slowly cause a tumor to develop. Smoking cigarettes, eating foods high in fat, and failure to exercise are behaviors that can support the conditions in the body that increase the risk that the cancer gene will be "turned on" and cause a tumor to grow.

The environment in which a person lives contributes directly and indirectly to that person's behavior, the choices the person makes, and the stress he or she experiences daily and over time.

For example, some of the conditions people live with in neighborhoods like Middle East Baltimore make them likely to exercise less than people living in other conditions do—or not at all. Middle East Baltimore does not have recreational spaces, parks, or green spaces; its sidewalks are uneven, making walking and running difficult; and the neighborhood is unsafe, so many people do not feel safe to walk alone.

Middle East Baltimore does not have a grocery store nearby. It has only convenience stores, which sell many inexpensive processed foods. At the nearest market, fruits and vegetables are costly. So individuals living in this community are likely to eat less healthy foods than those in neighborhoods with more options.

And living in an unhealthy environment like Middle East Baltimore, with its high crime rate, means living in fear of violence. The daily, chronic stress this puts on the body and mind affects an individual's health.

These are ways in which historically abandoned and low-income communities—communities of poverty—influence choices and behaviors and produce a continuous level of stress. While it appears from the outside that a person living in such a community simply chooses not to exercise or to eat only processed foods—basically, to be unhealthy—he or she has little choice in the matter.

Together, socioeconomic factors, biology, behavior, and environment result in an individual's health. Because individuals live in communities, the collective health of any community is greatly influenced by the environment or type of neighborhood in which they live, which in turn is influenced by their socioeconomic conditions, which together influence behaviors (see figure 9.1).[7]

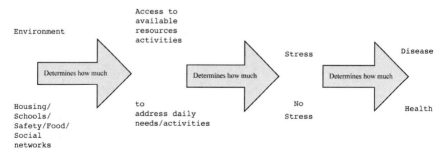

Figure 9.1. Social factors contributing to health or illness

POWER DETERMINES CHOICES, BEHAVIORS, AND ENVIRONMENT

We do not all have an equal degree of choice to decide on the environments in which we live, work, play, learn, and worship. Some have a great degree of choice in some or all of these matters. Others have none. This option to choose, the freedom of opportunity, is determined by the power we have, individually or collectively. And that power is in turn determined by social factors such as race or ethnicity, class or income, employment and education, gender, immigrant status, and religious identity.

These factors determine the social networks in which we are connected, which in turn help to shape our opportunities to "get ahead in this world": our power. Our power then determines the environments in which we find ourselves living, working, playing, learning, and worshipping—whether they are ones we chose or the only ones available to us.

The opportunity to choose, or the fear of having no choice, can have a profound effect on an individual's health. In 2001, when residents learned of the rebuilding plan to displace them from their homes, they had no choice about or control over leaving their homes. The decision had already been made without their participation. While SMEAC attempted to stop this plan, it was too late. Residents then attempted to affect the way the process would occur.

This lack of choice and the consistent fear from not knowing when the plans would change again have produced severe, sustained stress in the lives of Middle East Baltimore residents. For residents uprooted from their homes, the stress of this change continues to have chronic effects on their health.[8] The shock of being uprooted from home and community, the place once associated with one's identify, is traumatic and sometimes continues unhealed.[9]

SMEAC offered a temporary shelter from the stress of the unknown during the most challenging times for residents affected by the rebuilding of Middle East Baltimore. It offered a sanctuary where residents could share their concerns and feel supported, and it gave them some control in challenging a plan that produced discrimination and unsafe demolition practices and offered no opportunity to stay in the community, minimal benefits, and no reasonable opportunity for return to the community.

DISCRIMINATION RESULTS IN POOR HEALTH

In addition to the stress of displacement from one's home, for the community, whose majority is African American and low-income, the frequent experience of being treated differently because of skin color or a lack of material resources is already a chronic source of stress. Studies show that discrimination, prejudice, and stigmatization from being different result in physical and psychological stress.[10,11]

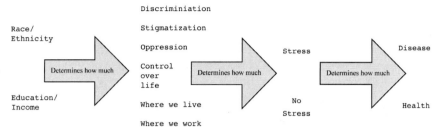

Figure 9.2. Race and class affects stress and health

When these differential perceptions and actions result in the denial of one's worth or humanity or the violent enforcement of one's position in society, the stressful consequences can be severe. This consistent pattern of stress for people of color and low-income people leads to chronic poor health conditions over their lifetimes.[12,13]

Stress results in changes in the physical and mental ability of the body to respond to daily challenges.[14] The chronic stress of being discriminated against, stigmatized, and treated in inferior ways results in a constant charged state of the body. This charged state is normal when an individual faces an acute stressful situation; it is the body's fight-or-flight response. But this state is healthy and normal only in acute situations. When the body remains in this state for an extended time, it begins to have negative effects on the organs. The body never relaxes or comes back to balance.

This chronic state of "being on" causes the body and mind to become weaker and more susceptible to illnesses of all forms, affecting the immune, nervous, and circulatory. Diseases such as lupus, asthma, depression, chronic fatigue syndrome, high blood pressure, strokes, arthritis, chronic pain syndrome, and all forms of cancer are more likely to develop due to the weakened organ systems and abnormal regulation of the immune and endocrine systems affected by chronic stress.[15]

The stress of stigmatization and discrimination against African Americans and the lack of resources and lack of choice resulting from living a life of a low-income person affect the acute and long-term health of individuals.[16]

In 2001, the daily charge of stress on residents of Middle East Baltimore increased when they learned that they would have to move to accommodate a rebuilding plan that did not include them. The resultant stress from the lack of power to participate or control how the rebuilding process in Middle Esat Baltimore directly and indirectly affected residents increased the risk for poor health outcomes now and in the future.

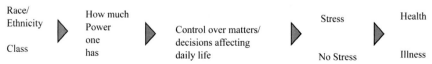

Figure 9.3. Power affects health

For low-income residents, whose daily lives may be spent in jobs that are more stressful and provide less security, impose higher demands, and provide less control than jobs at higher economic levels, facing additional stressful events in their home lives increases their risk of new illnesses or worsening existing ones.[17,18] This "weathering" or accumulation of stress effect from living in chronic challenging environments and situations also increase the risk of accumulating poor health outcomes.[19,20]

The judgment by the social norm of the United States through the decades has indicted "these" people—poor and African American—as morally weaker, less clean, less industrious, and less intelligent. These oppressive attitudes and perceptions have supported the continued discrimination witnessed by the way rebuilding of low-income and African American communities occurred historically and still does today. In Middle East Baltimore today, this pattern continues, of treating low-income African Americans living in abandoned communities as "unfit" for participating in decisions affecting their neighborhoods.

After displacement, some residents report being happy to be "away" from the JHMI, suggesting that now they can live in peace without worrying whether their homes will be taken someday. Relocating from Middle East Baltimore removed a chronic stress that contributed to their present and future health outcomes. This chronic feeling of powerlessness, or lack of control, results in stress and health effects in communities like Middle East Baltimore, where residents lived in fear that it was "just a matter of time when Hopkins would take our homes." The lack of control contributed to this fear and the subsequent stress.

SMEAC requested a health impact assessment (HIA) of the rebuilding process to EBDI and partners. There was no response to this, verbally or in writing. Including clear measures of health consequences during and after the rebuilding process would increase our understanding of how rebuilding efforts affect the health of already vulnerable communities. It would also increase our understanding of how prevention of abandonment and disinvestment may affect neighborhood conditions to lessen health disparities between low-income and African American communities and communities with other economic and racial profiles.

THE HEALTH OF ABANDONED COMMUNITIES IN BALTIMORE: PAST AND PRESENT

The health of residents of a community is affected by the social conditions of the individuals living in that community. Education affects the types of job one can fill, income determines the type of house one can afford, and both therefore determine the neighborhood one can afford to live in.

In the eighteenth and nineteenth centuries in Baltimore, the prevalence of infectious diseases was greatest in the lowest-income neighborhoods. The majority of African Americans lived in these neighborhoods. Families living in less housing space, earning less income, and working longer hours were more likely to have an infant die than those with more spacious housing, earning larger incomes, and working shorter hours.[21]

During the tuberculosis epidemic in Baltimore in the early 1900s, the common wisdom of that time viewed tuberculosis as "a disease of African Americans," leading to greater separation of the races. One historian wrote, "Along with the perception that African Americans were more susceptible to this disease, was the association that filth was something normal to them. No distinction was introduced as to the role of poverty in causing the squalid conditions leading to living in an unsanitary home, in areas of great congestion and poor ventilation."[22]

During a cholera epidemic, in the summer of 1832, 853 persons died of cholera. The public response to this was that the majority of the 853 cholera victims were the most "worthless sort".[23] Included in this "worthless" class were African American citizens and newly arrived immigrants who had not yet worked their way up the social ladder of land or business ownership.

The neglect of adequate housing, health care, and nutrition needs from being a segregated community left individuals in these neglected communities at greater risk for infectious diseases such as tuberculosis, typhoid fever, and cholera. The authorities of that time determined that to remove the causes of diseases meant removing the effects of poverty: overcrowding, poor sanitation, insufficient food.[24] There was no mention of removing the causes of poverty, overt and subtle racism and classism, which would end segregation and unequal distribution of resources and allow for healthy environments in which to live.

Coming into the twentieth and twenty-first centuries, low-income and African American communities in Baltimore have continued living in social and environmental conditions with less adequate housing, less sanitation services, greater drug trade and use, increased crime, and inadequate infrastructure compared to other communities.[25] In the twenty-first century, similar communities continue to suffer most severely from the diseases of today: chronic illnesses such as heart disease, high blood pressure, chronic lung diseases, diabetes, rheumatoid arthritis, cancers, sexually transmitted diseases, HIV/AIDS, drug addiction, mental illness, obesity, childhood asthma, and lead poisoning.[26]

In communities like East Baltimore, delinquent landlords did not adhere to the law requiring removal of lead-based paint from houses, and its removal was not systematically monitored. As a result, many low-income African American families with newborn and young children who lived in these houses were exposed to lead. In the mid-1990s, East Baltimore gained the name "zombie land" because of the highest rate of children with lead poisoning in Baltimore.

This direct effect of substandard housing and lack of public services to hold landlords accountable for lead-based paint removal is a clear indication of how places of poverty affect the individual and collective health of East Baltimore residents today. Because children exposed to lead have an increased likelihood of developmental, behavioral, and educational difficulties they are at increased risk for not completing higher education, not accessing employment and risk for violent behavior and

and decreased likelihood of subsequent movement out of a low-income status in the future.[27] This continuation of the cycle of poverty of people is affected by the poverty of the place: unhealthy communities as a risk factor for unhealthy people. Such an environmental effect of poverty on individual health is both a cause and a consequence of poverty and a clear indication of how our communities make us sick.

In 2000 in East Baltimore, rates of childhood immunization remained low compared to those of the city as a whole, while rates of childhood lead poisoning, asthma incidence, drug dependence, mental illness, death from homicide, infant mortality, diabetes, accidents, and HIV were high compared to those of Baltimore and of Maryland. It was therefore not surprising that the health of the area was declared "by most measures, appalling, making East Baltimore one of the least healthy communities in the United States".[28,29]

As in the 1900s, race and class status continue to determine the health of individuals while race and class segregation continue to determine the health of communities.[30,31,32] Today, poverty is the greatest predictor of poor health across the world.[33]

SEPARATE AND UNEQUAL COMMUNITIES, UNEQUAL HEALTH

Studies continue to show that in societies, states, and communities where there are greater gaps between the rich and the poor, greater degrees of health disparity exist. In general, the more unequal a society is in regard to wealth (income, education, assets), the more people die earlier, are obese, and have mental illness; more babies die in infancy; more teenagers become pregnant; more people are imprisoned, likely to use illegal drugs, do poorly in education, and commit murder; communities lack trust and cohesiveness; and communities experience more violence.[34,35,36]

This gap in power, and therefore resources, between communities with excess wealth and those with insufficient wealth determines the degree to which health and social outcomes differ between those communities, because access to wealth determines the degree of adequate housing, safety, recreation, sanitation, education, transportation, and access to appropriate health care services. Within communities, a gap in access to health care, socioeconomic status and risk factors for disease exist between racial and ethnic minorities and the general populations living in the same areas.[37]

The groups with less wealth are stigmatized and must continuously suffer the stress of this stigmatization. This results in negative consequences to their physical and mental health. A marginalization of self relative to the others who are more wealthy easily occurs. For example, in states with greater gaps between the rich and the poor, people with low income report more unhealthy days than those with larger incomes.[38] The greater the gap in income, the greater the disparity in health outcomes.

In 2000, residents in Middle East Baltimore had greater incidences of heart disease, diabetes, several cancers, sexually transmitted diseases, TB, and HIV, than did residents in any other part of the city or state. The crime rate was one of the worst in the city of Baltimore.[39] The gap in the rate of high school graduation, income, and property value between East Baltimore and the city and state of Maryland remains significant today as in the past.

The negative health effects on those in the groups with less wealth result not only from the stress of living in poverty or from being a member of a different race or ethnic group. Those with less and those marginalized due to being different also hold a negative self-perception.[40] This division results in distrust and a feeling of isolation, which in turn affects the health of a community.[41]

Such a relationship exists between the neighbors of East Baltimore: the Middle East Baltimore community and the JHMI community. The large economic and social disparity that has grown over the past century has fueled each community's negative perceptions of the other, separating them even further. Residents in Middle East Baltimore have consistently reported that it is the responsibility of the JHMI to be a better neighbor through helping with the upkeep of its less powerful neighbors.[42] Members of the JHMI community feel that their less wealthy neighbors are "unsafe" and contribute to the increased crime in their community. Each neighbor remains aware of the other's perception.

These perceptions of difference result in a similar process of isolation by both communities. In the low-income community of Middle East Baltimore, a community abandoned by the larger city, region, state, and country, residents had moved inward, becoming socially isolated and excluded. They continue to manage without the support of thriving community organizations and ties to systems of government as seen in similarly disinvested and abandoned communities.[43,44] This isolation and exclusion from those seen as having more abundance along with the demonizing as "criminal" and "unhealthy" by the same has a negative effect on the physical and social health of the community.[45]

Within the Johns Hopkins community, individuals are continuously warned of the safety concerns outside their boundaries. Today, many students, faculty, and staff park in the garages affiliated with the institutions and use institutional transportation to their destinations to ensure their safety.

Meanwhile, the JHMI and Middle East Baltimore, divided as they are by perceptions of "us and them," face the same safety concerns. Those driving through the East Baltimore neighborhoods to get to their Johns Hopkins destinations faced the same security issues residents have lived with 24 hours a day in East Baltimore. The crime did not begin at Madison Street because it marked the boundary of the JHMI's property. The same effects of abandoned houses, drug dealing and the crime that accompanies it, and all the other social outcomes that challenged the residents of East Baltimore 24 hours a day challenged the individuals entering and leaving the Johns Hopkins building.

Though not so apparent, there is a health effect on the more powerful neighbor, too. The powerful neighbor has also has fear: fear of its neighbors. The difference is that the more powerful communities, like the JHMI community, have sufficient resources to manage their fears, their feelings of insecurity. They have control over the perceived challenge, managing it with millions of dollars in security officers, off-duty police officers, camera surveillance systems, and auto surveillance systems. As the Middle East Baltimore community deteriorated, the JHMI's budget for security increased. Eventually, in the early 1990s, the institution developed its own guard force, Broadway Services. Its services now extend into the rebuilt area of Middle East Baltimore.

When these security measures become insufficient, as occurred in the late 1990s, the fear of their neighbors is managed through expansion into the "challenging areas." This control, available through the wealth of the institution, balances the potential negative effect of the fear of crime on their person or community.

Losing potential students and faculty to competitive institutions situated in more safe neighborhoods is also a fear to the highly ranked university and hospital system. Loss of research dollars can potentially accompany the loss of the "brightest minds" choosing to study and practice at the institution and builds fear. Prospective students, researchers, physicians, and faculty who visited the JHMI commented on the severe blight just north of the campus, stating that they could not work or go to school near such unsafe communities. Some questioned the relationship between the Johns Hopkins community and its neighbors to the north, wondering how such a world-renowned institution could coexist with neighbors in such states of deterioration and poverty. Others questioned how the world's leading institution on health, living next door to a community with the leading indicators of all forms of poor health—physical, mental, behavioral, economic, social, environmental—was helping to address these causes and consequences of poverty.[46]

Removing the cause of this fear, through removal of the people and rebuilding of the place, is supported by existing powerful relationships with other private institutions and government. Such powerful bridging relationships between private developers and government continue to disproportionately benefit the wealthy and widen the economic and health gap between institutions like JHMI and adjacent disinvested communities like East Baltimore.[47]

The less powerful neighbors do not have the resources to control their fears of isolation, exclusion, and stigmatization and therefore suffer the effect of these fears—resources of economic wealth or bridging relationships with government. Eventually, when these fears are realized by forced displacement, greater fear is created, maintaining continuous stress in the body and mind. This is the history of Middle East Baltimore and similar communities living near more powerful communities that continue to grow in wealth and privilege.

The current inequality ignites the memories of the historic way land owned by African Americans was taken by whites following the end of the Civil War. Residents today view this "taking" as a taste of the past, when even their ancestors' ownership of land wasn't enough to keep it out of the hands of white landholders.

One resident compared homeownership in Middle East Baltimore like farming the land of Hopkins, eventually taken when they are ready to use it for their own purpose: "It's like sharecropping, till they ready to take the land." He suggested that it is no different today, when more than 800 African American households are forced to leave their homes with no plan for return, for the desires of the primarily white stakeholders. The difference is that today, the promise of a "responsible relocation package" is offered as the twenty-first century model of "fair trade."

ORGANIZING, COMMUNITY PARTICIPATION, AND HEALTH

Communities with greater participation, organized around common interests, have better health than those with less community participation.[48] This healthy organizing within local communities leads to bonding and trust among neighbors, shared vision in the way a community changes, and a sense of being part of something greater than a single household. This "participation" and being part of a whole support the social connections, or cohesion, that result in healthy communities.[49] In communities with poor organizing or participation around common goals, a sense of isolation and fragmentation exists.[50] Neighbors may not know each other or may feel disconnected from each other, with no formal or informal bonding.[51]

During SMEAC's organizing processes, neighbors came to know each other. Door knocking by residents to inform each other of meetings resulted in some speaking to neighbors on their block for the first time, after more than 7 years of living near each other. The regular meetings of SMEAC, well-attended by residents, became a place where neighbors shared their fears, frustrations, and desires for themselves and their community. They experienced a sense of control from this social support that likely helped to reduce some of the harmful health effects of the stress of being forced to leave networks and homes.[52,53,54]

Such a dynamic also helps to counteract the possible negative health effects of the stress of feeling powerless in the face of EBDI and the JHMI. On a larger and historic scale, after the Civil Rights Movement of the 1950s and 1960s, the health inequality between African Americans and whites was the least ever reported. Investigation of potential causes for this change suggests that the effect of the organizational power and successes of African Americans coming together contributed to improved health status for the population as a whole.[55]

The bonding that occurred between residents ended as, one by one, they were relocated out of the neighborhood. Today, some residents wonder where their neighbors "ended up." Many express regret that they were not able to stay in contact. One elderly resident still living in Middle East Baltimore wished that SMEAC would reorganize: "so I can come to meetings again . . . I miss it." He did not have a specific issue that was on his mind, he wanted to "see the old faces again." This dislocation from community, the uprooting, and deterioration of social networks and support creates risk for acute and chronic negative health consequence for residents.[56,57,58]

The sense and security of seeing "old faces," a social network, is especially important for the elderly and those with disabilities. The elderly have greater difficulty adjusting to a new environment where the places and the people are not familiar. Several elderly residents died shortly after they were relocated. It is unclear how much the stress from having to disrupt their social networks and move from their homes of more than 40 or 50 years, the stress of "not knowing" a new neighborhood, and their existing chronic health conditions each contributed to their deaths: "They need to keep track of how many people keep dying." As one elderly resident reported, "Nobody knows me here." These stressors did not help whatever illnesses already existed.

For others, the understanding that their historic community was not worthy of being maintained did not diminish the chronic stress of feeling marginalized. As reported by a resident several years after relocation, "That project was never about us . . . they wanted us out the way so they could build their fancy buildings." Following up with residents affected by the relocation process is particularly important to begin to understand the short- and long-term effects on the mental and physical health of Middle East Baltimore residents.

While organizing brought residents together for support, the stress on residents from challenging the hierarchical model of rebuilding in Middle East Baltimore was severe. The continued attempt to respond to the powerful stakeholders' timeline and schedules placed a heavy burden on residents involved in SMEAC's leadership: "They call last-minute meetings just to try our nerves."

Many residents were fearful of taking time off from work to attend rebuilding meetings, hearings, or rallies. SMEAC members also had to attend internal leadership and organizational development trainings, board meetings, subcommittee meetings: "We should get paid for all these meetings . . . this is time." Residents attempted to review all the documents involved in relocation, demolition, and economic inclusion. During some months, there were meetings scheduled 4 days of the week, making it difficult for residents to attend them all.

While SMEAC coordinated different residents to attend different meetings, these residents were not compensated for their time, even though the positions of the organizer and executive director of SMEAC were compensated. Challenging the powerful stakeholders of EBDI and its partners, whose salaries compensated them according to what the market allowed, SMEAC was always at a disadvantage.

Residents had absolutely no control of the timeline for the rebuilding of Middle East Baltimore. What was clear was that a biotech park had to be delivered to the JHMI by a particular date: "All they care about is that . . . park." This clear knowledge of having no power to slow down the process of meetings and demolition and construction timelines, for the sake of building the first biotech building, maintained an attitude of stress throughout the lifetime of SMEAC. This chronic period of stress and lack of control continues for residents in the second phase and for those who may eventually want to return from the first phase.[59,60]

Today, residents in Middle East Baltimore who have been relocated report being tired and frustrated: ". . . can't even drive down there anymore." One resident said: "I got lost over there . . . can you believe it . . . it's not the same . . . made me cry." Others who have not been relocated continue to report feeling stressed in waiting to find out what else "they" will decide to change along the way. Without an organized force, existing residents feel even greater stress, lack of control, and powerlessness: "We just waiting for them [EBDI and Hopkins] to tell us what next . . . tired of this mess."

These stressors compound the existing chronic health consequences of being stigmatized for being African American, low-income residents living in disinvested neighborhoods. The effect of this 20-year rebuilding process on the health of individuals will remain undocumented but for self-reports such as these anecdotes. As one remaining resident put it, "I don't know how much longer I can fight them, they wearing me down." It is clear that a systematic analysis of the health consequences of this and similar mass displacement and demolition processes must be undertaken.[61]

MIDDLE EAST BALTIMORE'S CHILDREN ARE AT RISK

Increased experience of stressful events during childhood also increases the risk of developing chronic illnesses later in life.[62,63] This includes mental illness and effects on the ability to function in the workplace.[64] Stressful situations during pregnancy increase the risk of a child's being born with a low birth weight, which increases the risk of other illnesses during childhood and adulthood.[65] Pregnant mothers with less income are at increased risk of being exposed to stressful events, with resultant effect on the fetus and newborn.[66,67,68,69] Furthermore, chronic exposure to stress during childhood and adolescence can result in abnormal responses in the body later in life when faced with an acute stressful event.[70] Why is this important in this story?

It is important because children lived in 51 percent of the 800 households affected by the rebuilding process in Middle East Baltimore—approximately 400 households.[71] Of the total 800 households, more than 400 homes housed renters; a majority of those households were headed by women. A majority of these 400 renting households were relocated into neighborhoods with similar socioeconomic indicators, in East Baltimore.[72] Additionally, of the almost 400 rental households relocated by 2010, almost half (193) had received a supplemental relocation benefit that granted additional income for rental expense for 5 years.

By 2010, more than one third of these 193 households had reached the end of their supplemental period. These households are at risk of another relocation or of losing their homes unless they can find the income to replace the supplemental benefit. There is no formal plan by EBDI and partners to address this inevitable transition once the supplemental assistance expires.

Another 100 rental households had been transitioned to housing vouchers, with many expressing that it was challenging to meet the requirements of the landlords. This places them at risk for losing their leases if they are unable to meet these requirements. Many of the households affected by these challenges were not responding to outreach by EBDI staff and therefore were on their own in negotiating these financial risks.

Such difficult living environments are direct stressors for the parents and children who live in them. In pregnancies throughout this period of rebuilding, both mother and newborn remain at risk for acute and chronic health challenges.

The risk of another involuntary relocation, due to expired relocation benefits or poorly managed vouchers, places even more stress on a family already stressed by social factors that include race, class, and environment. This type of situation increases the risk for children of being exposed to adverse events and in turn developing acute and chronic health conditions, in childhood and later in life.

These stressors increase the risk of having poor health outcomes for another generation of low-income and African American families. The gap between the health of the wealthy and the health of those with low incomes in this rebuilding process in Middle East Baltimore is likely to grow, persisting into yet another generation. Studies of other large scale displacement and demolition projects suggest that children are affected negatively due to challenges in integrating in their new peer groups, disruption of their peer and social networks in their previous communities, and disruption of the social networks of their parents.[73]

MOVING BEYOND POVERTY OF HEALTH
WITH FREEDOM OF CHOICE

Residents of Middle East Baltimore had many poor health indicators—physically, mentally, and socially—before the rebuilding process began. Conditions that shape health or illness changed during the rebuilding process; some toward health, many toward illness. Residents did not choose these conditions. Neither did they choose the previous conditions, such as disinvestment, increasing poverty, and social isolation resulting from unjust laws of segregation.

In Middle East Baltimore, each resident is violated in not having the freedom or choice in deciding when to move and where to live when forced to move. They were deemed not worthy of being "strategic partners" in decisions affecting their homes and communities. Instead, outsiders with the resources and the power were the "strategic partners" and residents the "advisors" to the process.[74] This "normal" structural violence will influence residents' health outcomes, now and in the future. The result of the shock of losing a support system will affect the health of residents forced to move, now and in the future. Similarly, feeling that they have no reasonable choice in returning to their community will also influence health outcomes.

For residents in the communities peripheral to Middle East Baltimore, their fate remains unknown. Will they benefit from the rebuilt community or will the walls of separation simply be extended to their borders as in past rebuilding projects? This produces feelings of powerlessness, in which there is no freedom of choice and continued stress. A community of people who feel powerless have little inspiration to participate in the daily activities that lead to maintaining a healthy community, today or in the future.

This is the cycle of power, control, stress, and health that produces the poverty, or scarcity, of health. Power allows a person the security to make decisions about the big and little things of daily life. The amount of power we have determines how much control we have to manage the trauma and stresses we face in everyday life, and their resulting effects on ourselves and our communities. In East Baltimore, this power imbalance has grown, detracting from the past and present physical, mental, social, economic, and spiritual health of the people and the place.

An attempt to address this historic lack of power through community participation, transparency, and a plan aimed at equitable benefit in this rebuilding process can begin to turn around the current and projected poor health consequences of noninclusion, nontransparency and the unknown of future plans. Distributing decision making to all stakeholders would begin to narrow and bridge the gap between those with power and those without, thereby decreasing the stress of this rebuilding process on its most vulnerable stakeholders. The final chapter will address steps that may move toward a more participatory and comprehensive process with a goal of equitable benefit to all stakeholders involved.

NOTES

1. Galtung J. (1969) "Violence, peace and peace research." *J Peace Res.* 6:167.

2. Gomez M, Muntaner C. (2005) "Urban redevelopment and neighborhood health in East Baltimore, Maryland: The role of institutional and communitarian social capital." *Critical Pub. Health* 83:85.

3. Massey D, Denton NJ. (1993) *American apartheid: Segregation and the making of the underclass.* Harvard University Press, Boston, MA.

4. Wallace R. (1998) "A synergism of plagues: "planned shrinkage," contagious housing destruction and AIDS in the Bronx." *Environ Res.* 47:1.

5. Fullilove MT. (2004) *Root shock: how tearing up city neighborhoods hurts America, and what we can do about it.* Random House, NY.

6. Wallace R, Fullilove MT. (2008) *Collective consciousness and its discontents: Institutional distributed cognition, racial policy and public health in the United States.* Springer, NY.

7. Kreiger N. (2011) *Epidemiology and the people's health: theory and context.* Oxford University Press, UK.

8. Fullilove MT. (2004) *Root shock.*

9. Fullilove MT. (1996) "Psychiatric implications of displacement: contributions from the psychology of place." *Am J Psychiatry.* 153:1516.

10. Sternthal MJ, Slopen N. Williams DR. (2011). "Racial disparities in health: How much does stress really matter." *The Du Bois Review: Social Science Research on Race.* 8:95. journals.cambridge.org/action/displayJournal?jid=dbrOnline. Accessed April 2011.

11. Steele CM. (2010) *Whistling Vivaldi.* W.W. Norton & Co., NY.

12. Sternthal MJ, Slopen N. Williams DR. (2011) *Racial disparities in health.*

13. Steele CM. (2010) *Whistling Vivaldi.*

14. Cohen S, Janicki-Deverts D, Miller GE. (2007) "Psychological stress and disease." *JAMA* 298:1685.

15. Cohen S, Janicki-Deverts D, Miller GE. (2007) "Psychological stress and disease."

16. Marmot M, Wilkinson RG. (2005) *Social determinants of health.* 2nd. ed. Oxford University Press, UK.

17. Marmot M, Wilkinson RG. (2005) *Social determinants of health.*

18. Pearlin LI. (2010) "The life course and the stress process: some conceptual comparisons." *J Gerontol B Psychol Sci Soc Sci.* 65B:207.

19. Geronimus AT. (2001) "Understanding and eliminating racial inequalities in women's health in the United States: the role of the weathering conceptual framework." *J Am Med Womens Assoc.* 56:133.

20. Geronimus AT, Hicken M, Keene D, Bound J. (2006) "'Weathering' and age patterns of allostatic load scores among blacks and whites in the United States." *Am J Public Health.* 96:826.

21. Olson SH. (1997) *Baltimore: the building of an American city.* The Johns Hopkins University Press, Baltimore, MD.

22. Olson SH. (1997) *Baltimore: the building of an American city.*

23. Rosenberg CE. (1962) *The cholera years: the United States in 1832, 1849, 1866.* University of Chicago Press, Chicago, IL

24. Olson SH. (1997) *Baltimore: the building of an American city.*

25. Massey D, Denton NJ. (1993) *American apartheid.*

26. Kawachi I, Berman LS. (2003) *Neighborhoods and health.* Oxford University Press, UK.

27. Pruss-Ustun A, Fewtrell L, Landrigan PJ, Ayuso-Mateos JL. "Ch. 19. Lead exposure." *Comparative quantification of health risks.* WHO. www.who.int/healthinfo/global_burden_disease/cra/en/

28. Gomez M, Muntaner C. (2005) *Urban redevelopment and neighborhood health in East Baltimore, Maryland.*

29. JHU President's Council on Urban Health—report on an urban health initiative, 1999. www.jhu.edu/news_info/report/urbanhlt. Accessed November 2010.

30. Braveman P, Egerter S, An J, Williams D. (2009) *Issue Brief 5: Race and socioeconomic factors.* Princeton, NJ: Robert Wood Johnson Foundation.

31. Williams DR, Mohammed SA. (2009) "Discrimination and racial disparities in health: evidence and needed research." *J Behav Med.* 32:20.

32. Williams DR. (2011) *Moving upstream to the roots of health disparities: Wealth, education, race.* Robert Wood Johns Foundation.

33. World Health Organization. (2008) Closing the gap in a generation: Health equity through action on the social determinants of health. www.who.int/social_determinants/the commission/finalreport/en/index.html. Accessed December 2010.

34. World Health Organization. (2008) Closing the gap in a generation.

35. Wilkinson R, Pickett K. (2010) *The Spirit Level. Why greater equality makes societies stronger.* Bloomsbury Press, London.

36. Galea S, Tracy M, Hoggatt KJ, DiMaggio C, Karpati A. (2011) "Estimated deaths attributable to social factors in the United States." *AJPH.* 10:205.

37. Centers for Disease Control. (2009) Surveillance of health status in minority communities—Racial and Ethnic Approaches to Community Health Across the U.S. (REACH U.S.) Risk Factor Survey, United States, 2009. 2011 file:///Volumes/TOSHIBA/Rebuilding%20 book/Refs/Surveillance%20of%20Health% webarchive. Accessed July 2011.

38. Wilkinson R, Pickett K. (2010) *The Spirit Level.*

39. Gomez M, Muntaner C. (2005) *Urban redevelopment and neighborhood health in East Baltimore, Maryland.*

40. Williams DR, Mohammed SA. (2009) *Discrimination and racial disparities in health.*

41. Marmot M, Wilkinson RG. (2005) *Social determinants of health.*

42. Gomez M, Muntaner C. (2005) *Urban redevelopment and neighborhood health in East Baltimore, Maryland.*

43. Gomez M, Muntaner C. (2005) *Urban redevelopment and neighborhood health in East Baltimore, Maryland.*

44. Wilkinson R, Pickett K. (2010) *The Spirit Level.*

45. Williams DR, Collins C. (1995) "US socioeconomic and racial differences in health: patterns and explanations." *Annu Rev Sociology.* 21:349.

46. World Health Organization. (2008) Closing the gap in a generation.

47. Gomez M, Muntaner C. (2005) *Urban redevelopment and neighborhood health.*

48. Kawachi I, Subramanian SV, Kim D, eds. (2008) *Social capital and health.* Springer Science and Business Media, LLC., NY.

49. Gomez M, Muntaner C. (2005) *Urban redevelopment and neighborhood health.*

50. World Health Organization. (2008) WHO final report to the WHO Commission on social determinants of health from the Social Exclusion Knowledge Network. www.who.int/social_determinants/knowledge_networks/final_reports/sekn_final%20report_042008.pdf. Accessed January 2011.

51. Woolcock M, Narayan D. (2000) "Social capital: Implications for development theory, research, and policy." *World Bank Research Observer.* 15:225.

52. Wallace R. (1998) "A synergism of plagues: 'planned shrinkage,' contagious housing destruction and AIDS in the Bronx." *Environ Res.* 47:1.

53. Geronimus AT. (2000) "To mitigate, resist, or undo: addressing structural influences on the health of urban populations." *Am J Public Health.* 90:867.

54. Keene DE, Geronimus AT. (2011) "'Weathering' HOPE VI: the importance of evaluating the population health impact of public housing demolition and displacement." *J Urban Health.* 88:417.

55. Williams DR. (2011) *Moving upstream to the roots of health disparities.*

56. Wallace R. (1998) "A synergism of plagues: 'planned shrinkage,' contagious housing destruction and AIDS in the Bronx." *Environ Res.* 47:1.

57. Geronimus AT. (2000) "To mitigate, resist, or undo."

58. Keene DE, Geronimus AT. (2011) "'Weathering' HOPE VI."

59. Bosma H, Stansfeld SA, Marmot MG. (1998) "Job control, personal characteristics, and heart disease." *Occup Health Psychol.* 3:402.

60. Stansfeld S, Fuhrer R, Shipley MJ, Marmot MG. (1999) "Work characteristics predict psychiatric disorders: prospective results from the Whitehall II study." *Occup Environ Med.* 56:302.

61. Keene DE, Geronimus AT. (2011) "'Weathering' HOPE VI."

62. Bellinger DL, Lubahn C, Lorton D. (2008) "Maternal and early life stress effects on immune function: relevance to immunotoxicology." *J Immunotoxicol.* 5:419.

63. Graham JE, Christian LM, Kiecolt-Glaser JK. (2006) "Stress, age, and immune function: toward a lifespan approach." *J Behav Med.* 29:389.

64. Kristensen P, Gravseth HM, Bjerkedal T. (2010) "Influence of early life factors on social inequalities in psychiatric outcomes among young adult Norwegian men." *European J Pub Health.* 20:517.

65. Holland ML, Kitzman H, Veazie P. (2009) "The effects of stress on birth weight in low-income, unmarried black women." *Womens Health Issues.* 19:390.

66. Braveman P, Egerter S, An J, Williams D. (2009) Issue Brief 5.

67. Holland ML, Kitzman H, Veazie P. (2009)

68. Gluckman PD, Hanson MA, Beedle AS. (2007) "Early life events and their consequences for later disease: a life history and Chevolutionary perspective." *Am J Hum Biol.* 19:1.

69. Entringer S, Epel ES, Kumsta R, Lin J, Hellhammer DH, Blackburn EH, Wüst S, Wadhwa PD. (2011) "Stress exposure in intrauterine life is associated with shorter telomere length in young adulthood." *Proc Natl Acad Sci.* 108:E513.

70. Obradovic J, Bush NR, Stamperdahl J, Adler NE, Boyce WT. (2010) "Biological sensitivity to context: the interactive effects of stress reactivity and family adversity on socio-emotional behavior and school readiness." *Child Dev.* 81:270.

71. SMEAC (2004) Save Middle East Action Committee, Inc. Listening Project.

72. ABT. Associates. (2007) Final Report. East Baltimore Development Initiative. Post relocation satisfaction survey.

73. Keene DE, Geronimus AT. (2011) "'Weathering' HOPE VI."

74. ABT Associates (2008) East Baltimore Neighborhood Revitalization. Phase 1 Baseline Summary Report. 2001–2005.

10

The Next 10 Years: Moving Toward Equity or the Same Ole Experiment?

"Felt this [SMEAC] was a big victory, in getting people to be represented at the table; it made the project change its game." —Baltimore activist

". . . from each according to his abilities and to each according to his need." —Friedrich Engels

This final chapter will address potential steps moving forward into the next 10 years of rebuilding Middle East Baltimore.

THE INEQUALITY OF POWER AND THE INEQUITY IN BENEFIT

While the initiators of the plan to rebuild Middle East Baltimore did not set out to "organize misery," their plan did just that. And yet, this misery, chaos, uncertainty, and frustration for residents resulted in organizing and building of relationships among residents and bridging partnerships with outside organizations, until they were displaced. The networks that formed to challenge the power of the outside stakeholders were disrupted and removed, resulting in loss of the growing power residents had come to harness.[1] Residents agreed that their community needed great effort and many partners to help in rebuilding a more healthy community. Like anyone living in a neighborhood, they wanted to participate in and own the processes affecting their neighborhood. But those with power, and its ability to dictate what should be done, took the control out of the hands of residents. This is the "organized misery" of the first 10 years of rebuilding Middle East.

The current formula of displacing "the people of poverty"—low-income and working poor people—out of a "place of poverty"—a disinvested and abandoned place—is what has occurred in Middle East Baltimore to date. This formula displaced the people and demolished the place of disinvested homes, businesses, schools, and churches. In the cleared land is planned new homes, businesses, schools, and churches, for a different group of people, not the "people of poverty" who lived in the previously disinvested place. This is a rebuilding initiative akin to urban renewal—of the place and not of the people. For this to be a rebuilding process about the people, opportunities for increased income, education, entrepreneurship, and job skills must be incorporated into the plan for Middle East and East Baltimore, and follow those who do not return. There currently exists no visionary plan to address the root causes of poverty of people or place.

With the "people of poverty" removed, the powerful stakeholders no longer must see the daily result of growing income inequality—the stark differences between the rich and the poor. Because residents did not change in the process of displacement to other neighborhoods, their new neighbors may similarly judge them and discriminate against them. This rebuilding process has not changed the stigmatization and the effects of "feeling different" for these displaced low-income residents. These likely outcomes must be tracked.

The "place of poverty" was also changed over the first 10 years. After the removal of the people, and the eyesore of the houses and structures that had become the physical framework of a low-income and disinvested neighborhood, the place was changed. That place is now gentrified: new complexes with soft edges, a biotech park with lots of shiny and smooth exterior surfaces, new infrastructure of pipes and electrical equipment, private security guards—on bicycles, in cars, and surveilling through cameras—new street corners and improved sidewalks, manicured green spaces, increased lighting, and spacious small parks outlined with chairs for relaxing in.

There are few of the people of poverty congregating about, except at the bus stops, where remaining residents wait for change. In fact, as you walk or drive through the newly gentrified area, you feel as if you have entered the Johns Hopkins medical complex. Indeed you have.

So, having moved from poverty to gentrification, how do we finally move to balance? Perhaps this period of waiting, during which new buildings have been slow to materialize and new residents have been slow to show interest in living in them, has been necessary. It can offer historic residents, of Middle East Baltimore and East Baltimore alike, and the powerful stakeholders an opportunity to build bridges to each other and a framework for envisioning what type of balance—social, cultural, economic—may emerge.

As discussed earlier, planned mixed-income communities have not resulted in the outcomes expected, and in many places they have increased or maintained clear separation of the "old" and the "new." In this project, the historic distrust and the struggle for inclusion by residents have not increased the likelihood that this mixed-income experiment will result in a harmonious community. In fact, a community organization formed today between new and historic residents would likely be ineffective at best, and antagonistic at worst, given the events before and during the rebuilding of Middle East Baltimore.

The bitter taste of past exoduses of people and memories remains, as does this feeling of "same ole, same ole." Some older residents liken the new graduate student housing being constructed on Washington Street to construction of the 1960s graduate student housing on Broadway when "our land was taken by Hopkins." This continued physical expansion, reminiscent of past rebuilding efforts, must be addressed.

The next 10 years can offer a different type of rebuilding outcome, if the people directing the process look critically at the past 10 years and identify the areas in need of change and those worthy of continuation, remove existing barriers that maintain separation between the stakeholders, move away from places of defensiveness, and recognize that there is no one magic ingredient for success. Success in this rebuilding effort would strive toward a people and place based initiative focused on economic gain for both new and historic residents and businesses. Perhaps all stakeholders can agree upon what success is not: gross inequity between historic residents and the old and new powerful stakeholders; continued segregation of residents into peripheral neighborhoods already in decline; lack of opportunity for equitable economic gain; lack of an organized community base of impacted residents fully participating in rebuilding the larger East Baltimore.

FRAMEWORK FOR CHANGE

Healing

A healing process of mutual acknowledgment of past and current roles of each stakeholder in East Baltimore is necessary. This will allow transparency and new beginnings to develop toward equity of benefit, while showing a willingness of each stakeholder to "change the game" in the next 10 years of rebuilding.

It would benefit all involved in the rebuilding of Middle East Baltimore and East Baltimore to come together and heal the past: the myths, the facts, and the pains of both sides of the division. Such a process will offer a base from which negotiations can begin anew and allow for common goals to develop. Open discussion about the historic, present, and future imbalance of power between existing neighbors—and the systems that support it—which has and continues to drive the persistent path of gentrification of the community; and the lack of targeted resources to allow historic residents to participate in rebuilding and maintaining their community can begin to acknowledge the "elephant in the room" affecting everyone but not being addressed.

Because many of the residents affected by this rebuilding effort feel "unheard, disrespected, and not understood," it seems unfair to now expect them to swallow this history and hold open their hearts and minds to the new people and place of Middle

East Baltimore. It is important to acknowledge that this is usually the way the United States has conducted itself: with little regard to repairing past injustices. And yet, our abandoned communities and the current rebuilding effort in East Baltimore are stark examples of how the stress and trauma from injustices of racial and class oppression of the past continue to bear their fruits today.

Acknowledging the existence and consequences of a historic power imbalance can be difficult for those on both ends of the power differential. Still, looking at this honestly is a clear way to begin to collectively figure out ways to narrow this difference, moving toward a middle. For residents in Middle East Baltimore, having the powerful stakeholders acknowledge that residents have had little control in the disinvestment of their community, and in the rebuilding of it, is important.

Acknowledging that changes toward equity came from residents organizing and demanding justice would be part of a recognition by those in power of the power imbalance between themselves and the residents, which is rooted in laws and policies supporting segregation by race and class. There would have been no need for a movement against the inequities of the rebuilding plan if there had not been such clear injustices initiated and financially supported by these powerful stakeholders.

It is typical of the dynamics of such great inequality of power for those with power to expect gratitude from the less powerful when a redistribution of resources in line with justice is proposed or occurs. This paternalistic attitude runs deep in the interactions, public and private, in the rebuilding of Middle East Baltimore and if addressed diminishes another "elephant in the room."

Change is waiting to happen. The next 10 years of rebuilding Middle East Baltimore can be this change, the dawn of a new era in community rebuilding. With the lessons learned from previous rebuilding efforts in East Baltimore and other similarly disinvested and abandoned low-income and African American communities, and the first 10 years of this rebuilding effort, change can move all those involved toward healing. It is really up to us, individually and collectively, to move our society toward being a more just one. We can begin right here.

Organizing, Advising, and Deciding

Residents of Middle East Baltimore must organize themselves into a whole. A new advising body must be organized to include all stakeholders affected by the rebuilding of Middle East Baltimore and East Baltimore—a task force. And increased representation on the EBDI board of directors by informed community members of the entire East Baltimore area is necessary.

Community Organizing

Organizing from the East Baltimore resident base must be renewed. The revolution by residents through the vehicle of SMEAC challenged the intended "Negro removal." While SMEAC did not stop the process, or successfully change the gentrification of the first 31 acres, the individuals involved directly and indirectly with SMEAC transformed themselves. Affected residents identified their needs, demanded justice together, and effectively changed the relocation plan, the demolition plan, and the housing plan. There is hope that, in time, the physical result of the negotiated relocation and housing plans will materialize.

With the disbanding of SMEAC, the process of rebuilding has become even more of an experiment, on the people and the place. When residents organize, collectively identify the changes necessary to secure a community-owned rebuilding process, and then make them happen, the current top-down experiment on residents will end. Then they will become co-owners in setting the terms for a renewed Middle East Baltimore.

From a place of trust, an organized community can represent the collective voice of remaining residents and those who wish to return. A force to hold the stakeholders accountable for following the process, to ensure that all residents are informed of changes, and to maintain residents as a priority in the short- and long-term plan of rebuilding East Baltimore is necessary. An organized force can begin to identify short- and long-term goals that increase greater ownership in the rebuilding of Middle East Baltimore and East Baltimore.

Together, residents can challenge the current lack of local opportunity for small-business ownership; co-ownership and investment in new businesses, such as a retail square or supermarket; and lack of sufficient apprenticeship training programs for local residents in construction, biotechnology, technology, health care services, and the hotel industry; and other opportunities for increased income. This would support a future in which residents can maintain their rebuilt homes, new apartments, and rebuilt community and participate in the amenities offered by the new businesses that will slowly find their way into the community. A process that increases assets, through income and training, must guarantee the necessary resources for this to occur. This will directly benefit residents' ability to stay in the rebuilt community.

EBDI and partners must continue to be held accountable for the rehabilitation of houses for residents in Phase 2 through the House for a House and Home Repair Programs. Continued actions by EBDI and partners must ensure that one third of the houses built in each phase are affordable to low-income residents, equally distributed between ownership and rental opportunities.

There must be advocacy for a relocation policy for returning residents that describes the details of affordable return (including housing structure, cost, and taxes), supported by construction of housing that will accommodate those wanting to return—in cost, physical structure, tax incentives, and insurance. Until a larger task force is convened, a CBA or something similar may begin to hold the powerful stakeholders more accountable to spoken promises.

In addition to these economic, housing, and relocation benefits, stipulations to minimize the expansion of the Johns Hopkins community and its affiliates, with all their different names (Life Sciences Park at Johns Hopkins, Kennedy Krieger), must be put in writing and made legally binding.

The opportunity for their children to attend the new community school must be guaranteed in perpetuity for historic residents—relocated and returning. And criteria must be specified to ensure that the school's teaching programs meet all students where they are instead of teaching to a set of privileged standards devoid of the history of the local area.

In addition, a 50-year plan for affordable taxes for historic residents that would guarantee that residents are not taxed out of their community belongs in a CBA. Besides mass removal of residents, being taxed out of the rebuilt area seals the gentrification strategy in rebuilding abandoned communities.

Advising

The creation of a task force to address the overarching goal of eradicating the causes and consequences of poverty would be an inspiring change in the current rebuilding efforts.

Bridges must be built, and a task force may be the vehicle to begin this process. An intentional space, created to allow all participants to feel safe to acknowledge the "elephants in the room," can begin to open up space for a conversation about the differences as well as the similarities between the current stakeholders and the new residents. Acknowledging that people with different life experiences, economic backgrounds, and spiritual histories do have different values and behaviors is important. It allows a more intentional and open discussion about how they can live together harmoniously in the midst of the differences. Once the differences are exhausted, there is nothing left but the similarities, and over time an intentional movement toward the middle can occur, bridging the similarities and differences.

It also helps for the collective stakeholders to have similar knowledge about the intention and interest of all at the table. This type of transparency also sets the stage for more honest discussions when the effects of this power difference play out in daily activities. In a housing and relocation meeting, those leading the meetings are almost always white men, from EBDI or the Annie E. Casey Foundation. Acknowledging the power imbalance that is made manifest in these daily racial and class outcomes begins to offer more transparency and helps in moving toward changing them.

Once it is acknowledged openly and collectively, a discussion of whether it is acceptable to continue in these ways, and if not, what should be done about it can occur. This type of open acknowledgment would initiate a change in the way things have been done for the first 10 years in rebuilding Middle East Baltimore—and in the past 100 years. This acknowledgment of difference, without judgment, allows for healing old wounds and can prevent new ones from forming.

Currently there is no cross-conversation between residents and the powerful stakeholders that these institutional oppressive relationships occur, shaping individual relationships and affecting resident ownership of the rebuilding process. This lack of open communication and transparency among all stakeholders can and does result in a fearful and stressful environment for all involved.

Among themselves, residents acknowledge the power difference. But generally, within the ranks of the powerful stakeholders, there is no acknowledgment of these power imbalances. One likely reason is that when there is acknowledgment, noble intentions require doing something about it. The lack of awareness may therefore come from a "convenient ignorance" or "intentional blindness." Either way, discussions across this imbalance would begin to move the rebuilding process toward honest and authentic community transformation, personal and collective.

To get at common goals, stakeholders can begin to identify the goals they do not share, which often result from their having different life experiences, resources, and histories. Shining some light on these histories can begin to bridge the gap of nonunderstanding that currently exists between stakeholders. While these processes may seem to "waste" time in talking, developing collective awareness can begin to usher in transparency, trust, and acceptance of differences.

Decision Making

The context in which to ensure greater decision making by affected residents must be developed. Increasing the number of residents on the board of EBDI can begin to effect this. However, the way decisions currently are made, by two or three board members, must also change.

The open meetings addressing all aspects of the rebuilding process (subcommittees of the board for relocation, housing, demolition, economic inclusion, plan of return, follow-up, economic and business development (the last two are not currently in existence)—which are fulfilling the 2005 legislation for greater resident input— must continue. EBDI must make greater effort to reach out to affected residents and those in the peripheral community for participation and input. While these settings allow community participation, they do not affect decision making. A method may be developed where a process for consensus decision making occurs in these meetings in regard to issues discussed before taken to the EBDI board. Upon voting by the EBDI board, decisions can be brought back to the committee meetings with reasons for such decisions. If there is valid reason for challenging the board's decision in light of unsound reason or biased reason which shows disproportionate benefit for the community, decisions should be returned to the board for further clarification addressing the referenced challenges. While time-consuming, such a process allows greater transparency and decision making to residents who do not have decision making power. Such a process may also begin to "train" board members to be more effective in addressing the issue of equity in benefit to the community which is disproportionately represented on the board.

The board must have greater influence over initiatives carried out by the organization. Therefore, the board must be more involved from the beginning of a planned initiative, small or large. This means more communication between board members, ensuring that each is fully informed about a new initiative well before it has been pieced together for a final decision. The board must also be more aware of the decisions and actions of EBDI, the major developer, and the leadership of JHMI who are directly working with the major developer.

More transparency between board members regarding their individual motivations and expectations in each new initiative is also necessary. An analysis of benefit to all the stakeholders and their interests should accompany each new initiative, to ensure that decisions are fully informed with regard to who benefits—in the short term and in the long term. In contexts in which there are extreme power imbalances, fear of repercussions for specific decisions may exist. An anonymous method for decision making by board members can help ensure truthful processes.

The board of EBDI must set an example for the organization by being more publicly accountable. This can occur through public transparency of minutes. EBDI must be more publicly accountable by sharing its financial reports, audits, projections and actuaries, and plans.

A Comprehensive and Participatory Plan

A new and comprehensive plan—of physical, economic, social, health, educational, recreational, and security goals—must be envisioned, designed, defined, funded, implemented, and evaluated by all stakeholders. They must include historic and newly arrived residents and businesses. This planning must address the entire 88 acres of Middle East Baltimore and the larger East Baltimore area. Each of the domains just listed must be clearly developed with a timeline for the next 20 years, with 3-year strategic plans providing benchmarks by which to measure achievements and identify necessary changes over time.

Addressing the root causes of poverty and benefiting the public are inseparable. Once a process of reconciliation between the different stakeholders has occurred, and a task force or advisory group has formed—with healthy bonding and bridging relationships—a comprehensive plan can be developed. Addressing the whole community, all the aspects that define community, can be informed by this body through a sharing of experiences. This and the previous two recommendations can be funded by the current developers in the first 88 acres, from the continued asset increases these powerful partners of EBDI have gained through public financing and tax credits. Funneling portions of this benefit back into strategies to address poverty in East Baltimore is a clear public benefit. After all, it was the same poverty, pushed aside, that enabled them to develop and gain those assets.

Each domain of community change—physical, economic, social, health, educational, recreational, and security—must be carefully assessed for its current status, the causes thereof, and expected outcomes. Carefully identifying the benchmarks by which to assess what works and what requires change is critical to ensuring that a plan remains on track to its intended outcomes. Points of failure are opportunities for improvement and can be used to identify new ways to address old issues. An overall goal, to bring public and private dollars to address the consequences of poverty within the context of new cohesive forces, can begin to renew East Baltimore.

Old models of reliance on economic markets within the city that have done little to secure increased income and business ownership in the low-income and African American communities of Baltimore must be acknowledged and put aside. These old models continue to benefit the same powerful corporations, which expand and continue to hire workers at minimal pay and with minimal benefits. Self-sustaining models of economic sufficiency for previously abandoned communities can change the current free market of cheap labor always available to expanding corporations. Until economic sufficiency occurs in these communities, they remain the victims of the powerful engines that maintain the separation of the rich and the poor—as has occurred in East Baltimore.

Rebuilding communities from the inside, which aligns the processes that contribute to a healthy community with the practical physical changes that must occur, may lead to community transformation at the core. The sprit of the individual and the collective that has been abandoned can be simultaneously addressed, right alongside the structural and economic changes. Both have been neglected and therefore both must be taken care of, with equal dedication.

To remove a group of residents and then claim to have rebuilt the community is simply redevelopment of physical space. To rebuild a community with the participation of the historic residents, who provide direction in addressing the causes and the consequences of abandonment, is community transformation. This process, acknowledging the abandonment and decay of the community and their effects on the physical place and on the minds and bodies of the people, allows for a healing that can result in transformation.

From this point, as the community is rebuilt with buildings and with the systems and services that support a transformed people, we can state that we have rebuilt a community toward health and wholeness. The way redevelopment of abandoned communities has occurred in the United States—forced from the outside—does not foster respect, healing, and survival of healthy communities.

WHY CHANGE NOW?

Why should the current powerful stakeholders change the game, especially in the absence of any organized community force holding them accountable? There are several reasons. This book lays out the perspectives from inside the community: the people directly affected—forced to leave their homes, support systems, and generational history. And it shows what conditions were in place more than 100 years ago that set the stage for this type of community rebuilding to occur today—racist and classist laws and policies, fueled by current unjust housing and development policies and public-private partnerships which disproportionately benefit the wealthy. This history can inform the present, offering more clarity about proceeding into the future.

Those with power in this current rebuilding effort have the ability to help transform this history so that the past is healed and to set the stage for a new day. Many came to the table with good intentions, ignorant of the history and of the ways they benefit from it. Some came with selfish intentions, motivated by greed. Others became caught in the conditions, swayed by the power of the majority stakeholders. All are affected by and have participated in this process, and therefore all have an opportunity to change it.

Power does not have to be corrupt or oppressive or to continue behaviors ensuring race and class oppression, widening the gap between the rich and the poor. Power can transform for justice, just as the power of residents transformed the relocation, demolition, and housing processes. Collective power, of the community stakeholders side by side with the outside stakeholders, can create even greater change—change that benefits all more equitably.

A redistribution of power, in the form of assets and all the conditions that contribute to asset building, can occur if those currently driving this rebuilding process decide to do so. The JHMI is premier in health care, teaching, research, and public health. What it is not premier in, in its own hometown, is equitable distribution of this power, gained from the causes and consequences of poverty in its own backyard.

This rebuilding of 88 acres of Middle East Baltimore with equity can change that and bring the institution into the twenty-first century as a powerful institution that recognizes its past and plants the seeds for a new future. In time, it can become a premier institution in setting the example for similar expanding corporations—educational, health care, and other types. It can position itself as a leader not just through research, teaching, and direct health care, but also through action aimed at the greatest social determinant of health outcomes, poverty. It is up to the JHMI.

The city and state governments' participation in this project to date has been supportive of those already in power, with minimal effort or action to address the causes and conditions of poverty. The next 10 years offer the current and future administrations an opportunity to change this history and to remedy the previous 10, as well as the discriminatory policies and practices that have paved the way for continued separation of the rich and the poor. The current rebuilding process the administrations at city and state levels continue to support simply repeats the old "urban renewal" methods, with new labels and fancy programs that are insufficient to address the root causes of poverty. In fact, the hypocrisy of displacing low-income and working poor people and rebuilding the disinvested place they called home, replacing them with people who are different in class and race, is the "same ole same ole" in Baltimore.

Why should they change their game? The current governor of the state of Maryland was the mayor of Baltimore during the first years of the rebuilding of Middle East Baltimore. He led the initiative, partnered with the JHMI. He may one day decide to seek higher public office. And perhaps an administration capable of envisioning and supporting a new way of rebuilding cities, aimed at addressing the roots and consequences of poverty in a bold and revolutionary way, may be worthy of the support of the people of the United States.

There is great opportunity for change, to showcase how government can work for the people and be accountable to the people, bringing back the intended role of government in parts of the United States while addressing one of the biggest challenges to the country and the world: poverty.

The elected officials representing Middle East Baltimore and the larger East Baltimore can do better by its constituents. They have swung from both extremes in their private support and at times public actions. Several amendments to the Middle East Baltimore Urban Renewal plan were introduced during the first 5 years. However these same amendments which could hold the powerful stakeholders accountable to housing affordability, resident participation, a tangible plan for residents choosing to return, economic inclusion of local residents, and adequate follow up of displaced residents, have been subsequently ignored by current city, state, and federal elected officials.

Why should they change their game? They have a responsibility to the community they directly represent even while the power of the offices of the mayor and governor may challenge their freedom to act in residents' best interest. They approved the taking of land through eminent domain powers and therefore have a responsibility to assure that this public-private partnership fulfills the letter of the law in regard to "public benefit". Without measurable benefit to the historic community and return of residents they have condoned the continued growth of power and benefit inequality in East Baltimore. To begin to address this concern, they should immediately introduce legislation stopping the use of the powers of eminent domain for further development in East Baltimore.

The foundations have played a large role in the rebuilding effort. Why should they change their game? The first question to ask is, "Why did they become involved, in such a big way, in the first place?" If their intention was to produce balance between the government and the major developer, the JHMI, then they have to do better. Foundations are ultimately accountable to their funders or donors, through their boards of trustees. Donors want to know their dollars are benefiting "worthy causes," which often translate to populations that are vulnerable, and they reduce their taxes. Assisting populations to move out of poverty can only occur through asset development, whether in income, education, housing, or health. The current rebuilding effort requires restructuring that will rebuild communities through all these domains. Therefore, the foundations' dollars have not been well spent to date, to accomplish their donors' goals.

The donors must either hold the current foundations accountable for meeting these goals or ensure that there are sufficient resources for the foundations to accomplish them. The current foundations have advertised themselves as contributing to a noble cause. Yes, it is noble to address the causes and consequences of poverty. Unfortunately, the first 10 years of rebuilding Middle East Baltimore have addressed neither.

When they have acted in a way that contributes to fulfilling this noble intention, and not to further widening the gap between the rich and the poor of East Baltimore and beyond, then they will deserve such credit. Indeed, there is much for the foundations to gain in ushering in a new way to rebuild abandoned inner cities. It would set a new benchmark for the role of foundations in reinterpreting current discriminatory laws and practices and offer an example of successful public-private partnerships in accomplishing public service.

Community stakeholders have much to gain by changing the current game. Participation by residents, in an organized way, would begin to provide some accountability to the residents in the process again. Becoming informed about the successes and failures of efforts in other cities would help to broaden the conversation about equitable benefits for residents of the East Baltimore area. Decision making by resident stakeholders is key to addressing equity. An organized force is necessary to ensure that individual resident decision makers are informed by the larger community and that they inform the larger community of the process and of opportunities for participation.

The benefit to residents of the Middle East Baltimore and East Baltimore communities from an equitably planned and implemented rebuilding process would be great. Middle East Baltimore residents would see the benefit in housing equity and would realize an overall asset increase. East Baltimore residents would enjoy similar benefits and avoid having their communities become the refuge of the crime and grime that were pushed out of Middle East Baltimore.

With an organized force of the greater East Baltimore area holding the powerful stakeholders in this rebuilding process accountable for the tremendous public assistance and tax subsidies enjoyed by the private developers, a redistribution of assets can begin to materialize. Building stable and thriving communities throughout East Baltimore will ensure that continued speculation—buying and boarding up of houses—does not guarantee a continued cycle of abandonment, poverty, and gentrification. Such success can become models for other similar communities in Baltimore, the United States, and abroad.

EVALUATING THE FIRST 10 YEARS AND GETTING IT RIGHT IN THE NEXT 10 BENEFITS ALL

Though it does not evaluate the current rebuilding process, this book does review what has occurred so far and consider what may happen next. It has maintained a people-centered perspective in the hope of assisting all the stakeholders to look optimistically and realistically at the challenges ahead in rebuilding Middle East Baltimore in a way that benefits all.

The community stakeholders' understanding of a beneficial outcome often looks different from those of the EBDI board of directors and staff, the primary funders, the development organizations, the JHMI, the communities peripheral to Middle East Baltimore, the planning and development branches of the city and state government, and the foundations. And within each of these groups, there exists a mix of ideas of what successful may look like.

Based on these different ideal outcomes for each stakeholder, measuring the success achieved to date would reveal a mixed bag. Many ways of examining outcomes have been discussed, including survey and focus group results from those who have been displaced, before and after displacement and listening projects. Others include this author's analysis of interviews with and observations by the stakeholders involved in the process.

Together they reflect varied indicators and outcomes, including an organized community, the health outcomes of forced relocation, the lack of control in housing choice, the evolution of a community organization, the personal transformation of organized residents, the healing effect of a community organization, data regarding the neighborhoods that residents have been relocated into, the dollar amount that residents received in relocation assistance, the dollar value of the homes that residents were relocated into, consistency in promises and practice by all stakeholders, residents who want to return, residents who don't want to return, residents who died, residents who reported greater joy after displacement, the dollar value of the renovated homes that some residents chose, the change in demolition protocol and subsequent policy compelling safe demolition in the state of Maryland, the change in housing rehabilitation in the second phase, the lack of residents returning to the rebuilt community, the tension that exists between the residents and other stakeholders, the general discontent that many residents continue to report, the lack of co-ownership in decision making in the rebuilding of Middle East Baltimore, the lack of a community organization representing Middle East residents, racist and classist attitudes that frame the current process, increased house equity, increased property tax payments, safer neighborhoods, better schools, nearby supermarket, further transportation to work, snobbish neighbors, temporary jobs, housing vouchers, supplemental housing assistance, end of supplemental housing assistance, not being listened to, helpful relocation assistance, unhelpful relocation assistance, and many others.

These indicators or outcomes, individually and together, offer a snapshot of what has been the process and the result of this rebuilding process in Middle East Baltimore. Each stakeholder has an opinion about whether any or all of them are the appropriate ones to use to determine success. Reaching some agreed-upon common indicators of success would in itself be a successful outcome.

The current outcomes made public by EBDI and its partners are ones they alone chose. All stakeholders must be at the table in deciding what are the goals of this rebuilding effort: address the causes and consequences of poverty in East Baltimore, expand an already powerful corporation, build self-sufficiency in local business ownership and income increase, build new houses East Baltimore residents cannot afford, move the poor out of the community, bring new people in, assure there is 80 percent white people living in Middle East Baltimore, increase temporary and low-wage employment in East Baltimore, set local hiring goals, assure minority and women businesses are qualified to apply for contracts, relocate residents into houses they cannot afford in the long run, assist residents in maintaining equity in their new homes, build a new school for JHMI staff and students, build a new school for all of East Baltimore and displaced residents, build a new park, build a new park that will be gated, make the streets safe for the JHMI students, staff, and visitors, make the streets safe for historic residents, bring in restaurants residents cannot afford, build equal numbers of low, moderate, and market rate housing, establish a multicultural/ethnic/income community organization?

Over the next 10 years, the process will continue to change and the indicators will need to change. Identifying common goals will help in keeping the outcomes consistent, even as the indicators change over time.

Is a community rebuilding process portable? Can a good process that emerges in Middle East Baltimore be used in other communities in Baltimore and Maryland and other states across and outside the United States? What would determine whether it could become a model for rebuilding historically abandoned communities? A series of evaluations would be required, to look into the practical way that this process could be adapted to fit smaller and larger communities.

The rebuilding of historically abandoned communities might take a long-range vision of 20 to 30 years and include a) planned rehabbing and new construction to avoid relocation; b) equity in relocation benefits—when necessary; c) accessing governmental resources for support and implementation of healthy demolition processes; d) involving diverse stakeholders, including planning, development, transportation, preservation, health, education, recreation, environment, private, nonprofit, security, government, philanthropy, and residents; e) engaging residents (with adequate resources to compensate for time) to ensure co-ownership of all aspects of rebuilding; f) economic planning to address generational low income and underemployment; g) identifying resources to ensure the maintenance and growth of rebuilt communities; h) identifying a plan that addresses the risk of being taxed out of the rebuilt area; and i) identifying common and dissimilar goals of diverse stakeholders.

A strategy that fits one community will not fit another community exactly. Each community has its own culture and norms; the same is true for each set of stakeholders involved in a rebuilding process. A plan that keeps equity as its platform and requires all of the following could serve as a general framework of any new rebuilding process: community participation and ownership as parts of rebuilding from start to finish; transparency of interests, values, and goals of the key stakeholders; and respect for historic place and people. Adapting the specifics of each local community and its stakeholders into this framework could likely continue the process of rebuilding on the road of greater participatory and equitable practices.

The historic Middle East Baltimore community was a community defined by culture, physical boundaries, and memories. Because it was a "community of memory," residents will not forget the past.[2] This "nonforgetting" offers some hope that a vibrant and renewed Middle East Baltimore can still happen—by all the people, and for all the people.

The "socially engineered" community that is in the process of becoming the new Middle East Baltimore community, renamed to erase the memory of the past, is a community of physical boundaries. With intentional shifts in the current planning and implementing of the rebuilding process, Middle East Baltimore can refresh itself, in people and place, without a complete cleansing of its history and memory. In fact, there are vast opportunities for equitable change to occur—with political will, an organized community, and equitable participation from all stakeholders. And yes the money is there, once America places equal value on the poor and African American people of its land.

REBUILDING ABANDONED COMMUNITIES IN AMERICA

This writing has focused on one example of rebuilding our abandoned communities in America and offered both a microscopic and macroscopic view of how this occurs. It offers us insight into the processes that occur outside the public eye after the public announcements. The daily activities which determine how an affected community benefits during and after a rebuilding project is critical if we are to truly address equity in benefit to stakeholders involved in rebuilding our abandoned communities. If a major goal of our rebuilding practices is to address the root causes of generational poverty, our practices must change.

In general the planning and processes of rebuilding abandoned communities in America must be more inclusive from its planning to its evaluation stages. Input must be sought from all sectors including planning, community development, economic development, housing, transportation, environment, health, parks and recreation, education, safety, social services, engineering, architecture, and urban design. Most importantly the community must be included in all its parts—residents, businesses, places of worship. Urban plannners must be educated formally and informally as to the role of healthy community organizations in participating in development plans, before development occurs. Their offices should maintain strong linkages with community organizations to inform them of current trends and needs of the community. Such relationships will allow for easy participation of community voice when plans for development begin, informed from inside and outside the affected community.

Development plans should be linked to direct and indirect outcomes for the community. These plans should indicate number of jobs, timeline, employment benefits, number of ownership and rental housing, housing cost, financial structure to assure affordability for residents. Plans should project and compare how assets gained by powerful developers are comparable to assets gained for local residents, those who remain or are displaced. And environmental and health impact assessments should be completed before and after rebuilding of a community occurs.

Federal grants used for rebuilding abandoned communities must be more stringently assessed for compliance with standards of expected outcome. These standards must be developed through rigorous assessment of the communities being rebuilt and not settle for general outcomes which may not apply to different communities and cities. For example, if federal dollars dictate community participation how does the office of Housing and Urban Development assure that there is real community participation and not puppet organizations consisting of people handpicked by the developer?

Community redevelopment policies must address the whole community with outcomes that reflect specific improvement in the overall health of the community—employment, safety, housing, education, recreation, social inclusion and networking. Laws and policies which allows public-private partnerships to disproportionately benefit private developers should be changed to reflect balanced benefit to all stakeholders. For example tax credits to developers may require a payback which contributes to residents' remaining and thriving in their community through tax-relief programs or mortgage or rental assistance, ownership in corporate shares, investment in community-owned businesses.

Communities must organize themselves before, during, and after plans for rebuilding. An organized community increases the likelihood of maintaining communication with city departments which participate in preventing community abandonment and disinvestment. In addition, community organizations provide a structure for members to develop their vision of their community through direct input from its members. The larger the membership the greater likelihood of communication and response from city departments and elected officials in regard to resident concerns in their community. Voting for representatives who respond to the needs of the community also increases the likelihood that residents concerns are addressed by city departments.

During rebuilding processes residents must be involved in all aspects to assure the community remains a major stakeholder in the rebuilding plan. A continued presence of formal and informal community organizations at meetings may assure that the needs of the community is consistently on the table and concrete plans are made and implemented to address these needs throughout the rebuilding processes. An organized community can increase the likelihood that their voice are not only advisors to the process but decision makers in determining their community.

In addressing the root causes of growing disinvestment and abandonment, housing, real estate, and lending policies which continue to result in racial and class segregation must be critically assessed for their intended or unintended consequences and changed and followed to evaluate the results of these changes. City housing inspection programs must be adequately funded to assure speculation does not result in patterns of abandonment and identify early signs of abandonment. City government polices can institutionalize processes between housing and community development and planning offices alerting each to signs of abandonment which could lead to early remedies to stem continued abandonment. For example one boarded-up house can be documented by a housing inspector and trigger activity from community development and planning or environmental department personnel for a beautification strategy, increased pest control, or environmental inspection and sanitation. Slum landlords must be identified and targeted through mandates which forbid them to continue doing business in communities they have previously targeted. Land banking practices which lead to greater abandonment must be made illegal and remedied through forced sale or effective use that contributes to a thriving community.

While this story of rebuilding in East Baltimore has discussed these issues on a local level, they occur in varying degrees in similarly abandoned communities in America. It offers us opportunity to learn from those aspects we find are helpful and prevent those we find are not.

NOTES

1. Greenbaum S. (2008) "Poverty and the willful destruction of social capital: displacement and dispossession in African American communities." *Rethinking Marxism.* 20:42.

2. Baum, HS. 1983. *The organization of hope. Communities planning themselves.* State University of NY Press, NY.

Epilogue

Most people have had their bond with their childhood home compromised by moving out at some point. But Jesse Johnson, who has stayed with her 86-year-old father, Stanley, in the house where she grew up, has retained an intimate sense of her past. Everything around her is laden with personal history—from the delicate pink china that the senior Johnson picked up in Japan during World War II to the mantel full of family photos. The baby granddaughter in one picture has just gotten married.

Jesse Johnson, 37, takes a seat at her dining-room table after a long day working at Towson University's post office, sweeps aside her weariness, and tries to explain what the relocation process means to her and her father.

"There was no electric wiring in the house when he purchased it in 1948," Johnson says. "He did the paneling, the floors, and the concrete in the backyard. He built a garden there. He had kids here, sent them off to school, sent them off to war, sent them off to college. My mother died here.

"This isn't just a house—it's a home," Johnson says with a faint smile. "There are memories here that you can't take with you."

For an hour, Stanley Johnson opts not to speak, explaining to his daughter through hand gestures that the idea of displacement is just too much for him to discuss. She speaks for him and other elderly people who don't have a child living with them.

"A lot of [older people] are sitting there and they are worried about it," she says. "They don't have work to go to, children to take care of, and things to distract them from sitting there hours and hours. 'When are they going to put me out of my house? When are they going to take away my home?' This is it for them. This is their house. They didn't plan to go any place else."

As the conversation meanders around to the house's marble front steps, a standout architectural feature in a block of brick and cement stoops, Stanley Johnson suddenly speaks up, his voice shredded by an 18-year struggle with shingles. He describes how he built the steps himself, fixed them on top of a brick foundation. As a laborer in Sparrows Point for more than 40 years, Johnson knew how to lay brick, and his workmanship was tested when a car smashed into the steps. But the marble was just—his hand sweeps the air—"scratched."

Stanley Johnson takes over the conversation and tells tales of Baltimore in the jazz era, a time when he sang, a time when he and a woman named Billie Holiday sat backstage sharing some drinks in a club on Bond Street. Shaking off any appearance of infirmity, he chugs across the room and slides the new CD player off his old record-player console, ready to play some 78s.

But when asked how he feels about his impending forced move. Stanley Johnson stops suddenly, the boyish elasticity draining from his face, his eyes looking into nowhere.

"Oh man," he says, his voice scratched like an old record. "That's rough. That's rough."

There's a pause.

"I worked my whole life for this house."*

*Excerpt from *Baltimore City Paper*. "A bitter pill." November 12, 2003. The names of the persons have been changed. This piece was the report of an interview with one of the families affected by the rebuilding of Middle East Baltimore. Mr. Johnson died before moving into his replacement house.[1]

NOTE

1. *Baltimore City Paper*. November 12, 2003. Cohen C. "A bitter pill. A new biotech park promises to cure what ails."

Bibliography

ABT Associates. (2007) Final Report. East Baltimore Development Initiative. Post relocation satisfaction survey. January 17, 2007.

ABT Associates. (2008) East Baltimore Neighborhood Revitalization. Phase 1 Baseline Summary Report. 2001–2005. March.

Acevedo-Garcia D, Osypuk T, Werbel R, Meara E, Cutler D, Berkman L. (2004) "Does housing mobility improve health?" *Housing Policy Debate.* 15:49.

Afro-American. May 15, 1982. "East Baltimore Community Corp. make things happen on the Eastside."

Annie E. Casey Foundation. (2001) "The Sandtown-Winchester neighborhood transformation initiative: lessons learned about community building and implementation." www .chapinhall.org/sites/default/files/old_reports/104.pdf. Accessed January 2011.

Baltimore Business Journal. September 16, 2002. "City names Hopkins Biotech Park board." www.bizjournals.com/baltimore/stories/2002/09/16/daily42.html. Accessed January 2011.

Baltimore City Paper. May 31, 2000. "Testing ground."

Baltimore City Paper. November 12, 2003. Cohen C. "A bitter pill. A new biotech park promises to cure what ails."

Baltimore City Paper. March 16, 2005. "Danger zone."

Baltimore City Paper. February 22, 2006. "Moved and shaken."

Baltimore City Paper. May 2, 2007. "Don't you be my neighbor."

Baltimore Council of Social Agencies. (1937) Frances H. Morton. Social study of Wards 5 and 10 in Baltimore Maryland.

Baltimore Engineer. January 1934. 8:6.

Baltimore Metropolitan Council. 2000 Census tract data. Baltimore neighborhoods. www .baltometro.org/C2K/SF3medincome.pdf. Accessed May 2011.

Baltimore Sun. July 9, 1929. "Across town."

Baltimore Sun. April 22, 1935. "City urged to aid Hopkins campaign."

Baltimore Sun. July 16, 1943. "Johns Hopkins Hospital Hampton House."

Baltimore Sun. November 18, 1945. "Hopkins hospital seeks $3,000,000."

Baltimore Sun. June 11, 1946. "Johns Hopkins Hospital drive underway."

Baltimore Sun. June 11, 1946. "Your debt to the Hopkins."

Baltimore Sun. May 24, 1950. "Slum clearance projects here approved."

Baltimore Sun. July 19, 1951. "Hospital addition being built."

Baltimore Sun. April 27, 1953. "Hemmed in, hospital grows up."

Baltimore Sun. January 18, 1955. "Broadway slum housing plan unsettled."

Baltimore Sun. January 20, 1955. "The Broadway. Pig in a poke."

Baltimore Sun. March 16, 1956. "U.S. approves of Broadway Project fund."

Baltimore Sun. September 6, 1957. "Hospital plans include motel, shopping unit."

Baltimore Evening Sun. February 11, 1958. "Development near Hopkins Hospital hits council snag."

Baltimore Sun. April 6, 1958. "Unit defends relocation of Broadway families."

Baltimore Sun. July 1, 1959. "City renewal check paid."

Baltimore Sun. September 1960. "Ground broken for $2,000,000 Hopkins building."

Baltimore Sun. March 9, 1967. "Residents in renewal area voice fears about project."

Baltimore Sun. October 17, 1968. "Area to east of Green Mount like a graveyard for buildings."

Baltimore Sun. December 15, 1968. "Renewal with a difference."

Baltimore Sun. March 9, 1969. "An extraordinary way to plan a school."

Baltimore Sun. October 26, 1969. "Whatever happened to model cities?"

Baltimore Sun. October 8, 1973. "We live here."

Baltimore Sun. August 5, 1978. "Group plans to buy, recycle 20 houses."

Baltimore Sun. October 17, 1978. "City plans for 1979 outlined."

Baltimore Sun. August 15, 1982. "East Baltimore Community Corp. make things happen on the Eastside."

Baltimore Sun. August 15, 1982. "She gave the Middle East neighborhood a name and a dream."

Baltimore Sun. December 22, 1982. "Resident groups tif."

Baltimore Sun. August 9, 1992. "City's blight outpaces housing inspectors."

Baltimore Sun. February 7, 1994. "Renewal set for East Baltimore."

Baltimore Sun. March 5, 1994. "Fast-track in Sandtown-Winchester."

Baltimore Sun. April 8, 1998. "A neighborhood hospital; Hopkins."

Baltimore Sun. April 26, 1998. "Homeowners angered by Hopkins bids."

Baltimore Sun. October 15, 2000. "Eastside loses ground in effort to stem blight."

Baltimore Sun. January 11, 2001. "City, Hopkins weigh plan for east-side development."

Baltimore Sun. January 16, 2001. "City plan for troubled area alarms some residents divided over plan to raze homes near Hopkins."

Baltimore Sun. May 31, 2001. "Planned Hopkins biotech park draws guarded response from community."

Baltimore Sun. July 26, 2001. "Hopkins neighbors react to its recent struggles."

Baltimore Sun. May 22, 2002. "A business plan for biotech park."

Baltimore Sun. February 17, 2004. "Official notices of move are met with resignation."

Baltimore Sun. December 26, 2004. "Goals met but not hopes; Development."

Baltimore Sun. August 26, 2007. "Residents back 'House for a House.'"

Baltimore Sun. July 27, 2010. "The art of activism."

Baltimore Sun. July 29, 2011. "Residents give cool reception for new vision in East Baltimore."

Baltimore Sun. August 26, 2011. "Hopkins, Morgan take the reins in Eastside school."

Baltimore Urban Renewal and Housing Agency. 1967. "The Residents. Their characteristics, houses, needs, attitudes. Gay Street I."

Barbush E. (2009) *Middle East Baltimore Stories: Images and words from a displaced community.* SMEAC, Art on Purpose.

Baum HS. 1983. *The organization of hope. Communities planning themselves.* State University of NY Press, NY.

Bellinger DL, Lubahn C, Lorton D. (2008) "Maternal and early life stress effects on immune function: relevance to immunotoxicology." *J Immunotoxicol.* 5:419.

Bioethical Commission Report on Guatemala Research. 1946–48 inoculation STD studies in Guatemala. www.bioethics.gov. Accessed September 2011.

Blomley N. (2004) *Unsettling the City: Urban land and the politics of property.* Routledge, NY.

Bosma H, Stansfeld SA, Marmot MG. (1998) "Job control, personal characteristics, and heart disease." *Occup Health Psychol.* 3:402.

Bostic RW, Lewis LV, Sloane DC. (2006) "The neighborhood dynamics of hospitals as large landowners." community-wealth.com/_pdfs/articles-publications/anchors/. Accessed March 2011.

Braveman P, Egerter S, An J, Williams D. (2009) *Issue Brief 5: Race and socioeconomic factors.* Princeton, NJ: Robert Wood Johnson Foundation.

Brown NLM, Stentiford BM. (2008) *The Jim Crow encyclopedia. Greenwood milestones in African American History. Vol 2.* Greenwood Press. San Francisco, CA.

Bullard, R. (2007) *The Black metropolis in the twenty-first century: Race, power, and politics of place.* Rowman & Littlefield Publishers, Inc., Lanham, MD.

Carpenter DM, Ross JK. (2009) "Testing O'Connor and Thomas: Does the use of eminent domain target poor and minority communities?" *Urban Studies.* 46:2447.

Centers for Disease Control. (2009) Surveillance of health status in minority communities—racial and ethnic approaches to community health across the U.S. (REACH U.S.) Risk Factor Survey, United States, 2009. 2011 file:///Volumes/TOSHIBA/Rebuilding%20book/Refs/Surveillance%20of%20Health% webarchive. Accessed July 2011.

Centers for Disease Control. U.S. Public Health Service Syphilis study at Tuskegee. www.cdc.gov/tuskegee/timeline.htm. Accessed March 2011.

Change4-Real. (2009) The community's response to the Oldtown Redevelopment Plan. June 4, 2009-Draft.

Chesney AM. (1943) *The Johns Hopkins Hospital and the Johns Hopkins University School of Medicine. Vol 1. 1887–1888.* Johns Hopkins University Press, Baltimore, MD.

Cohen S, Janicki-Deverts D, Miller GE. 2007. "Psychological stress and disease." *JAMA.* 298:1685.

Commission on City Plan. (1945) The Hubbard Report. Redevelopment of blighted residential areas in Baltimore.

Community 2168 Working Parties. www.liverpool.nsw.gov.au/LCC/INTERNET/me.get site.sectionshow&PAGE1815. Accessed April 2011.

Crowder PA. (2007) "Ain't No sunshine: Examining informality and state open meeting acts as the anti-public norm in inner-city redevelopment deal making." University of Tulsa Legal Studies Research Paper No. 2008–01. *Tennessee Law Review.* 74:4.

Cutrona CE, Wallace G, Wessner KA. (2006) "Neighborhood characteristics and depression: An examination of stress processes." *Curr Dir Psychol Sci.* 15:188.

Daily Record. January 30, 2008. "East Baltimore community school will displace at least 25 homeowners, 47 renters."

Daily Record. January 31, 2011. "A dream derailed."

Daily Record. February 1, 2011. "The muddled money trail."

Daily Record. February 2, 2011. "Seeking a new vision."

Daily Record. February 3, 2011. "The education solution."

Daily Record. February 4, 2011. "An uncertain future."

Daily Record. February 7, 2011. "Resolution on New East Baltimore hearings pass unanimously."

Daily Record. July 28, 2011. "Residents rebuke EBDI developer."

Daily Record. August 1, 2011. "Miles out as East Baltimore Community School's head."

Daily Record. August 1, 2011. "New EBDI plan increases size."

Daily Record. August 10, 2011. "Board of Public Works sell bonds for state health lab."

Daily Record. August 28, 2011. "Hopkins poised to take over East Baltimore Community School."

Daily Record. September 18, 2011. "Baltimore finds funds for EBDI TIF."

Department of Housing and Community Development. July 15, 1968. Information Services.

Diamond Neighborhoods. www.jacobscenter.org. Accessed October 2010.

Dudley Street Neighborhood Initiative. www.dsni.org. Accessed September 2010.

East Baltimore Demolition Protocol. 2005.

EBDI (2001) Draft of Historical East Baltimore Community Relocation Policy and Benefits. November 2001.

EBDI (2002) Statement . . . of the EBDI Special Committee on Relocation. September 2002.

EBDI (2002) Homeowner Acquisition/Relocation Process Guide. December 2002.

EBDI (2004) Relocation Policy.

EBDI (2011) Revised Master Plan. July 28, 2011.

EBDI (2009) The workforce supply and demand characteristics of the East Baltimore Development Inc. redevelopment effort.

EBDI. (2011) Housing and relocation report.

Entringer S, Epel ES, Kumsta R, Lin J, Hellhammer DH, Blackburn EH, Wüst S, Wadhwa PD. (2011) "Stress exposure in intrauterine life is associated with shorter telomere length in young adulthood." *Proc Natl Acad Sci.* 108:E513.

Farfel MR, Orlova AO, Lees PS, Rohde C, Ashley PJ, Chisolm JJ Jr. (2003) "A study of urban housing demolitions as sources of lead in ambient dust: demolition practices and exterior dust fall." *Environ Health Perspect.* 111:1228.

Fraser JC, Kick EL. (2007) "The role of public, private, non-profit and community sectors in shaping mixed-income housing outcomes in the US." *Urban Studies.* 44:2357.

Fullilove MT. (1996) "Psychiatric implications of displacement: contributions from the psychology of place." *Am J Psychiatry.* 153:1516.

Fullilove M. (2001) "Root Shock: the consequences of African American dispossession." *J Urban Health.* 78:72.

Fullilove MT. (2004) *Root Shock: how tearing up city neighborhoods hurts America, and what we can do about it.* Random House, NY.

Fullilove MT. *Elements of urban restoration: Rebuilding America's cities after blight, flight and disinvestment.* In press. 2011.

Galea S, Tracy M, Hoggatt KJ, DiMaggio C, Karpati A. (2011) "Estimated deaths attributable to social factors in the United States." *AJPH.* 10:205.

Galtung J. (1969) "Violence, peace and peace research." *J Peace Res.* 6:167.

Geronimus AT. (2000) "To mitigate, resist, or undo: addressing structural influences on the health of urban populations." *Am J Public Health.* 90:867.

Geronimus AT. (2001) "Understanding and eliminating racial inequalities in women's health in the United States: the role of the weathering conceptual framework." *J Am Med Womens Assoc.* 56:133–136, 149.

Geronimus AT, Hicken M, Keene D, Bound J. (2006) "'Weathering' and age patterns of allostatic load scores among blacks and whites in the United States." *Am J Public Health.* 96:826.

Gibson K. (2007) "The relocation of the Columbia Villa community: views from residents." *J Plann Educ Research.* 27:5.

Gluckman PD, Hanson MA, Beedle AS. (2007) "Early life events and their consequences for later disease: a life history and Chevolutionary perspective." *Am J Hum Biol.* 19:1.

Gomez M. (2005) "Demanding a better deal." *Shelter Force.* November/December #144.

Gomez MB, Muntaner C. (2005) "Urban redevelopment and neighborhood health in East Baltimore, Maryland: The role of institutional andcCommunitarian social capital." *J Critical Public Health.* 15:83.

Graham JE, Christian LM, Kiecolt-Glaser JK. (2006) Stress, age, and immune function: toward a lifespan approach. *J Behav Med.* 29:389.

Greenbaum S. (2008) Poverty and the willful destruction of social capital: displacement and dispossession in African American communities. *Rethinking Marxism.* 20: 42.

Harris E. (2008) Community 2168 Stakeholder Interviews. Centre for Health Equity Training Research and Evaluation and Community 2168, Liverpool NSW.

Harvey D. (2000) *Spaces of hope.* U California Press, California.

Hesseltine WB. (1962) *The tragic conflict: the civil war and reconstruction.* George Braziller, NY.

Historic East Baltimore Community Action Coalition. May 1994. Community Revitalization Plan. Baltimore, MD.

Holland ML, Kitzman H, Veazie P. (2009) "The effects of stress on birth weight in low-income, unmarried black women." *Women's Health Issues.* 19:390.

Hopkins Magazine. February 1952. "Hopkins-Broadway area getting tailor-made reconstruction."

Hopkins Medicine. Spring/Summer 2011. "A new prescription for partnerships."

Housing Authority of Portland. (2007) New Columbia: Report on development goals. December.

Housing Authority of Portland. (2010) Report to the community. Measuring success 2002–2009.

Indypendent Reader. Summer 2006. "#1 Baltimore: A conversation between David Harvey and Marisela Gomez."

Inside Story. inside.org.au/understanding-miller/. Accessed March 2011.

Jacobs DE, Mucha A, Stites N, MacRoy P, Evens A, Rafferty P, Phoenix J, Persky V. (2007) Preliminary results of lead particulate deposition from housing demolition. American Industrial Hygiene Conference and Exposition. June 2007.

JHU President's Council on Urban Health—report on an urban health initiative, 1999 www .jhu.edu/news_info/report/urbanhlt. Accessed November 2010.

Johns Hopkins Medicine. www.hopkinsmedicine.org/about. Accessed June 2011.

Johns Hopkins Medicine. www.hopkinsmedicine.org/about. Accessed November 2010.

Johns Hopkins Medicine. www.hopkinsmedicine.org/graduateprograms/campus.cfm. Accessed May 2011.

Johnstone Q. "Federal Urban Renewal Program" (1958). Faculty Scholarship Series. Paper 1896. digitalcommons.law.yale.edu/fss_papers/1896. Accessed January 2011.

Kawachi I, Berman LS. (2003) *Neighborhoods and health.* Oxford University Press, UK.

Kawachi I, Subramanian SV, Kim D, eds. (2008) *Social capital and health.* Springer Science and Business Media, LLC., NY.

Keene D, Padilla M, Geronimus AT. (2010) "Leaving Chicago for Iowa's 'Fields of opportunity': community dispossession, rootlessness and the quest for somewhere to 'Be OK.'" *Hum Organ.* 69:275.

Keene DA, Geronimus AT. (2011) "'Weathering' HOPE VI: The Importance of evaluating the population health impact of public housing demolition and displacement." *J Urban Health.* 88:417.

Kelly Jr., JJ. (2006) "'We shall not be moved': Urban communities, eminent domain and the socioeconomics of just compensation." *St. Johns's L. Rev.* 80:923.

Kelly Jr., JJ. (2008) "Taming eminent domain." *Shelter Force.* Spring #153.

Kennedy M, Leonard P. (2001) *Dealing with neighborhood change: A primer on gentrification and policy choices.* www.policylink.org/pdfs/BrookingsGentrification.pdf. Accessed January 2001.

Kreiger N. (2011) *Epidemiology and the people's health: theory and context.* Oxford University Press, UK.

Kristensen P, Gravseth HM, Bjerkedal T. (2010) "Influence of early life factors on social inequalities in psychiatric outcomes among young adult Norwegian men." *European J Pub Health.* 20:517.

Lees L. (2008) "Gentrification and social mixing: Towards an inclusive urban renaissance?" *Urban Studies.* 45:2449.

Levy D, Kaye D. (2004) *How are HOPE VI families faring? Income and employment.* Washington, DC: Urban Institute.

Lopez, A. (2006) Weighing and reweighing eminent domain's political philosophies post-Kelo, 41 *Wake Forest L. Rev.* 237:243.

Marmot M, Wilkinson RG. (2005) *Social determinants of health.* 2nd. ed. Oxford University Press, UK.

Manjarrez C, Popkin S, Guernsey E. (2007) *Poor health: Adding insult to injury for HOPE VI families.* The Urban Institute Press, Washington, DC.

Mcdougall HA. (1993) *Black Baltimore. A new theory of community.* Temple University Press, Philadelphia, PA.

Medoff P, Sklar H. (1994) *Streets of Hope. The fall and rise of an urban neighborhood.* South End Press, Cambridge, MA.

MD. Real Property Code Ann. § 12-101. General provisions.

MD. Real Property Code Ann. § 12-102. Relocation and assistance.

MD. Real Property Code Ann. § 12-105.1; 12.202; 12.204; 12-205.1. Real Property—Condemnation-Procedures and compensation.

Miami Herald.com. June 9, 2008. UM bets on biotech future. www.miamiherald.com. Accessed March 2011.

Morningside Post at Columbia University. Columbia Signs Benefits Agreement. themorningsidepost.com/2011/03/columbia-promises-benefits-agreement/. Accessed May 2011.

National Housing Law Project. (2002) False Hope: A critical assessment of the Hope VI Public Housing Redevelopment Program.

Nelson DW. *Simply Put. Selected speeches of Douglas W. Nelson, the Annie E. Casey foundation president & CEO, 1990–2010.* (2010) www.aecf.org/~/media/Pubs/Other/S/SimplyPut SelectedSpeechesofDouglasWNelson/Nelson_simply_put.pdf. Accessed March 2010.

News American. September 2, 1973. "EBMP offers adequate care despite strife."

News American. August 15, 1981. "Striking health workers want wage hike."

New York Times. 1910. "Baltimore tries drastic plan of race segregation."

New York Times. August 6, 2008. "Building a biotechnology park in Baltimore by rehabilitating a neighborhood."

NPR National Public Radio. July 12, 2011. "As income gap balloons, is it holding back growth?" www.npr.org/2011/07/10/137744694/as-income-gap-balloons-is-it-holding-back-growth?ft=1&f=1001. Accessed July 2011.

Olson SH. (1997) *Baltimore: the building of an American City.* The Johns Hopkins University Press, Baltimore, MD.

The Oregonian. June 20, 2007. "Old mind-set hobbles New Columbia."

The Oregonian. June 23, 2010. "Killing spurs increase in security at Portland's New Columbia."

Obradovic J, Bush NR, Stamperdahl J, Adler NE, Boyce WT. (2010) "Biological sensitivity to context: the interactive effects of stress reactivity and family adversity on socioemotional behavior and school readiness." *Child Dev.* 81:270.

Overtown Alliance. (2011) Sustainable Community Benefits Agreement. A visionary partnership between Overtown, University of Miami Life Science and Technology Park & Wexford Science and Technology 2011.

Pearlin LI. (2010) "The life course and the stress process: some conceptual comparisons." *J Gerontol B Psychol Sci Soc Sci.* 65B:207.

Perez G. (2002) "The other "real world": gentrification and the social construction of place." *Urban Antropology.* 31:37.

Philadelphia Neighborhoods. March 4, 2010 "Nicetown-Tioga: Temple hospital changed the neighborhood and not necessarily for the better." sct.temple.edu/blogs/murl/2010/03/04/nicetown. Accessed March 2011.

Pietila A. (2010) *Not in my neighborhood. How bigotry shaped a great American city.* Ivan R. Dee, Chicago.

Popkin S, Katz B, Cunningham M. (2004) *A decade of Hope VI: Research findings and policy challenges.* Urban Institute, Washington, DC.

Portland State University Magazine. Winter 2006. "A new way home."

Power Pictorial & Gas Graphic #6. April 1926.

Price D, Popkin S. (2010) *The Health Crisis for CHA Families.* Urban Institute, Washington, DC.

Pruss-Ustun A, Fewtrell L, Landrigan PJ, Ayuso-Mateos JL. "Ch. 19. Lead exposure." *Comparative quantification of health risks.* WHO: www.who.int/healthinfo/global_burden_disease/cra/en/

Rosenberg CE. (1962) *The cholera years: the United States in 1832, 1849, 1866.* University of Chicago Press, Chicago, IL.

Rubin RL. Spring. (2008) *Shelter Force.* "Take and give."

SMEAC (2004) Save Middle East Action Committee, Inc. Listening Project 2004.

Sasaki Associates Inc. (2006) East Baltimore Neighborhood Project. 2006.

Sheridan PG. (2005) Kelo v. City of New London: New Jersey's Take on Takings. 38.113.83.199/Students/academics/journals/law-review/Issues/archives/upload/sheridan.pdf. Accessed May 2011.

Sherry G. (1957) *Catholic Reporter*. "Part 1 Urban renewal project concerns all citizens."

Sicher P. (2010) "Hopkins and other institutions pay Baltimore $20.4 million to avoid tax increases." *The News-Letter*. July 15, 2010. Accessed March 2011.

Skloot R. (2010) *The immortal life of Henrietta Lacks*. 2010. Random House, New York.

Smith N, Caris P, Wyly E. (2001) "The 'Camden Syndrome' and the menace of suburban decline: Residential disinvestment and its discontents in Camden County, New Jersey." *Urban Affairs Review*. 36:497.

Sojourner-Douglass College. 2001. Fundraising letter.

South Florida Business Journal. June 2, 2010. "Overtown residents demand UM commitment."

Stansfeld S, Fuhrer R, Shipley MJ, Marmot MG. (1999) "Work characteristics predict psychiatric disorders: prospective results from the Whitehall II study." *Occup Environ Med*. 56:302.

Steele CM. (2010) *Whistling Vivaldi*. W.W. Norton & Co., NY.

Steinberg S. (2010) "The myth of concentrated poverty." *The integration debate: Competing futures for American cities*, ed. by Chester Hartman C, Squires GD. Routledge, NY.

Sternthal MJ, Slopen N. Williams DR. (2011) "Racial disparities in health: How much does stress really matter." *The Du Bois Review: Social Science Research on Race*. 8:95. journals.cambridge.org/action/displayJournal?jid=dbrOnline. Accessed April 2011.

Talley B. (2005) Restraining eminent domain through just compensation: Kelo v. City of New London, 125 S. Ct. 2655.

Urban Design Associates. East Baltimore Study. May 2001.

Urban Design Associates. East Baltimore Study. December 2001.

Urban Renewal Plan, East Baltimore, Amendment 3. 1994.

Urban Renewal Plan, Middle East Baltimore, Amendment 6. 2000.

Urban Renewal Plan, Middle East Baltimore, Amendment 7. 2002.

Urban Renewal Plan, Middle East Baltimore, Amendment 8. 2005.

U.S. Government Printing Office. Trials of war criminals before the Nuremberg Military Tribunals under Control Council. 1949 Law No. 10, Vol. 2, pp. 181–82. Washington, D.C.

Valparioso. "Judicial Review of Displacee Relocation in Federal Urban Renewal Projects: A New Approach?" (1969) 3. *Val. U. L. Rev.* 258. Available at: scholar.valpo.edu/vulr/vol3/iss2/7. Accessed November 2010.

Voices from Within. A displaced community speaks out. Wide Angle Video. 2004.

Wallace R. (1998) A synergism of plagues: "planned shrinkage," contagious housing destruction and AIDS in the Bronx. *Environ Res*. 47:1.

Wallace R, Fullilove MT. (2008) *Collective consciousness and its discontents: Institutional distributed cognition, racial policy and public health in the United States*. Springer, NY.

Washington Post. August 24, 2001. "My kids were used as guinea pigs." www.gwu.edu/~pad/202/readings/lead-hopkins.htm. Accessed November 2010.

WBAL News. October 2010. "East Baltimore Tax District Plan concerns some."

WBAL News. March 30, 2011. "EBD-Ire-Residents of Middle East (an E. Balto. neighborhood) attack quasi-public corporation renovating their community, at City Council hearing."

WEAA radio show. January 2011. Marc Steiner.

WEACT for Environmental Justice. Columbia University Expansion Project. www.weact.org/Programs/SustainableDevelopment/ColumbiaUniversityExpansionProject/tabid/216/Default.aspx. Accessed February 2011.

Wilkinson R, Pickett K. (2010) *The Spirit Level. Why greater equality makes societies stronger*. Bloomsbury Press, London.

Williams DR, Collins C. (1995) "US socioeconomic and racial differences in health: patterns and explanations." *Annu Rev Sociology.* 21:349.

Williams DR, Mohammed SA. (2009) "Discrimination and racial disparities in health: evidence and needed research." *J Behav Med.* 32:20.

Williams DR. (2011) *Moving upstream to the roots of health disparities: Wealth, education, race.* Robert Wood Johns Foundation.

Williams RY. (2011) *The politics of public housing: Black women struggle against urban inequality.* Oxford University Press, UK.

Wilson WJ. (1996) *When work disappears: The world of the new urban poor.* Random House, NY.

Woolcock M, Narayan D. (2000) "Social capital: Implications for development theory, research, and policy." *World Bank Research Observer.* 15:225.

World Health Organization. (2008) "Closing the gap in a generation: Health equity through action on the social determinants of health." www.who.int/social_determinants/the commission/finalreport/en/index.html Accessed December 2010.

World Health Organization. (2008) WHO Final Report to the WHO Commission on social determinants of health from the Social Exclusion Knowledge Network. www.who.int/social_determinants/knowledge_networks/final_reports/sekn_final%20report_042008.pdf. Accessed January 2011.

Index

About the Author

Marisela B. Gomez is a community activist, author, public health professional, and physician scientist. She received a BS and MS from the University of New Mexico in Albuquerque—during and after completing 4 years enlistment in the U.S. Airforce—a PhD, MD, and MPh from the Johns Hopkins University. She spent 17 years as an activist/researcher or participant/observer in East Baltimore during and after training at the Johns Hopkins Schools of Medicine and Public Health. Past and current writings address social determinants and health, social capital and urban health, disparities in mental health care in incarcerated populations, disparities in substance use treatment, mental health care in the primary health care setting, community organizing and development, and mindfulness practices in organizing. She spends her time between the city and counties of Baltimore, Maryland.